Phonological Studies in
Four Languages of Maluku

Summer Institute of Linguistics and
The University of Texas at Arlington
Publications in Linguistics

Publication 108

Editors

Donald A. Burquest
University of Texas
at Arlington

William R. Merrifield
Summer Institute of
Linguistics

Assistant Editors

Rhonda L. Hartell

Marilyn A. Mayers

Consulting Editors

Doris A. Bartholomew
Pamela M. Bendor-Samuel
Desmond C. Derbyshire
Robert A. Dooley
Jerold A. Edmondson

Austin Hale
Robert E. Longacre
Eugene E. Loos
Kenneth L. Pike
Viola G. Waterhouse

Phonological Studies in Four Languages of Maluku

Donald A. Burquest and Wyn D. Laidig
Editors

A Publication of
The Summer Institute of Linguistics,
The University of Texas at Arlington,
and
Pattimura University
1992

© 1992 by the Summer Institute of Linguistics, Inc.
Library of Congress Catalog No: 92–80562
ISBN: 0–88312–803–9
ISSN: 1040–0850

All Rights Reserved

No part of this publication may be reproduced, stored in a retrieval system, or transmitted in any form or by any means—electronic, mechanical, photocopy, recording, or otherwise—without the express permission of the Summer Institute of Linguistics, with the exception of brief excerpts in journal articles or reviews.

Cover sketch and design by Hazel Shorey
Cover design depicts Maluku hand-woven fabric

Copies of this and other publications of the Summer Institute of Linguistics may be obtained from

International Academic Bookstore
7500 W. Camp Wisdom Road
Dallas, TX 75236

Contents

Preface	vii
Introduction	1
Phonology of Sawai *Ronald Whisler*	7
1. Phonology	8
2. Morphophonemics	23
3. The Sawai seven-vowel system	28
References	32
Kisar Phonology *John Christensen and Sylvia Christensen*	33
1. Stress	34
2. System of phonemes	41
3. Ambivalent phonemes	50
4. Distribution of phonemes	56
5. Morphophonemics	58
6. Conclusion	65
References	65
Segments, Syllables, and Stress in Larike *Carol J. Laidig*	67
1. Segments	72
2. Syllables	92
3. Stress and the phonological word	97
4. Stress in contractions and compounds	105
5. Stress shift at clause level	116
6. Summary	119
7. Interlinearized text	121
References	126

A Lexical Phonology of West Tarangan *Richard Nivens* 127
  1. Stress 129
  2. Phonemes 137
  3. Syllable and root structure 159
  4. Lexical rules for affixation 164
  5. Reduplication 185
  6. Cliticization and other syntactic processes 200
  7. Postsyntactic processes 206
  8. Summary of rules 209
  9. Summary of River dialect phonology 217
  References 226

Preface

It is one of the privileges of Pattimura University to be able to share with the rest of the world a part of Maluku's linguistic heritage. Each of the dozens of languages in Maluku is but one manifestation of just as many local cultures; in a sense, an audible symbol of our peoples' ethnic pride and identity. Pattimura University, while functioning as a vehicle of national unification, also recognizes the importance of identifying the cultural and linguistic diversity of its population. As history as shown us time and time again, lasting and stable unification at the national level can never really be achieved without an open recognition and acceptance of the inherent cultural diversity of that nation's peoples. This is a part of the task set before Pattimura University, and it is within this framework that our cooperative effort with the Summer Institute of Linguistics takes place.

Over the past several years, it has been a pleasure to have those from the Summer Institute of Linguistics work as faculty members of Pattimura University. This interaction has been rewarding for all concerned, both at the professional level, as well as at the personal level. The recent establishment of the Center for Maluku Studies and Development at Pattimura University, currently coordinating this cooperative effort, should further facilitate such interaction in the future.

It is my pleasure to be a part of the linguistic research presented in this volume. I view these tangible results of our work together not as a culmination, but rather as a beginning. I am grateful for the opportunity to be involved in the documentation and preservation of Maluku's cultural heritage, and am excited about the leadership role which Pattimura University is able to play.

Dr. Ir. J. L. Nanere, MSc.
Rector, Pattimura University
Ambon, Maluku, Indonesia
September, 1990

Introduction

Donald A. Burquest
University of Texas Arlington and The Summer Institute of Linguistics
and
Wyn D. Laidig
Pattimura University and The Summer Institute of Linguistics

These papers result from an ongoing cooperative research program with the Pattimura University, located in Ambon, the provincial capital of Maluku, Indonesia, and the Summer Institute of Linguistics. It was the editors' privilege to be part of a workshop conducted on the campus of Pattimura University in May and June of 1990, during which time these papers were put into final form. The editors are grateful to our colleagues at Pattimura University, and especially to Rector J. L. Nanere, for their part in making this work possible.

Although the papers can speak for themselves, it may be helpful to include a few introductory remarks to place them in their proper setting and to draw attention to some of the specific points of interest in the descriptions.

There is still a significant amount of disagreement regarding the classification of Austronesian languages in Maluku. Dahl (1976) places the languages in the west Austronesian subgroup, distinct from the Oceanic (east Austronesian) languages. Dyen (1978) also places the Austronesian languages of Maluku together with those of western Indonesia, although he includes the Formosan languages with them in a group he calls Hesperonesian.

However, according to Blust (1978, 1980) the languages of Maluku are more closely related to the Oceanic languages than they are to the Formosan languages and the languages of western Indonesia. Blust proposes the following classification for these language families:

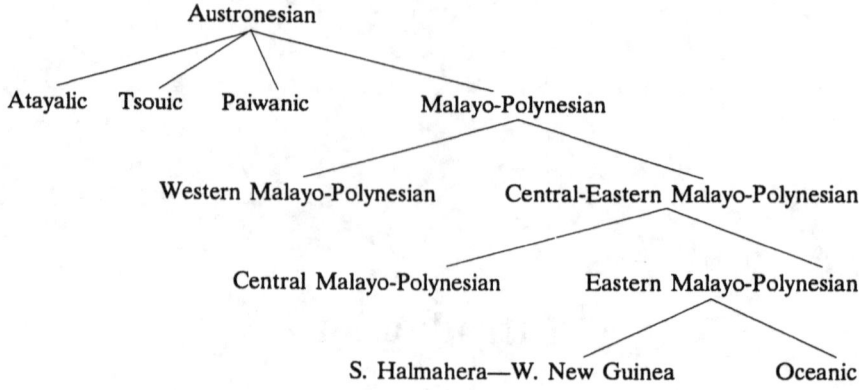

Under this classification Larike, Kisar, and West Tarangan are members of the Central Malayo-Polynesian group, while Sawai belongs to the South Halmahera-West New Guinea subgroup of Eastern Malayo-Polynesian. A more detailed discussion regarding the genetic relationships between the Austronesian languages of Maluku is found in Collins (1982, 1983). The papers in this volume are arranged so as to present Sawai first, with the languages of the Central Malayo-Polynesian group following. The overall geographical ordering is generally from north to south.

Before briefly summarizing the major facts of each language, a few points of general interest may be appropriate. Austronesian languages typically have a system of five vowels. Two of the languages described here (Sawai and West Tarangan) exhibit seven-vowel systems; they represent two different branches of Austronesian, and they are relatively remote from each other geographically, which may add some significance to this finding. The consonant inventories of these languages vary in interesting ways, especially in the obstruents. The treatment of glottal stop as being in some contexts contrastive and in others not, is also of interest. As expected, morphophonemic alternations exhibit the remnants of sound change, but in different ways in the different languages. Finally, the matter of reduplication is of particular interest in terms of proposals in Metrical Phonology; these papers provide an interesting cross-section of reduplicative processes which invite both synchronic and diachronic analyses.

Sawai (Whisler) is a member of the South Halmahera-West New Guinea branch of the Austronesian language family. It is spoken on the island of Halmahera, in northern Maluku. It is also known by the name Weda.

Sawai has fourteen consonants in native vocabulary, including full contrastive sets of voiced and voiceless stops (neutralized morphophonemically

Introduction

in favor of voiceless stops in cluster with following voiceless stops) and a three-way contrast in nasals. Sawai is unusual in that it has seven contrastive vowels: /i e ɛ a ɔ o u/. Limitations on vowel distribution suggest an earlier more-restricted inventory, and the unusual nature of the vowel system receives extensive discussion in the paper. The vowel /ɛ/ has characteristics setting it apart from all other vowels: it is inserted to maintain phonotactic patterns at higher levels at the ends of words ending in a consonant or glide, either pre-pause or before words beginning with a voiced continuant; it is inserted to break up clusters of three consonants across word boundaries; it is deleted in some other contexts by a rule which applies after the voicing assimilation rule for stops (resulting in clusters that do not agree in voicing); finally, it is a common template vowel in reduplication.

The following reduplication patterns are found in Sawai: temporal duration of adjectives and verbs (CV + stem); nominalization of verbs (CVC + stem); and reciprocal verbs (CVC + stem). In the last case, the final consonant of the reduplicative template is in fact the second consonant of the stem, which follows naturally if it is assumed that the initial consonant of the stem cannot be realized because the initial position of the reduplicative template is already filled by /f/.

Larike, Kisar, and South Tarangan are all languages of the Central Malayo-Polynesian branch of Austronesian. Kisar (Christensen and Christensen), spoken on the island of Kisar in southwest Maluku, is also known by the name Meher.

Kisar has thirteen consonants, including a voiceless retroflexed alveolar stop, which is suggested as being a reflex of the historical voiced alveolar stop (there are no voiced stops in Kisar), its retroflexed articulation corresponding to the alveolar point of articulation of voiced coronal stops in the daughter languages as opposed to the dental articulation of voiceless coronal stops. The glottal stop in Kisar is phonologically significant medially; initially it has two possible statuses, analyzed as sometimes phonologically significant, at other times the result of a phonetic rule inserting it in initial position of vowel-initial words. These two opposing interpretations of the same phonetic entity find support in the fact that some stems with initial phonetic glottal stop function as consonant-initial stems (these are interpreted as having an underlying glottal stop), while others (those with only a phonetic glottal stop) function differently and are analyzed as vowel-initial. The same opposition shows itself also in reduplication, where the phonological glottal stop appears in the reduplicated form and the phonetic glottal stop does not.

There are the expected five vowels in Kisar: /i e a o u/. The vowels /e a/ have lax variants, occurring mostly in syllables immediately preceding the stressed syllable of the word. Consonant clusters are not infrequent across syllable boundaries; vowel sequences are always interpreted as sequences of separate syllables, an analysis for which several arguments are advanced.

Stress is highly predictable in Kisar, falling on the penultimate syllable of the root. Monosyllabic roots are stressed on the root syllable unless prefixed, in which case stress is penultimate on the word; prefixes do not cause stress to shift on multisyllabic roots. Monosyllabic suffixes have no effect on stress; disyllabic suffixes (possibly historically separate words) receive the primary stress of the word as if they were roots. Secondary stress occurs on alternating syllables of longer words. A metrical analysis of stress is presented, analyzing Kisar as having left-headed binary feet and right-headed n-ary phonological words (monosyllabic suffixes under this analysis are considered extrametrical).

Reduplication is mentioned only briefly in this paper but is apparently of two general types: full reduplication (the final vowel of the prefixed copy is sometimes deleted), and reduplication of the initial CV of the stem.

Larike (Laidig) is spoken on the island of Ambon, in central Maluku. Like most languages of the area, borrowing has had a significant impact on its phonological structure. In native vocabulary it manifests thirteen consonants (/d/ is the only voiced stop). Glottal stop functions in some contexts as a legitimate phoneme in its own right, in other contexts (before vowel-initial words and between geminate vowels) being only a surface phone, the result of phonetic epenthesis. The five vowels are the classic /i e a o u/, with /i e a/ manifesting lax (interpreted as [-Advanced Tongue Root]) variants in statable contexts (often involving a nearby front vowel). Consonant clusters in native vocabulary are rare, the result of affixation of the possessive marker -r or the stative marker -n, or application of an optional rule of vowel elision. Vowel sequences are frequent, interpreted by Laidig as sequences of syllables.

There is an interesting pair of morphophonemic alternations involving obstruents. Most verbal forms with initial /k/ or /p/ show a variant with glottal stop instead in morphologically defined contexts. In exactly complementary contexts, forms with /t/ or /s/ show a variant with /r/. Laidig refers to a proposal by Collins, who reports similar alternations in other languages of central Maluku, and finds the explanation for these alternations in the diachronic assimilation of an obligatory subject agreement marker.

Stress is highly predictable in Larike, occurring on the penultimate syllable of the root in its underlying representation; affixes do not affect

Introduction

stress placement. Apparent exceptions can be largely explained on the following grounds: (1) A few words manifest final stress and can be interpreted as being historically compound words in which the second element was monosyllabic and attracted stress as is characteristic of the second stem in compounds. (2) A few other words manifest antepenultimate stress when the surface form is considered, but the surface form can be seen as a result of a rule of vowel epenthesis applying after penultimate stress placement. (3) A few further apparent exceptions are accounted for with reference to a process characteristic of compounding (vowels in sequence across morpheme boundaries are combined into a single syllable in such structures, followed by reapplication of rules of syllabification and stress placement), and a general rule of deletion of the first of two identical vowels (the result of juxtaposition of pronominal morphemes in specific syntactic contexts). (4) Finally, there are three clause-level morphemes which obligatorily attract stress and override the general rules defining word-level stress.

Reduplication in Larike is of two types: total reduplication, in which the entire stem is reduplicated; and reduplication of the initial consonant of the stem (including rule-produced glottal stop) followed by the vowel /a/.

The presentation of West Tarangan phonology by Nivens is by far the most ambitious and the most theoretically related of the set. Although Nivens sets forth an analysis making use of metrical trees within the framework of lexical phonology, at several points he insightfully discusses the specific theoretical issues involved in analyzing the facts of the language. In addition to the value of the analysis itself, this paper provides a good introduction to lexical and metrical approaches to phonology and their application. Although the presentation focuses on the facts of the Coast dialect, in an appendix Nivens includes a brief analysis of the River dialect, in which he compares the two.

West Tarangan is spoken on the island of Tarangan, Southern Aru, in south Maluku. The language has thirteen consonants in the underlying representation. Glides /w/ and /y/ have obstruent variants [g] and [dʒ], respectively, word initially and in the onset of stressed noninitial syllables. Fricatives have stop variants in syllable-final position. The velar stop /k/ has an optional glottal stop variant (which may subsequently be deleted) between nonhigh vowels. Voiced obstruents do not occur syllable-finally; morpheme-initial consonant clusters require the first member to be a liquid or a glide (of the latter only /y/ occurs).

West Tarangan has seven vowels: /i e ɛ a ɔ o u/. The vowel /a/ has special status: it is by far the most frequent; it is inserted and deleted by rule; and it is obligatory as one of the vowels in a vowel cluster. There are no further apparent restrictions on vowel clusters except that geminates do not occur in underlying representation. High vowels /i u/ have lax variants (analyzed here as [-Advanced Tongue Root]) in closed syllables; /a/ is often laxed to [ə] when unstressed.

Geminates of both consonants and vowels, arising from affixation and cliticization, are commonly degeminated.

Stress in West Tarangan is generally penultimate on the root. Most exceptions are roots which have a mid vowel in the final syllable, which attracts stress. Affixes and clitics neither carry stress nor affect stress placement. A metrical analysis of stress is proposed in which (in general terms) phonological feet are binary and left-headed, and phonological words are binary and right-headed. There is some degree of weight sensitivity involved in the construction of feet (including interpreting syllables with mid vowels, which are always closed in final syllables, as heavy), which accounts for final stress with few exceptions. Secondary stress occurs on any syllable dominant in a foot which does not receive primary stress; it is not always alternating.

A most interesting set of phenomena in West Tarangan has to do with allomorphy. Nivens provides extensive and insightful discussion of various sorts of facts, demonstrating how lexical phonology provides an understanding of them (although a few points of difficulty remain). Examples include prefix vowel deletion before vowel-initial roots, lowering of prefixal /i u/ to [ɛ ɔ], and various morpheme-specific rules of deletion of consonants and vowels in specific contexts. Each rule is identified as to its stratum of application, and numerous derivations are presented illustrating the use of metrical trees in a lexical phonology treatment.

References

Blust, Robert A. 1978. Eastern Malayo-Polynesian: A subgrouping argument. Pacific Linguistics C-61:181–221.

———. 1980. Austronesian etymologies. Oceanic Linguistics 19:1–181.

Collins, James T. 1982. Linguistic research in Maluku: A report of recent field work. Oceanic Linguistics 21:73–146.

———. 1983. The historical relationships of the languages of Central Maluku, Indonesia. Pacific Linguistics D-47.

Dahl, Otto C. 1976. Proto-Austronesian. Scandinavian Institute of Asian Studies monograph series 15. Lund: Studentlitteratur.

Dyen, Isidore. 1978. The position of the languages of Eastern Indonesia. Pacific Linguistics C-61:235–254.

Phonology of Sawai

Ronald Whisler
Pattimura University and The Summer Institute of Linguistics

This paper presents a brief description of the phonology and morphophonemics of the Sawai language. Sawai is an Austronesian language of the South Halmahera-Western New Guinea language family (Blust 1978). It is spoken in the districts (*kecamatan*) of Weda and Gane Timor in southern Halmahera, northern Maluku Province, Indonesia. Sawai, sometimes referred to as Weda, has approximately 10–12,000 speakers.

There is dialect chaining among the Austronesian languages of south Halmahera (Whisler 1989). This chaining effect is also seen from village to village within the Sawai language. In addition, villages that have the same religion (either Muslim or Christian), also have a higher percentage of lexical similarities than villages of the alternate religion, even though they might be farther apart geographically. It is generally held among the Sawai speakers that the most original dialect of Sawai is spoken in the three Kobe villages (Kobe Tanjung, Kobe Gunung, and Kobe Peplis).

Very little has been published on this Austronesian language. Michael Thomas lived in the village of Kobe Gunung for approximately one year and wrote on Sawai pronominal prefixes (Thomas 1983), and a Pattimura University research team has written on Sawai grammar (Latupapua et al. 1981–82).

Research for the present paper was done in the villages of Lelilef Woyebulan and Kobe Peplis. The Kobe dialect is the source of the data in this paper.

1. Phonology

1.1. Word stress

Word stress is generally on the penultimate syllable of multisyllabic roots.

(1) /yɛgɛt/   ['yɛgɛt]   'oil'
    /lobɛn/   ['lobɛn]   'net'
    /bobane/   [bo'bane]   'bay'
    /salanipɛ/ [sala'nipɛ] 'wasp'

However, if the penultimate vowel is a mid front lax vowel /ɛ/ and the final vowel is other than /ɛ/, the stress falls on the ultimate syllable.

(2) /lɛlit/   [lɛ'lit]   'mango'
    /fɛfo/   [fɛ'fo]   'lemon'
    /dɛlut/   [dɛ'lut]   'parents'
    /musɛla/ [musɛ'la] 'woven mat'
    /kɛet/   [kɛ'et]   'prevent'

Word stress is not affected by affixation.[1] Because stress is predictable, it is considered nonphonemic and will not be written in this paper except when necessary to the discussion.

1.2. Phonemes

Consonant inventory. Sawai has a total of fourteen consonants: six stops, two fricatives, three nasals, one liquid, and two semivowels. In addition to the phonemes shown in (3), /h/ is found in borrowings from Indonesian and neighboring Papuan languages, but it will not be considered part of this phonemic inventory because of its borrowed nature.

---

[1]There are five known words which do not conform to this rule, probably explainable historically. Also, the possessive enclitic /mam/ causes a stress shift; however, this unusual enclitic is most likely a borrowing from the local Malay (see footnote 5).

Phonology of Sawai

(3) Consonants

	labial	alveolar/palatal	velar/glottal
stops voiceless	p	t	k
voiced	b	d	g
fricatives	f	s	
nasals	m	n	ŋ
lateral		l	
semivowels	w	y	

Consonant description. All stops occur in syllable-initial position. The voiceless stops are the only stops to occur frequently in syllable-final position. Syllable-final contrast is rare among stops.

/p/ [p] voiceless unaspirated bilabial stop

(4) [paɾi] 'or' [f-tapɛn] '2p-to burn'[2]
    [pɛspɔsɛ] 'cloudy' [ŋalɛp] 'cloth'

/b/ [b] voiced bilabial stop

(5) [balɛt] 'DIR left' [bɛboko] 'head'
    [bɛtbɛt] 'soil' [ɾub] 'thunder'

/t/ [t] voiceless unaspirated alveolar stop

(6) [t-ɔ] '3s-to eat' [yotɛf] 'sago thatch'
    [mɛtɛt] 'hill' [n-tɛlɔt] '3s-hungry'

/d/ [ɾ] voiced alveolar vibrant flap; occurs intervocalically in roots; occurs as the first of two consonants in clusters; occurs syllable finally; and occurs occasionally word initially. There are some exceptions to these environments, in that occasionally [ɾ] will occur in

---

[2] Abbreviations used in the examples in this paper: 1p first-person plural, 1pe first-person exclusive, 1pi first-person inclusive, 1s first-person singular, 2p second-person plural, 2s second-person singular, 3p third-person plural, 3s third-person singular, ART article, ASP aspect, CAU causative, DIR direction, NEG negative, pl plural, PL ART plural article, RECP reciprocal, REL relativizer, ST stative, TR transitivizer.

unpredictable environments. There are, however, no clear contrasts between [d] and [ɾ].³

(7) [ɾakɛn] 'close' [n-dɛɾɛɾɛ] '3s-to follow'
    [m-diɾkɛ] '2s-to move' [n-ɛɾoɾ] '3s-to ask'

[d] voiced alveolar stop; occurs elsewhere

(8) [deko] 'friend' [mdi] 'tree trunk'
    [dodego] 'sugar press' [t-dɛ] '1p-to go along'

/k/ [k] voiceless unaspirated velar stop

(9) [kyat] 'person' [kɛkalɛ] 'worm'
    [ɾ-tukɛl] '3p-to buy' [n-tok] '3s-to pound'

/g/ [g] voiced velar stop

(10) [gɛlat] 'worm' [lɛgaɛ] 'older man'
     [n-gɛgisɛ] '3s-skinny' [n-ɛgag] '3s-to scratch'

The fricatives /f/ and /s/ both occur syllable initially and syllable finally. The glottal fricative /h/, because it occurs with a very low frequency and is a result of borrowing from non-Austronesian languages in the area, is not considered a part of the Sawai phoneme inventory.

/f/ [f] voiceless labio-dental fricative

(11) [fawa] 'how many' [fakfuk] 'curly, tangled'
     [k-ɛfliŋɛn] '1s-to check' [wɛf] 'island'

/s/ [s] voiceless alveolar grooved fricative; occurs elsewhere

(12) [sni] 'month, moon' [nase] 'ASP will'
     [k-ɔsɛl] '1s-to stand' [k-ɛus] '1s-to wash'

---

[3]In this paper, except when phonetic brackets are used, [ɾ] is represented orthographically with a separate symbol r, even though [ɾ] is actually an allophone of /d/. For example /dakɛn/ [ɾakɛn] 'close' is represented orthographically as rakɛn.

Phonology of Sawai

[tʃ] voiceless alveopalatal affricate, an allophone of /s/; occurs when preceded by a nonliquid alveolar at a morpheme break

(13) preceded by velar   preceded by non-liquid alveolar

[k-suŋ]   '1p-to enter'   [n-tʃuŋ]   '3s-to enter'
[k-sep]   '1s-to bathe'   [n-tʃep]   '3s-to bathe'
[k-solɛt]   '1s-to go upstream'   [r-tʃolɛt]   '3p-to go upstream'
[k-sopɛn]   '1s-to go outside'   [r-tʃopɛn]   '3p-to go out'

This same affrication occurs in a different manner when the transitivizer -o is added verb finally. In some words syllable-final /ɛ/ separating /t/ and /s/ is deleted, bringing together the /ts/ combination, which in turn is affricated.

(14) /i n-wetɛs-o/   'he 3s-to go by-TR'
     [i nwetso]   ɛ deletion (discussed below)
     [i nwetʃo]   phonetic realization

The examples below of a verb root having an initial /s/ demonstrate how affrication does not occur with the attachment of nonalveolar proclitic markers, but does occur with alveolar proclitic markers.

(15) [m-suŋɛ]   '2s-to enter'   [n-tʃuŋɛ]   '3s-to enter'
     [f-solɛtɛ] '2p-to go upstream'   [t-tʃolɛtɛ] '1p-to go upstream'
     [k-sepɛ]   '1s-to bathe'   [r-tʃepɛ]   '3p-to bathe'

Evidence for an underlying form for the voiced alveopalatal affricate is not as strong as for its voiceless counterpart. I postulate that when /y/ is preceded by a nonliquid alveolar consonant, it affricates in a manner similar to /s/, as discussed above. In spoken Sawai, these two sounds (nonliquid alveolar consonant followed by /y/) never form a sequence phonetically, a fact that seems to support this affricate hypothesis.

There is additional support for this analysis in that the rule for voiceless affrication listed above can occasionally apply to its voiced counterpart. In the villages of Weda and Lelilef (although rarely in the Kobe villages), when the third person plural proclitic marker d- is attached to a verb that begins with /y/, the result is sometimes a [dʒ] sound, as shown by the following example.

(16) /d-yɛnɛf/   [r-dʒɛnɛf]   '3p-to sleep'

One additional piece of evidence for the affrication of /y/ as [dʒ], is that the morpheme *ndyɛ* [ndʒɛ] 'that' is sometimes, especially in fast speech, pronounced as [nyɛ]. This would suggest that a sequence of an underlying alveolar followed by /y/ may be realized as [dʒ]. If the underlying alveolar is dropped, the /y/ is explicitly manifested phonetically in the surface representation [nyɛ].

The nasals /m/, /n/, and /ŋ/ and the liquid /l/ all occur syllable initially as well as syllable finally. They are described below.

/m/   [m] voiced bilabial nasal

(17)   [manɛ]   'chicken, bird'   [mɛɾmɛɾ]   'a plant'
       [n-boɛm]   '3s-to fish'   [pelɛm]   'sago container'

/n/   [n] voiced alveolar nasal

(18)   [ninɛ]   'mosquito'   [manɛ]   'chicken, bird'
       [nti-g]   'child-1s'   [in]   'fish'

/ŋ/   [ŋ] voiced velar nasal

(19)   [ŋalɛp]   'cloth'   [ŋɛnŋan]   'sun, day'
       [k-iŋɛt]   '1s-to lift'   [maŋ]   'dry'

/l/   [l] voiced alveolar lateral

(20)   [lapo]   'edge'   [dɛlut]   'parents'
       [βlu]   'leaves'   [yawɛl]   'fish hook'

The semivowels /y/ and /w/ both occur word initially, intervocalically, and in cluster with a consonant.

/y/   [dʒ] voiced alveopalatal affricate; occurs as the realization of an underlying voiced alveolar (presumably /d/) directly preceding /y/ (see discussion above)

(21)   [ndʒɛ]   'that'   [n-ɛdʒel]   '3s-to go around'
       [fadʒe]   'like this'   [n-fa-dʒol]   '3s-CAU-to gather'

       [y] voiced high front unrounded semivowel; occurs elsewhere

(22)   [yama]   'over there'   [n-fayal]   '3s-to know'
       [kyat]   'person'   [n-ɛfɛyɛ]   '3s-to dry'

/w/   [β] voiced bilabial fricative; occurs word initially when in cluster with a consonant

(23) [βlu]   'leaves'   [βlo]   'heart, emotion'
     [βlon]   'leader, owner'   [βyɔi]   'youngest child'

[w] voiced high back rounded semivowel; occurs elsewhere

(24) [wɔfɛ]   'deer trap'   [fawa]   'how many'
     [gwɔ]   'satan'   [n-pɔw] '3s-to split'

Consonant contrasts.

p/b   contrast both syllable initially and syllable finally

(25) pɔtɛn   'Patani (people)'   po   'to; on'
     bɔtɛn   'land'   bo   'ASP want, will'

     pɛkpuk   'lump, mound'   puŋ   'heart'
     bɛkbuk   'bubbles, foam'   n-buŋ   'ST-to add'

     n-ɛbyaf   '3s-blind'   tapɛn   'to burn'
     pyai   'alligator'   abɛn   (COUNTER)

     t-fa-pɛs   '1p-CAU-to shatter' m-ɛsɔp   '2s-to unstitch'
     t-fa-bɛs   '1p-CAU-competition' m-ɛsɔb '2s-hanging'

p/f   contrast both syllable initially and syllable finally

(26) n-ɛfɛtɛn   '3s-to tell'   n-yɛpɛn '3s-to hold'
     n-pɛtɛn   '3s-to suspect'   yɛfɛn   'street'

     n-po   '3s-to give'   f-ai   '2p-to steal'
     n-fo   '3s-to wring out'   pai   'who'

     pɔt   'geloba fruit'   nop   'bottom'
     f-ɔt   '2p-to catch'   nof   'type of fish'

b/m   contrast both syllable initially and syllable finally

(27)
bɔ	'type of bamboo'	bɛt	'garden'
m-ɔ	'2s-to eat'	mɛt	'cloud'
bɛtbɔt	'type of fish'	blik	'eel'
mɛtmɔt	'corpse'	m-lik	'2s-to bow'
n-ɛtibɛ	'2s-to plant'	dub	'thunder'
n-ɛtim	'2s-to patch'	d-um	'3p-to rebel'

b/w   contrast both syllable initially and less frequently syllable finally

(28)
bɔ	'sago branch'	bobo	'edge'
wɔ	'big bowl'	wɔwɔ	'root'
n-bɔlɛt	'3s-to tie'	n-bai	'3s-to visit'
wɔlɛt	'ocean'	n-wai	'3s-to bother'
n-fa-kabelɛ	'3s-CAU-to bend'	n-ɛsɔbɛ	'3s-to hang'
n-fa-kawelɛ	'3s-CAU-to fix'	n-ɛfsɔwɛ	'3s-to marry'

m/w   contrast both syllable initially and syllable finally

(29)
mɔdɛ	'ripe'	n-mɔɛ	'3s-shy'
wɔdɛ	'ready'	wɔɛ	'water'
lɛmlɛm	'lightning'	yama	'DIR top to bottom'
lɔwlɔw	'patience'	dʒawa	'thick part of oil'
mamɛt	'type of fruit'	n-lam	'3s-to throw out'
m-awɛt	'2s-to go up'	nɛlaw	'DIR oceanward'
gɛglɛm	'small thorn'	n-ɛtim	'3s-to patch'
gɛglɛw	'to shine'	n-tiw	'3s-to spear'

t/d   contrast syllable initially

(30)
| tɛl | 'three' | n-tɛ | '3s-to throw' |
| dɛl | 'friend' | n-dɛ | '3s-to go, follow' |

Phonology of Sawai

	m-tirɛ	'2s-to poke'	*toma*	'from the outside'
	m-dirɛ	'sT-to sink'	*doŋa*	'joint'
	tua	'uncle'	*n-ɛtim*	'3s-to plug (hole)'
	n-dua	'3s-to ask'	*n-dimɛ*	'3s-to crash'
	kɛ-tokɛ	'1s-to pound'		
	kɛ-dokɛ	'1s-to make a hole'		

t/s contrast both syllable initially and syllable finally

(31)
	ta	(relativizer)	*tu*	'true, real'
	sa	'submerged reef'	*su*	'now'
	m-ɛtuɛ	'sT-to be hard'	*k-ɔtɛl*	'1s-to itch'
	m-ɛsuɛ	'2s-to back up'	*k-ɔsɛl*	'1s-to stand'
	n-ɛblut	'3s-to pluck'	*fɔt*	'four'
	n-ɛblus	'3s-to have a nightmare'	*fɔs*	'rice'

d/n contrast as the proclitic subject marker on the verb, and syllable initially and syllable finally

(32)
	d-fan	'3p-to go'	*wɔdɛ*	'ASP already'
	n-fan	'3s-to go'	*wɔnɛy*	'right'
	n-pidɛ	'3s-dry, low tide'	*t-duwɛn*	'3p-to go down'
	n-pinɛ	'3s-to hide'	*nuɛn*	'many times'
	doudou	'dock'	*madɛy*	'bitter'
	nɛunou	'small waves'	*manɛ*	'bird, chicken'
	mɔdɛ	'ripe'	*wlɔ-d*	'to breathe-1p'
	mɔnɛ	'tomorrow'	*wlɔn*	'village leader'

d/l contrast syllable initially

(33)
	de	'and, with'	*dub*	'thunder'
	le	'only'	*nlub*	'hang down'
	dɛde	'wall'	*wɔdɛ*	'ASP already'
	lɛle	'coconut grater'	*wɔle*	'string, rope'

	n-dɛ	'3s-to go'	doɲa	'joint'
	n-lɛ	'3s-bad'	m-loɲɛ	'2s-to hear'

n/l contrast syllable initially or following another consonant

(34) nɛ (PL ART) nɔw 'type of tree'
 lɛ 'bad' lɔw 'far'

 n-uf '3s-to blow' ɛtnɛ 'every'
 luf 'mouse' ɛtlɛ 'leftovers, extras'

 pnu 'village' n-ɛftɔn '3s-to wait'
 plu 'feathers, hair' n-tol '3s-to kick'

k/g contrast both syllable initally, and syllable finally in a reduplicated syllable

(35) kit 'squid' Ku 'name of river'
 git 'gum' gu 'snake'

 n-ɛkas '3s-to split' n-ɛsakɛ '3s-to spear'
 n-ɛgas '3s-to clear throat' n-ɛsagɛ '3s-to strike'

 sɛksakɛ 'between legs' kel 'sago crumbs'
 sɛgsagɛ 'spear' gele 'grandmother'

k/ŋ contrast both syllable initally and syllable finally

(36) k-ɔ '1s-to eat' k-anɛ '1s-to order'
 ŋɔ 'star' ŋanɛ 'day'

 n-faɲfɔŋ '3s-to cut down' n-loɲɛ '3s-to hear'
 fakfuk 'tangled' lokɛ 'banana'

 n-tok '3s-to pound' kel 'sago crumbs'
 toŋ 'rattan' ŋele (COUNTER)

k/w contrast both syllable initially and syllable finally

(37) k-ɔ '1s-to eat' n-akɛt '3s-to close'
 wɔ 'soup bowl' n-awɛt '3s-to go up'

Phonology of Sawai

        n-tɛlak   '3s-to divorce'   n-ɛlik   '3s-to bow'
        ntɛlaw   (DIR ocean)   n-ɛliw   '3s-to pass up'

        n-ɛspɔk   '3s-on its back'
        n-tɛpɔw   '3s-to be split'

ŋ/w   contrast both syllable initially and syllable finally

(38)   ŋɔlo   'chin'   ŋɔ   'star'
        wɔwo   'root'   wɔ   'big bowl'

        ŋale   'meaning'   fafŋai   'mustache'
        n-wale   '3s-to swing'   fadwai   'to stir, to trouble'

        sɛŋsoŋ   'branch'   bɔŋ   'to add'
        sɛwsow   'wet sago'   bɔw   'pig'

n/ŋ   contrast both syllable initially and syllable finally

(39)   n-anɛ   '3s-to order'   n-ɔ   '3s-to eat'
        ŋanɛ   'day'   ŋɔ   'star'

        n-ai   '3s-to steal, take' nɔn   'pus'
        ŋai   'strand (of hair)'   ŋɔŋ   'type of mussel'

        manɛ   'bird, chicken'   fɔn   'skin disease'
        maŋ   'dry'   n-fɔŋ   '3s-to cut down'

Vowel inventory. Sawai has a seven-vowel system, which is unusual for an Austronesian language of Maluku and Irian Jaya. A simple description is given here. A more detailed argument for a seven-vowel analysis is given in §3, where I also present a hypothesis regarding a phonemic change from a five-vowel to seven-vowel system.

(40)   Vowels

	front	central	back
high	i		u
mid	e		o
low	ɛ	a	ɔ

Note that both /ɛ/ and /ɔ/ have been classified as low vowels: the morphophonemic rule of vowel fronting (see §2.1) treats /a/ as a fronted form of /ɔ/, and by analogy /ɛ/ is also treated as a low vowel.

Vowel description. The front vowels /i/, /e/, and /ɛ/ all occur in stressed and unstressed syllables, and in open and closed syllables.

/i/   [i] high front tense unrounded vowel

(41)   ['itɛ]   'we'   ['ntiŋ]   'tight'
       [lo'lahi]   'curse'   [ka'lawi]   'spear'

/e/   [e] mid front tense unrounded vowel

(42)   ['delɛk]   'bay'   ['leg]   'cave'
       ['lawe]   'thread'   ['pote]   'here'

/ɛ/   [ɛ] mid front lax unrounded vowel

(43)   [m-sɛ'lok]   '2s-to receive'   [nɛ-m-'dɛl]   '3s-ST-to go fast'
       [k-ɛ'ftɔn]   '1s-to wait'   ['lokɛ]   'banana'

The central vowel /a/ occurs in both stressed and unstressed syllables, and in open and closed syllables.

/a/   [a] low mid lax unrounded vowel

(44)   ['abɛn-lu]   'COUNTER-two'   [n-'fan]   '3s-to go'
       [so'gado]   'until'   ['lima]   'DIR here'

The back vowels /u/, /o/ and /ɔ/ occur in stressed and unstressed syllables, and in open and closed syllables.

/u/   [u] high back tense rounded vowel

(45)   ['utɛ]   'hair'   ['k-ut]   '1s-to carry'
       [pa'fule]   'not yet'   ['n-busu]   '3p-lazy'

/o/   [o] mid back tense rounded vowel

(46)   ['bobo]   'edge of something'   ['pocɛ]   'there'
       [k-ɛ'kwop]   '1s-to tip over'   ['lapo]   'edge'

Phonology of Sawai

/ɔ/ [ɔ] mid back lax rounded vowel

(47) ['n-ɔsɛl] '3s-to stand' [mɛ'lɔwɛ] 'light'
['kmɔn] 'axe' ['pɔtnɔ] 'living room'

Vowel contrasts.

e/i contrast in both open and closed syllables

(48) lema 'toward land' ŋale 'meaning'
lima 'toward speaker' k-ŋali '1s-to repent'

e-sɔ 'inanimate COUNTER-one' se 'therefore'
i-sɔ 'animate COUNTER-one' si 'they'

min 'inside'
n-men '3s-spins'

ɛ/ɔ contrast in both open and closed syllables

(49) gɛwgɛw 'sifter' fɛn 'turtle'
gɛwgɔw 'place' fɔn 'a skin disease'

nɛ 'these, those' f-ɛtɛn '2p-to count'
n-ɔ '3s-to eat' n-fɔtɛn '3s-to sniff'

faftɛn 'same sex sibling' Wedɛ 'town of Weda'
n-faftɔn '3s-to wait' wɔde 'ASP completive'

e/ɛ contrast in both open and closed syllables

(50) moke 'father' ndʒe 'this'
mokɛ 'sea cucumber' ndʒɛ 'that'

lɛmlem 'dew' n-tebɛ '3s-to get down'
lɛmlɛm 'lightning' n-tɛbɛ '3s-to cut'

le 'only, just' tɛptep 'edge of river'
lɛ '3s no good' tɛptɛp 'drop of blood'

a/ɛ   contrast in both open and closed syllables; in multi-syllabic roots they contrast only in the final syllable

(51) ga   'ASP just, and'   n-fan   '3s-to go'
      gɛ   'broth'   fɛn   'turtle'

      pua   'where'   ta   (REL)
      puɛ   'type of fish'   n-tɛ   '3s-to throw'

      isa   'fence'   sila   'folktale'
      isɛ   'rib'   silɛ   'sailfish'

a/ɔ   contrast in both open and closed syllables

(52) manɛ   'chicken'   n-ap   '3s-to row'
      mɔnɛ   'tomorrow'   nɔp   'to the bottom'

      n-fan   '3s-to go'   sɛnat   'mat'
      fɔn   'skin disease'   n-ɔt   '3s-to catch fish'

      n-ɛfay '3s-to feed'   t-ɔ   '1p-to eat'
      n-ɛfɔy '3s-to ignite'   ta   (REL)

      na   'do not'   isa   'fence'
      n-ɔ   '3s-to eat'   i-sɔ   'thing-one'

o/ɔ   contrast in both open and closed syllables; in multi-syllabic roots they contrast only in the final syllable

(53) n-po   '3s-to give'   bo   'want, desire'
      n-pɔ   '3s-to carry'   bɔ   'sago branch'

      wlo-di 'heart-3p'   m-loŋɛ   '2s-to hear'
      wlɔ-di 'breath-3p'   m-lɔŋɛ   'ST-to be long'

      yof   'sago'   wo   'alcoholic drink'
      yɔf   'withered limb'   wɔ   'big plate'

      n-ɛsow '3s-to sprinkle'   n-ɛror   '3s-to ask'
      n-ɛsɔw '3s-to loosen'   n-ɛrɔr   '3s-to spill'

Phonology of Sawai

u/o contrast in both open and closed syllables:

(54)
bubu	'tail of fish'	dulo	'type of shell'
bobo	'edge of something'	dolo	'like, same as'
n-busu	'3s-lazy'	luf	'mouse, rat'
bɛboso	'taboo'	n-lof	'3s-to be next to'
n-tuwɛl	'3s-to bend over'	k-ut	'1s-to carry'
t-owɛl	'3p-to boil'	kot	'magical statue'
bɛkbuk	'bubbles'	wlu	'leaves of tree'
bɛkbok	'fat'	wlo	'heart-3s'

1.3. Syllable structure

The minimal structure for a single syllable is V, while the most complex is CCVC. An example of each syllable type follows.

(55)
V	[i]	'he, she, it'
VC	[in]	'fish'
CV	[fa]	'stingray'
CVC	[ɾub]	'thunder'
CCVC	[kmɔn]	'axe'

The two-syllable root structures CV.CVC and CV.CV are the most common, although monosyllabic and trisyllabic roots are also common. The largest word found to date consists of five syllables.

Consonant clusters occur not only within the syllable but also across syllable boundaries. Vowel clusters occur word medially and finally.

1.4. Phonotactic constraints

Consonant constraints. Frozen or fossilized forms are artifacts of a morphophonemic process that was productive at a previous time. There are a number of such roots in Sawai, recognizable by their unique syllable structure. Almost without exception, when /ɛ/ follows a stem-initial consonant, the consonant that precedes the /ɛ/ also follows the vowel; apparently that consonant was at one time a reduplicated consonant followed by a front lax vowel but is now a frozen form.[4] A similar type of morphophonemic process is currently active in the language, although it occurs only with verbs (see §2.6).

(56) bɛbobɛl   'cold'   gɛgɛtɛs   'muddy'
     kɛkalɛ   'worm'   pɛplɛn   'fly'
     sɛslɔn   'standing water'   tɛtaŋo   'ear'

A list of all consonant clusters that have been found to occur is given in (57). The consonants in the column on the left specify the first member of each cluster, while the consonants in the row across the top specify the second member. All the possible phonological consonant clusters, both within roots and also due to morphological combinations, are listed.

(57)   Consonant clusters

	p	b	t	d	k	g	f	s	m	n	ŋ	l	w	y
p			pt	pd	pk			ps		pn		pl		py
b				bd	bk			bs		bn		bl		by
t	tp	tb	tt	td	tk	tg	tf	ts	tm	tn	tŋ	tl	tw	ty
d	dp	db	dt	dd	dk	dg	df	ds	dm				dw	dy
k	kp	kb	kt	kd	kk	kg	kf	ks	km	kn	kŋ	kl	kw	ky
g		gb		gr				gs		gn		gl	gw	gy
f	fp	fb	ft	fd	fk	fg		fs	fm	fn	fŋ	fl	fw	fy
s	sp	sb	st	sd	sk	sg			sm	sn		sl		sy
m	mp	mb	mt	md	mk	mg	mf	ms	mm	mn	mŋ	ml	mw	my
n	np	nb	nt	nd	nk	ng	nf	ns	nm	nm	nŋ	nl	nw	ny
ŋ			ŋt		ŋk		ŋf	ŋs	ŋm	ŋn	ŋŋ			
l	lp	lb	lt	ld	lk	lg	lf	ls	lm	ln	lŋ	ll	lw	ly
w	wp		wt	wr	wk	wg		ws		wn		wl		wy
y			yt	yd				ys		yn				

Of the consonant clusters listed above, all geminate clusters are reduced to one (see §2.5), and as mentioned earlier, an allophone of /s/ is [tʃ].

Vowel constraints. When /i/ or /e/ occurs in a root, no other instance of /i/ or /e/ occurs in that root, whereas /ɛ/ occurs with itself and all other vowels. The vowel /a/ is never preceded by /ɔ/ in the same word. Vowels /u/ and /ɔ/ never occur together in the same word.

---

[4] A few of the rare exceptions to this are listed below.
   dɛrɛrɛ   'to follow'   mɛlikɛ   'clouds'
   tɛbɔn   'a trap'   mɛpin   'women'

With few exceptions, /ɛ/ and /a/ are the only vowels to occur in the antepenultimate position of a root, as in (58).

(58) mamɛlɛl   'sleepy'   kalalimɛ   'soft'
      pɛgɛlɛ   'women'   bɛklinɛn   'quiet'

Exceptions are seen in (59) where the vowels /i/, /u/, and /o/ do occur in the antepenultimate, but very infrequently. The vowels /e/ and /ɔ/ never occur in the antepenultimate.

(59) mɛlikobɛn 'edible plant'   sogado   'until'
      n-gogoro   '3s-to love'   bubane   'harbor'

In an open syllable that precedes a stressed syllable, /ɛ/ and /a/ are in free variation. That the underlying form is /ɛ/ can be inferred from application of the stress rule (see §1.1), which in all other cases is totally general, i.e., if the penultimate vowel is /ɛ/ and the final vowel is other than /ɛ/, stress falls on the ultimate syllable.

(60) rɛ're   ~ ra're   'wall'
      n-ɛ'spɔk   ~ n-a'spɔk   '3s-on back side'
      n-ɛ'ror   ~ n-a'ror   '3s-to ask'
      rɛ'mag   ~ ra'mag   'sibling of same sex'

2. Morphophonemics

2.1. Vowel fronting. A subgroup of body parts and kinship terms (often classified as inalienable-possessed nouns) takes a possessive enclitic.[5]

(61) | 1s | 2s | 3s | 1pe | 1pi | 2p | 3p |
      | -g | -m | — | -mam | -r | -mi | -ri |

A root-final back vowel is fronted when a first or second person singular enclitic is attached to the root. This can be seen in the examples in (62).

---

[5]The possessive enclitic -mam does not act like other possessive enclitics: (a) it does not conform to the assimilation rule (see §2.2), (b) it is used for both edible and nonedible possession, and (c) it is the only suffix to cause a stress shift. Therefore, I have postulated that this is a borrowing, perhaps from the local Malay *kami*.

(62)

	child	heart	eye	opposite sex sibling
root	ntu	wlo	mtɔ	rɛmɔn (no true root)
1s	nti-g	wle-g	mta-g	rɛma-g
2s	nti-m	wle-m	mta-m	rɛma-m
3s	ntu	wlo	mtɔ	rɛmɔ
1pe	ntu-mam	wlo-mam	mtɔ-mam	rɛmɔ-mam
1pi	ntu-r	wlo-r	mtɔ-r	rɛmɔ-r
2p	ntu-mi	wlo-mi	mtɔ-mi	rɛmɔ-mi
3p	ntu-ri	wlo-ri	mtɔ-ri	rɛmɔ-ri

A word-final back vowel /o/ is inserted before the enclitic on this subgroup of body parts and kinship terms if there is not already a final back vowel in the root. Furthermore, the root that has the /o/ addition is not affected by the fronting rule; therefore, neither the /o/ nor the preceding vowel is fronted.

(63)

	hand	tooth	head	finger
root	fa	ŋaɲɛ	bɛbokɛ	kɛkolɛ
1s	fao-g	ŋaŋo-g	bɛboko-g	kɛkolo-g
2s	fao-m	ŋaŋo-m	bɛboko-m	kɛkolo-m
3s	fao	ŋaŋo	bɛboko	kɛkolo
1pe	fao-mam	ŋaŋo-mam	bɛboko-mam	kɛkolo-mam
1pi	fao-r	ŋaŋo-r	bɛboko-r	kɛkolo-r
2p	fao-mi	ŋaŋo-mi	bɛboko-mi	kɛkolo-mi
3p	fao-ri	ŋaŋo-ri	bɛboko-ri	kɛkolo-ri

2.2. Assimilation

Contrast between other types of possession is marked by the following possessive classifiers: *nɔ-* for edibles and hand tools, and *ni-* for other objects. When a first-person plural inclusive or third-person plural pronominal enclitic attaches to one of these possessive classifiers, the *n* of the classifier assimilates to the *r* of the enclitic.

(64) nɔ-r → [rɔ-r] 'our INCL edible'
　　 nɔ-ri → [rɔ-ri] 'their edible'
　　 ni-r → [ri-r] 'our INCL nonedible'
　　 ni-ri → [ri-ri] 'their nonedible'

A voiced stop assimilates to the voicelessness of a following voiceless obstruent.

Phonology of Sawai

(65)   tɛb + tubo   /tɛptubo/   'the top'
       sɛb + sibɛ   /sɛpsibɛ/   'knapsack'
       ntɛg + tig   /n-tɛktig/   '3s-to hop'
       tɛg + tegɛl   /tɛktegɛl/   'a place to step on'

2.3. Paragoge addition

The paragoge /ɛ/ is added to clause- and pause-final consonants and semivowels. The paragoge aids in the analysis of a phone as a high vowel or as a semivowel, because the paragoge is added only to consonants and semivowels.[6] In general, Sawai tends to end the phonological sentence with a CV syllable; if the final syllable is other than CV, /ɛ/ is added.

(66)   um   →   umɛ   'house'
       mɛkɔt   →   mɛkɔtɛ   'red'
       ay   →   ayɛ   'wood'
       aw   →   awɛ   'you'

The paragoge /ɛ/ is also added to final consonants and semivowels when the following word begins with a voiced continuant, and also to break up any potential three-consonant clusters at word breaks. (There are certain grammatical contexts that prohibit this rule from applying, which will be dealt with more thoroughly in a future paper on Sawai grammar.)

2.4. Deletion of syllable-final /ɛ/

In a root-final closed syllable of a bisyllabic root, /ɛ/ is deleted when followed by the suffixes -ɛ and -o. This rule must precede the voiced stop assimilation (§2.2) because this deletion brings about the only occurrence of a voiced stop following a voiceless one.

(67)   dupɛl-o   →   duplo   'to water, pour'
       tɔfɛn-o   →   tɔfno   'to try'
       babɛk-o   →   babko   'to wrap'
       tɔlɛn-o   →   tɔlno   'to live, sit'

---

[6]The addition of the paragoge also aids in the audible distinction between a high vowel and corresponding semivowel that it follows. In other words, the /ɛ/ in conjunction with /y/ and /w/ is realized as [yɛ] and [wɛ], a pronunciation which is distinguished from /i/ and /u/, respectively.

2.5. Geminate reduction

Geminate clusters can occur when either proclitics or reduplicative morphemes are preposed to a verb. When such a cluster occurs, the two identical consonants reduce to one. For example:

(68)

t-telɔtɛ	→	tɛlɔtɛ	'1pi-hungry'
f-fan	→	fan	'2p-to go'
k-kɛlak	→	kɛlak	'1s-to report'
m-mɛsiɛ	→	mɛsiɛ	'2s-to care for, to love'
kɛk-kakɛt	→	kɛkakɛt	'wooden door bolt' (reduplication)
tɛt-titɛf	→	tɛtitɛf	'spittle' (reduplication)

2.6. Reduplication rules

Duration. Temporal duration of adjectives and verbs can be expressed by the reduplication of the first consonant plus the front lax vowel /ɛ/. This type of reduplication is very limited, almost nonexistent, most likely having been replaced by other forms of temporal and durative markers. The metrical templates proposed are based upon the proposals by Marantz (1982). Because the reduplicative vowel is always /ɛ/, it is preassociated in the template; the stem vowel also becomes associated, but it receives no manifestation because the preassociated /ɛ/ takes priority.

(69) gɛlay + gɛlay   'to scream'
     CV   + CVCVC → gɛgɛlay   'wailing'
     ɛ

(70) dorɛm + dorɛm   'dark'
     CV   + CVCVC → dɛdorɛm   'night time'[7]
     ɛ

Nominalization. Nouns are derived from verbs by reduplicating the first two consonants of the verb root, separated by the mid front lax vowel /ɛ/.

---

[7] Note that the intermediate form *dɛdorɛm* is phonetically realized as [dɛɾorɛm], since [ɾ] is an allophone of /d/, and orthographically represented as *dɛrorɛm* according to the convention used in this paper (see footnote 3).

Phonology of Sawai

Note that the devoicing rule (§2.2) and geminate reduction rule (§2.5) apply to the new noun. In metrical terms, nominalization is achieved by reduplication using a prefixed CVC template with /ɛ/ as the preassociated vowel.

(71) tolɛn + tolɛn   '3s-to sit'
     ||| |||||
     CVC + CVCVC = tɛltolɛn   'chair'
      |
      ɛ

(72) gɔs + gɔs   'to scratch'
     ||| |||
     CVC + CVC → gɛsgɔs   'line, scratch'
      |
      ɛ

Further examples (intermediate forms are before devoicing and degemination):

(73) tib   'to stake'   /tɛbtib/ → tɛptib   'stake' (devoicing)
     titɛf 'to spit'   /tɛttitɛf/ → tɛtitɛf 'spittle' (geminate reduction)
     lɛsɛn 'to sweep'   → lɛslɛsɛn 'broom'
     gɛw   'to sift'   → gɛwgɛw   'sifter'
     sɛŋ   'to be happy'   → sɛŋsɛŋ   'happiness'

Reciprocal. A reciprocal verb is marked by initial *fa-* plus the reduplication of the second consonant of the verb root. Again the CVC reduplication prefix template can be used, but with both /f/ and /a/ preattached (together the sequence *fa-* matches the form of the causative prefix). Note that this preattachment means that it is only the second consonant of the stem that is realized in the reduplication, a fact which otherwise lacks ready explanation.

(74) ŋamo + ŋamo   'to argue'
     ||| ||||
     CVC + CVCV → famŋamo   'to argue with one another'
     ||
     fa

(75) duk + duk   'to meet'
      ||| |||
      CVC + CVC → fakduk 'to meet one another'
      ||
      fa

Other examples include the following reciprocal forms.

(76) fa-C RECP + eŋɔtɔ 'to see' → fateŋɔtɔ 'to see one another'
      fa-C RECP + gali   'to help' → falgali   'to help one another'
      fa-C RECP + pitno 'to tie' → fatɛpitno 'to tie to something else'

3. The Sawai seven-vowel system

Although there is strong evidence showing that Sawai is a seven-vowel system, there are a few factors which may make the linguist uneasy in this analysis. For instance:

1. Sawai is the only attested seven-vowel system among its language family (South Halmahera-Western New Guinea), the rest of which have the five-vowel system /i e a o u/ (with the possible exception of Buli, discussed below).
2. The vowels /ɛ/ and /a/ contrast only in single syllable words and in the final syllable of multisyllabic words.
3. /ɛ/ and /a/ are neutralized in prestressed syllables.
4. /ɔ/ occurs most often in stressed syllables.

Language data from the surrounding languages can help to explain some of the uniqueness of the Sawai vowel system. The neighboring languages of Gane and Kayoa are both approximately fifty to sixty percent cognate with Sawai. Gane (Teljur 1982) has an apparent five-vowel system /i e a o u/; there has been no analysis of Kayoa that I am aware of. The sequence of /oa/ in Gane and Kayoa words that are cognate with Sawai are commonly manifested with the low back vowel /ɔ/ in Sawai.

Phonology of Sawai

(77)   Gane   Sawai
       loal   pɛlɔy   'big'

       Kayoa   Sawai
       woya   wɔɛ   'water'
       ŋoan   ŋɔwɛn   'door'

       Tidore[8]   Sawai
       ŋoma   ŋɔ   'star'

Also, Gane words that have a final stressed syllable with /o/ as the nucleus, when preceded by /a/, are manifested by /ɔ/ in Sawai.

(78)   Gane   Sawai
       ha'on   mnɔm   'food'
       ma'on   mɔn   'boy'

It could be argued, therefore, that Sawai /ɔ/ is a result of coalescence of /o/ and /a/. Support for such a manifestation due to labial influence is also seen when the semivowel /w/ in Gane precedes a back vowel. This sequence is realized as the semivowel plus a low back vowel /ɔ/ in Sawai.

(79)   Gane   Sawai
       wosal   wɔsɛl   'to stand'
       wam   wɔm   'to come'
       wanto   wɔŋto   'meat'

This same phenomenon can be seen with an initial labial nasal followed by a back vowel. Sawai manifests this sequence as the nasal followed by the low back vowel /ɔ/.

(80)   Gane   Sawai
       mat   mɔt   'to die'

       Indonesian Sawai
       mata   mtɔ   'eye'

In addition to the comparative evidence, this coalescence of the phoneme sequence /oa/ is supported by the fact that /ɔ/ is the only vowel

---

[8]Tidore, a geographical neighbor of Sawai, is a Papuan language. Cognates are due to borrowing.

in Sawai not to occur as the final vowel of a vowel sequence. Also, the sequence /oa/ never occurs. Although the data is insufficient and the hypothesis cannot be established from Sawai alone, it appears that coalescence of some type occurred historically.

There is no clear evidence that the Sawai /ɛ/ has a vowel sequence counterpart in any of the neighboring languages. However, once again from the Teljur word list, Gane words that are cognate with Sawai shed some light on the Sawai vowel system. From these comparisons it can be seen that an unstressed closed final syllable in Gane is often manifested as an open final syllable in Sawai, with all final vowels realized in Sawai as the lax front vowel /ɛ/.

(81) | Gane | Sawai | |
|---|---|---|
| | katobat | kɛtobɛ | 'short' |
| | kunek | kunɛ | 'to know' |
| | mtubek | mtubɛ | 'to go first' |
| | manik | manɛ | 'chicken, bird' |

Other examples of unstressed Gane vowels being represented by the vowel /ɛ/ in Sawai include the following:

(82) | Gane | Sawai | |
|---|---|---|
| | ma'pin | mɛpin | 'girl, woman' |
| | m'loŋa | mloŋɛ | 'long' |
| | 'moda | morɛ | 'wind' |

The examples above seem to indicate that in unstressed syllables, the low back vowel /a/ of Gane is manifested by /ɛ/ in Sawai, the most neutral Sawai vowel.

In Maan's grammar of Buli (Maan 1951), a closely related language just to the north of Sawai, he states that there are five vowels in Buli /a e i o u/, and /a e o/ each occur with two variants. However, he states that the rules for the occurrence of the variants were not clear to him after a period of years in the language. From his grammar it is not clear if these vowels were ultimately analyzed as phonemes or allophones. The conclusion one gets from Maan's grammar is that he recognized at least a five-vowel system, with the possibility of eight vowels.

Although the Sawai system has developed historically from five vowels, there is no doubt that the present system has seven vowels. Among the arguments that can be given in support of a seven-vowel system are the following:

Phonology of Sawai

1. Both /ɛ/ and /ɔ/ have a substantial number of minimal pairs with their corresponding tense counterparts (see §1.2, Vowels).
2. Both /ɛ/ and /ɔ/ readily contrast in similar environments with /a/. Furthermore the vowel /ɛ/ is by far the most frequent vowel in Sawai, with /a/ the second most frequent. If /ɛ/ were somehow analyzed as an allophone of /a/, the phoneme /a/ would constitute fifty-five percent of Sawai vowel occurrences in my 2,300 word dictionary. The potential frequency of these two, if put together as one vowel, makes it an unlikely possibility.
3. If /ɛ/ or /ɔ/ were the result of synchronic vowel coalescence, their phonological presence would in some instances create a new situation of a three-vowel sequence, of which there are none in Sawai. Thus, such a source is not available.
4. /ɔ/ acts as a low back vowel in terms of the vowel fronting rule (see §2.1).
5. /ɛ/ is the only vowel that does not receive stress in the penultimate syllable, unless the syllable-final nucleus also has /ɛ/. If /ɛ/ is an allophone rather than a phoneme, the writing of the stress rule, which is very simple under the phoneme analysis (see §1.1), becomes more complex, due to the necessary ordering between the rule (yet to be specified) accounting for [ɛ], and the rule of stress placement. Otherwise stress can be stated solely on the basis of the syllable structure and the stem in the underlying representation.
6. Maan recognized at least a five-vowel system and possibly an eight-vowel system in the neighboring language of Buli, giving support for the possibility of a system that is quite similar to the seven-vowel analysis that I am suggesting for Sawai.

The Sawai phonological system is particularly interesting because of the seven-vowel system which characterizes it. The fact that it is the lax front vowel /ɛ/ which is apparently the unmarked vowel commonly inserted or deleted by phonological rule is especially striking. Reduplication is also very interesting, especially the reciprocal pattern utilizing a reduplicative template with two segments preassociated, a pattern apparently rare in languages of the world. While many questions remain, it is hoped that this brief introductory study will provide useful information for other scholars in the field.

References

Blust, Robert A. 1978. Eastern Malayo-Polynesian: A subgrouping argument. Pacific Linguistics C-61:181–234.

Latupapua, Z. J., Hasyim Rahman, F. A. X. Bixby, C. Lilipaty, and J. Th. S. Pattiselano. 1981–82. Struktur Bahasa Weda. Proyek Pendidikan Bahasa dan Sastra Indonesia dan Daerah Maluku. Jakarta: Dept. Pendidikan dan Kebudayaan.

Maan, G. 1951. Proeve Van Een Bulische Spraakkunst. S-Gravenhage Martinus Nijhoff.

Marantz, Alec. 1982. Re reduplication. Linguistic Inquiry 13:435–482.

Teljeur, Dik. 1982. Short wordlists from South Halmahera, Kayoa, Makian, Ternate, Tidore, and Bacan. Pacific Linguistics D-46:129–150.

Thomas, Michael. 1983. Pronominal prefixes in Sawai, a Bulic language. Pacific Linguistics C-77:285–289.

Whisler, Ronald. 1989. A dialect survey of Sawai. ms.

Kisar Phonology

John Christensen and Sylvia Christensen
Pattimura University and The Summer Institute of Linguistics

This paper gives a brief description of the phonology of the Kisar language as spoken in the village of Lebelau on the island of Kisar.[1] There are approximately 10,000 speakers living in twenty villages on the island which is located in the southwestern part of the Maluku province of Indonesia. In addition, Kisar-speaking people have migrated to the nearby islands of Wetar, Roma, Timor, and one village on the south coast of Seram. There are also a significant number of Kisar people living in Ambon, the provincial capital.

Kisar is an Austronesian language of Central Malayo-Polynesian (following Blust 1977). The most closely related languages are Roma and Luang which have a lexical similarity of sixty-two percent and fifty-five percent respectively to Kisar.[2] There are six main dialects spoken on the island of Kisar, but as the lexical similarity among them is between ninety-five percent to one hundred percent, the main distinction between the dialects seems to be intonation, rhythm, and lexical preference. One interesting

---

[1] On the island of Kisar there are two languages spoken: Kisar, spoken by the majority of people, and Oirata, a Papuan language, spoken by the people living in the two villages of East and West Oirata. The Kisar language is sometimes referred to as Meher, which is said to be derived from the name of the village these people originated from on the island of Timor Timur. Kisar speakers sometimes call their language Yotowawa, which is the Kisar word for the name of the island Kisar.

[2] See Taber (1990).

feature of this language is that it does not have any voiced stops and it has five contrastive voiceless stops.[3]

1. Stress

1.1. Stress on root words

Stress is not phonemic in this language. It occurs on the penultimate syllable of multisyllabic roots.[4] Periods are used to denote syllable boundaries unless they are already indicated by the presence of a stress mark.

(1)   ['ho.ro]   /horo/   'cough'
        ['ra.in]   /rain/   'dress'
        [ma'we.ke]   /maweke/   'girl'

In unaffixed monosyllabic roots the stress occurs on the ultimate syllable.

---

[3]Research for this paper was carried out under the auspices of Pattimura University and the Summer Institute of Linguistics. We lived in the village of Lebelau and studied this dialect from June 1988 to June 1990. Our main language resource people have been: Mia Mozes (60 year-old woman, wife of the traditional-customs leader), Leo Mozes (40 year-old man, local farmer), Cau Lainata (35 year-old man, school teacher), Di Lainata (35 year-old woman, school teacher), Cak Maromon (40 year-old man, local farmer), and Agu Maanana (young mother). We would like to express our thanks to these people and others who have helped us study their language. Examples for this paper are taken from a beginning lexicon of 1,000+ words, a number of texts and conversations, and our field data notebooks.

[4]There are a few words that apparently do not follow the stress rule. Some of these words are frozen contractions of two or more words in which stress has become attached to the antepenultimate syllable.

     ['namɛne]   /namene/   'before that'
     ['nanu]   +   ['mɛne] →   ['namɛne]
     before   that

     [ha'romɛne]   /haromene/   'probably'
     ['ha]   +   ['romo]   +   ['mɛne] →   [ha'romɛne]
     things   different   before

A few other words (and variations of these words) end in disyllabic /ia/ and do not follow the penultimate stress rule:

     [ɛn'pɛnia]   /enpenia/   'therefore'
     [naʔa'hɛnia]   /naʔahenia/   'he said it like this'

Further research is expected to prove that the final /a/ is a suffix or clitic since both words can occur without the final /a/. At this point there are not enough exceptions to merit positing phonemic stress.

(2) ['min]   /min/   'stay'
     ['ka]   /ka/   'not'

1.2. Stress on affixed forms

Prefixed and infixed forms. Stress occurs consistently on the penultimate syllable of prefixed and infixed forms. In prefixed monosyllabic roots stress does not occur on the root, rather it occurs on the penultimate syllable of the prefixed form.

(3)
    ['na-. ʔak]   /naʔak/   'he eats'
      3s   VI[5]
    ['no-. mun]   /nomun/   'he drinks'
      3s   VT
    ['na-. hur]   /nahur/   'he carries'
      3s   VT

In prefixed multisyllabic roots stress occurs on the penultimate syllable of the prefixed form. A secondary stress occurs on the second syllable to the left of the main stressed syllable, shown here by a double stress mark.

(4)
    [na-. 'ʔa.han]   /naʔahan/   'he is angry'
      3s   VI
    [na-. 'la.u]   /nalau/   'he laughs'
      3s   VI
    ["nam-. ku'ku.ru]   /namkukuru/   'he is sleeping'
      3s   RED VI

When a root is infixed, the stress occurs on the penultimate syllable of the infixed form.

---

[5]Abbreviations used in the examples of this article: 1p first-person plural, 1s first-person singular, 2s second-person singular, 3s third-person singular, DEF definite, INCL inclusive, INA POSS inalienable possession, N noun, NOM nominalizer, pl plural, POSS possessive marker, RED reduplication, TNS tense marker, VI verb intransitive, VT verb transitive.

(5) ['ho.wok] + [-nv-] → [ho'no.wok] /honowok/ 'the work'
     to work   NOM

   ['hɛ.lɛm] + [-nv-] → [hɛ'nɛ.lɛm] /henelem/ 'the setting'
     to set   NOM

   ['ko.wos] + [-nv-] → [ko'no.wos] /konowos/ 'sheath'
     to sheathe NOM

Suffixed forms. Stress occurs on the antepenultimate syllable of the suffixed form when the suffix is one syllable. When the suffix consists of two syllables the stress occurs on the penultimate syllable of the suffixed form. These two patterns are discussed separately.

Pattern 1. Monosyllabic suffix

When a monosyllabic suffix is added to a root, stress placement does not change to the new penultimate syllable of the suffixed form, but remains on the penultimate syllable of that root which is the antepenultimate syllable of the suffixed form.

(6) ['ra.in] + [-e] → ['raine] 'his dress'
      N   POSS

     [a'nu.lu] + [-e] → [a'nulue] 'his elder sibling'
      N   POSS

     ['o.hor] + [-ne] → ['ohorne] 'his navel'
      N   INA POSS

Final consonants may have an optional vocalic release which duplicates the preceding vowel. As in the case of monosyllabic suffixes, this additional vowel does not cause the stress to shift. The pronunciation of the vocalic release is optional.

(7) ['ka.ʔuk] ~ ['ka.ʔu.ku] 'afraid'
     ['na.kar] ~ ['na.ka.ra] 'house'

Pattern 2. Disyllabic suffix

Adding a disyllabic suffix causes stress to move to the penultimate syllable of the new suffixed form.[6] If the stressed syllable is consonant-final and the suffix is vowel-initial, resyllabification also occurs and the final-syllable coda of the stem becomes the onset of the first syllable in the suffix.

(8)   ['no.mun]   +   ['-ɛ.ui]
         VT   TNS
       [no.mu'nɛ.ui]   /nomuneui/   'drank'

       ['mo.u]   +   ['-ɛ.ui]
         VT   TNS
       [mo.u'ɛ.ui]   /moueui/   'cleaned'[7]

1.3. A metrical look at Kisar stress

Stress placement in Kisar appears to be sensitive to units of two because an addition of a monosyllabic suffix does not change stress placement but an addition of a disyllabic suffix does. Because of this binary sensitivity in this language, the metrical model provides a simple way to describe Kisar stress placement.

---

[6]It is likely that historically this disyllabic suffix was a separate word. Therefore a simple explanation could be proposed that stress is not shifted by a monosyllabic suffix, but does occur on compound words on the penultimate syllable of the second word. However, in the language as it is today this disyllabic suffix patterns as a suffix, not as a grammatical word.

[7]When a disyllabic word followed by a monosyllabic word is attached phonologically to a root word, a new stress group is formed.

       [ta'tana]   +   [-'ɛni]   +   [-'he]
       child   DEF   pl

First, the disyllabic word affects the root word according to Pattern 2 which states that stress will be penultimate.

       [ta'tana]   +   [-'ɛni]
       [tata'nɛni]   'this child'

Then the monosyllabic word is attached to the new phonological word according to Pattern 1 which states that a monosyllabic suffix results in stress on the antepenultimate syllable of the new phonological word.

       [tata'nɛni]   +   [-'he]
       [tata'nɛnihe]   'these children'

Hogg and McCully (1987:65), in their model of metrical stress, observe that stress strength is only measurable in relationship to sister syllables. This leads to the concept of metrical trees which are binary in nature and consist of weak and strong nodes. Stress placement in a given language is discussed in terms of foot and word levels. Two parameters are mentioned at each level: which node receives greater stress (right-headed versus left-headed), and which node receives lesser stress (left-branching or right-branching). One other important parameter is the side of the word from which the foot level and word level trees are built, left or right. The concept of extrametricality refers to syllables which lexically do not affect stress placement (Hogg and McCully 1987:109).

Three rules for Kisar stress placement are as follows.
1. All monosyllabic suffixes are extrametrical. This rule is applied before the other stress rules. Because monosyllabic suffixes are extrametrical they are not included in building the foot- and word-level trees and do not affect stress placement.
2. The foot-level tree is left-headed and right-branching binary. Trees are formed from the right edge of the word and the left node is strong.
3. The word-level tree is right-headed and left-branching n-ary. Therefore the right node is stressed more than any of the syllables branching to the left. The trees are formed from the right edge of the word.

Kisar Phonology

(9) Nonsuffixed examples

na.ʔa.han   'he is angry'

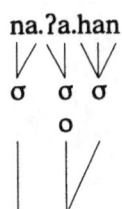

σ   σ   σ   syllable level

Rule 2. Foot level—left headed and right branching

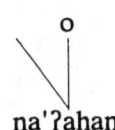

Rule 3. Word level—right headed and left branching

na'ʔahan

wa.na.ku.nu   'talk'

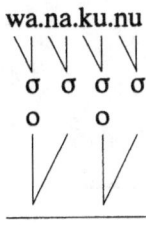

σ   σ   σ   σ   syllable level

Rule 2. Foot level—left headed and right branching

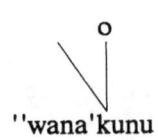

Rule 3. Word level—right headed and left branching

''wana'kunu

(10) Simple root + extrametrical monosyllabic suffix

o.hor.(-ne)   'naval'

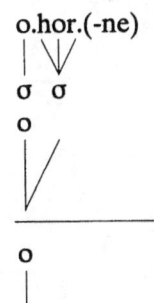

Rule 1. (ne) is extrametrical

σ   σ   syllable level

Rule 2. Foot level—ignores extrametrical syllable (ne)

Rule 3. Word level—ignores extrametrical syllable

'ohorne

(11) Root + polysyllabic affixes

ta'ta.na	-'e.ni	'this child'
ta.ta.n	-e.ni	v-deletion
ta.ta.	-'ne.ni	resyllabification

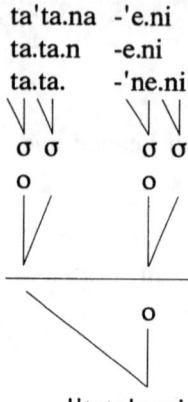

syllable level

Rule 2. Foot level

Rule 3. Word level

''tata'neni

tata.na	-'e.ni.	(-he)	'these children'
ta.ta.n	-'e.ni.	(-he)	v-deletion
ta.ta.	-'ne.ni.	(-he)	resyllabification
			Rule 1. (-he) is extrametrical

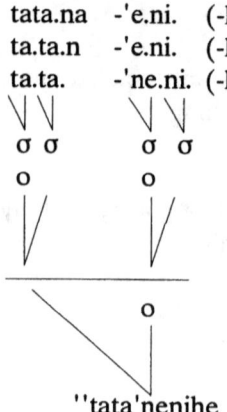

syllable level

Rule 2. Foot level—ignores extrametrical syllable (-he)

Rule 3. Word level—note word stress is on disyllabic suffix

''tata'nenihe

Kisar Phonology

2. System of phonemes

The system of phonemes in Kisar is displayed below.

(12) Consonants[8]

	labial	alveolar	alveopalatal	velar	glottal
stops	p	t	ț	k	ʔ
fricatives		s			h
nasals	m	n			
vibrant		r			
lateral		l			
semivowels	w		y		

(13) Vowels

	front	central	back
high	i		u
low	e	a	o

2.1. Consonants

Stops. Kisar has no voiced stops, however there are five contrastive voiceless stops. All stops are unaspirated. /ț/ and /ʔ/ occur word initially and medially. /p/, /t/ and /k/ occur in all positions.

/p/   [p] voiceless bilabial unaspirated stop

(14)   ['paku]   /paku/   'help'
       [na'pali]   /napali/   'cook'
       ['hap]   /hap/   'plant'

/t/   [t] voiceless alveolar unaspirated stop

(15)   [ta'tana]   /tatana/   'child'
       [man'tori]   /mantori/   'barber'
       ['tilu]   /tilu/   'on top of'

---

[8] /b/ occurs only in a few Indonesian borrowings. In many words borrowed from Indonesian this /b/ has become /p/.

/ṭ/ [ṭ] voiceless retroflexed alveolar stop[9]

(16) ['tɛrne]   /ṭerne/   'hear'
      [ʔi'ṭewe]   /iṭewe/   'directly'
      [ṭo'meku]   /ṭomeku/   'week'
      [mak'romoṭ]   /makromoṭ/   'strong one'

/k/ [k] voiceless unaspirated velar stop

(17) [nam'kaʔuk]   /namkaʔuk/   'afraid'
      ['kahi]   /kahi/   'salt water'
      [nak'niʔir]   /nakniʔir/   'sick'

/ʔ/ [ʔ] glottal stop. The glottal stop occurs word initially and medially. Word medially the glottal stop is phonemic. Word initially the glottal stop may be phonetic or phonemic which becomes evident only after the morphophonemic processes are applied. If the glottal stop is phonemic, morphophonemically it will surface as a consonant (see §5.5). If the glottal stop is phonetic it will not be inserted until all morphophonemic processes are complete; the word is treated as vowel-initial. Then the following late glottal insertion rule applies.

(18) Glottal insertion rule
     ∅ → ʔ/# _v

This rule inserts glottals before all free standing v-initial words. (See §5.4 for a more complete discussion on the initial glottal.)[10]

---

[9]This stop phoneme /ṭ/ is probably a reflex of an historical voiced alveolar, which contrasted with a voiceless dental stop. When the voicing contrast became neutralized, the point of articulation became contrastive.

[10]All v-initial words appear to have an initial phonetic glottal because there are no examples of minimal contrast with an initial glottal and without an initial glottal; the phonetic distinction between [ʔewi] and [ewi] does not exist in this language. However, although all v-initial words have the same glottal onset, not all v-initial words respond to morphophonemic processes in the same manner. Therefore we must posit a phonemic initial glottal for the v-initial words where the initial glottal surfaces during morphophonemic processes and a phonetic glottal for those v-initial words where the initial glottal does not surface during morphophonemic processes (see §5.5).

(19) ['yaʔu]   /yaʔu/   (1s)
    [maʔa'ruru]   /maʔaruru/   'great'
    [nak'niʔir]   /nakniʔir/   'sick'
    [ʔapun]   /ʔapun/   'pregnant'
    [ʔɛlɛk]   /ʔelek/   'close'

Fricatives. Both fricatives are voiceless and occur in all positions.

/s/   [s] voiceless alveolar grooved fricative

(20) ['sapu]   /sapu/   'orange, citrus'
    [sa'polu]   /sapolu/   'pants'
    ['ɛsne]   /esne/   'pineapple'
    ['lopos]   /lopos/   'to boil'

/h/   [h] voiceless glottal fricative

(21) ['ha]   /ha/   'stuff'
    ['maha]   /maha/   'tired'
    ['manha]   /manha/   'hot'
    ['paʔah]   /paʔah/   'break'

Nasals. Both nasals occur in all positions.

/m/   [m] voiced bilabial nasal

(22) ['meʔe]   /meʔe/   'again'
    [nam'wali]   /namwali/   'becomes'
    ['kɛmɛn]   /kemen/   'body'
    ['hɛlɛm]   /helem/   'dive'

/n/   [n] voiced alveolar nasal

(23) ['noro]   /noro/   'with'
    ['ɛsne]   /esne/   'pineapple'
    ['manha]   /manha/   'hot'
    ['naʔan]   /naʔan/   'eat'

Vibrant. The vibrant /r/ occurs in all positions.

/r/   [ɾ] voiced alveolar flap
[r] voiced alveolar trill occurs in free variation with [ɾ]. This is a short trill involving two or three tongue taps. It is most pronounced when the geminate /r/ occurs, but may also occur as syllable onset and coda.

(24)   ['ɾi]   ~   ['ri]   /ri/   'person'
        ['toɾi]   ~   ['tori]   /tori/   'cut'
        [wa'liuɾ] ~ [wa'liur]   /waliur/   'return'

Lateral. The lateral /l/ occurs in all positions.

/l/   [l] voiced alveolar lateral

(25)   ['liwar]   /liwar/   'fly'
        [ʔɛli'moʔo]   /elimoʔo/   'dirt'
        ['ʈeʔul]   /ʈeʔul/   'short'

Semivowels. Both semivowels occur word initially and medially.

/w/   [w] voiced bilabial nonsyllabic semivowel

(26)   ['wawi]   /wawi/   'pig'
        ['yawa]   /yawa/   'bottom'
        ['siwar]   /siwar/   'leak'

[β] voiced bilabial fricative, occurs in free variation with [w] before front vowels. The friction is more pronounced when /w/ precedes /i/.

(27)   [wɛ'wɛre]   ~   [wɛ'βɛre]   /wewere/   'together'
        ['weli]   ~   ['βeli]   /weli/   'buy'
        [oi'rawi]   ~   [oi'raβi]   /oirawi/   'yesterday'

/y/   [y] voiced alveopalatal nonsyllabic semivocoid

(28)   ['yaʔu]   /yaʔu/   (1s)
        [kali'yoro]   /kaliyoro/   'star'
        [yak'yaka]   /yakyaka/   'really damaged'

Consonant contrasts.

/p/ and /w/

(29) ['paku]   /paku/   'help'
      ['waku]   /waku/   'rock'

      ['poʔon]   /poʔon/   'look'
      ['woʔor]   /woʔor/   'mountain'

      ['hopon]   /hopon/   'order'
      ['howok]   /howok/   'work'

/t/ and /ṭ/

(30) ['take]   /take/   'hit'
      ['ṭalu]   /ṭalu/   'stallion'

      [ra'pita]   /rapita/   'to fight'
      [ʔou'kiṭa]   /oukiṭa/   'anywhere'

      ['tatan]   /tatana/   'small'
      ['waṭan]   /waṭan/   'cut'

/k/ and /ʔ/

(31) ['kuku]   /kuku/   'pound'
      ['kuʔu]   /kuʔu/   'immerse'

      [wa'keke]   /wakeke/   'chisel'
      [wa'keʔe]   /wakeʔe/   'very'

      ['wokor]   /wokor/   'mix'
      ['woʔor]   /woʔor/   'mountain'

/h/ and /ʔ/

(32) ['haha]   /haha/   'stuff'
     ['haʔa]   /haʔa/   'to climb'

     ['ʔihin] /ihin/   'contents'
     ['ʔiʔin] /iʔin/   'fish'

     ['rahu]   /rahu/   'one hundred'
     ['raʔu]   /raʔu/   'dish'

/r/ and /l/

(33) ['raʔu]   /raʔu/   'dish'
     ['laʔu]   /laʔu/   'marten'

     ['roʔo]   /roʔo/   'corral'
     ['loʔo]   /loʔo/   'maybe'

     ['hara]   /hara/   'to blossom'
     ['hala]   /hala/   'matter'

/t/ and /r/

(34) ['tolle] /tolle/ 'watch'
     ['rolle] /rolle/ 'pet'

     ['tate]   /tate/   'older sibling'
     ['rahu]   /rahu/   'hundred'

     [tə'tana] /tatan/ 'child'
     [tə'rana] /tara/   'little'

/ṭ/ and /r/

(35) ['ṭaʔuk]   /ṭaʔuk/   'wild'
      ['raʔuk]   /raʔuk/   'pick up'

      ['ṭiuk]   /ṭiuk/   'toss'
      ['riuk]   /riuk/   'hour'

      ['kaṭi]   /kaṭi/   'stab'
      ['hari]   /hari/   'open'

2.2. Vowels.

Front. All front vowels occur word initially, medially, and finally.

/i/   [i] voiced high close front unrounded vocoid

(36) ['ʔiṭa]   /iṭa/   'one'
      ['ʔiʔin]   /iʔin/   'fish'
      ['ʔoṭi]   /oṭi/   'bring'

/e/   [e] voiced mid close front unrounded vocoid. Occurs word finally and before all vowels. [e] tends to occur before /w/, /k/, /ʔ/, and /h/ in open syllables, but is in free variation with [ɛ] in this environment in some words.

(37) ['meki]   /meki/   'low tide'
      [ʔal'wɛrhe]   /alwerhe/   'rice'
      [kə'leʔuk]   /keleʔuk/   'corn'
      ['mei]   /mei/   'table'

[ɛ] voiced mid open front unrounded vocoid. Occurs in closed syllables and does not occur word finally. [ɛ] tends to occur before /p/, /m/, /y/, /ṭ/, and all alveolars in open syllables, but is in free variation with [e] in this environment.

(38) ['ʔɛsne]   /esne/   'pineapple'
      [na'ṭɛṭɛm]   /naṭeṭem/   'to be used to'
      [na'hɛre]   /nahere/   'to cry'
      [ʔal'wɛrhe]   /alwerhe/   'rice'

[e] and [ɛ] in free variation:

(39) [hehenamɛne] ~ [hɛhɛnamɛne]   'until'
     [wɛli]   ~ [weli]   'to buy'
     [mɛʔe]   ~ [meʔe]   'also'
     [nahehe]   ~ [nahɛhɛ]   'to try hard'

[ə] voiced mid close central unrounded vocoid. This occurs in fast speech in unstressed syllables preceding stressed syllables.

(40) [kə'leʔuk]   /keleʔuk/   'corn'
     [mə'mɛre]   /memere/   'red'

Central. This vowel occurs word initially, medially, and finally.

/a/ [a] voiced low open central unrounded vocoid

(41) ['ʔahu]   /ahu/   'dog'
     ['wali]   /wali/   'return'
     ['kakan] /kakan/   'to boil'
     [wo'aka] /woaka/   'four'

[ə] voiced mid close central unrounded vocoid. This occurs in fast speech in unstressed syllables preceding stressed syllables.[11]

(42) [tə'rana]   /tarana/   'little'
     [nə'naʔan] /nanaʔan/   'food'

Back. These vowels occur word initially, medially, and finally.

/u/ [u] voiced high close back rounded vocoid

(43) [ʔulu'wakun] /uluwakun/ 'head'
     [ʔum'ʔumu]   /ʔumʔumu/   'brush'
     [wa'kuku]   /wakuku/   'study'
     ['rahu]   /rahu/   'hundred'

---

[11]Both /e/ and /a/ become [ə] in fast speech in unstressed syllables preceding stressed syllables. In slow speech the distinction between /e/ and /a/ is maintained thus providing evidence that [ə] is a allophone of both /e/ and /a/.

Kisar Phonology

/o/ [o] voiced mid close back rounded vocoid

(44) ['ʔoir]   /oir/   'water'
     ['poʔon]   /poʔon/ 'look'
     ['noro]   /noro/   'with'
     ['porho]   /porho/ 'smell'

Vowel contrasts.

/i/ and /e/

(45) ['hir]   /hir/   'they'
     ['hɛr]   /her/   'beach'

     ['kali]   /kali/   'rope'
     ['kale]   /kale/   'gone'

     ['mori]   /mori/   'live'
     ['more]   /more/   'together'

/e/ and /a/

(46) ['ʔein]   /ein/   'foot'
     ['ʔain]   /ain/   (3s)

     ['meki]   /meki/   'low tide'
     ['maki]   /maki/   'die'

     ['wɛli]   /weli/   'buy'
     ['wali]   /wali/   'return'

/a/ and /o/

(47) ['ʔaur]   /aur/   'lime, citrus'
     ['ʔour]   /our/   'bamboo'

     ['rahu]   /rahu/   'hundred'
     ['rohu]   /rohu/   'cut'

     ['haʔa]   /haʔa/   'to climb'
     ['hoʔo]   /hoʔo/   'return'

/o/ and /u/

(48) ['hopon]   /hopon/   'order'
     ['hopun]   /hopun/   'meeting'

     ['koʔo]   /koʔo/   'palm wine'
     ['koʔu]   /koʔu/   'far'

     ['nano]   /nano/   'from'
     ['nanu]   /nanu/   'before'

3. Ambivalent phonemes

3.1. Semivowels

The front and back high-vocoids [i] and [u] are interpreted as the semivowels /y/ and /w/ when they occur in the syllable onset position and are therefore nonsyllabic. They do not occur in the syllable-coda position.

(49) ['yono]   /yono/   'don't!'
     ['wani]   /wani/   'bee'
     [kali'yoro] /kaliyoro/ 'star'
     ['wawan]   /wawan/   'on top'

3.2. Vowel sequences

There are sequences of vowels which can be interpreted either as separate segments, each vowel filling a peak slot in its own syllable, as diphthongs, or as sequences of consonant plus vowel. These ambivalent vowel sequences are, [ai], [au], [ei], [eu], [oi], [ou], [iu], [ui], [io], and [ia].

Kisar Phonology

(50) [ˈʔa.im]   /aim/   (1p)
      [ʔarˈpa.u]   /arpau/   'buffalo'
      [ˈne.i]   /nei/   'snake'
      [ˈle.u]   /leu/   'bed'
      [ˈʔo.ir]   /oir/   'water'
      [ˈlo.ur]   /lour/   'ocean'
      [ˈri.uk]   /riuk/   'hit'
      [mɛrˈwu.i]   /merwui/   'wild'
      [riˈor.ha]   /riorha/   'God'
      [la.riˈa.la] /lariala/   'please'

These vowel sequences are analyzed as separate fillers of individual peak slots of different syllables for the following reasons:

Nonsuspect vowel sequences. There are nonsuspect vowel sequences in Kisar. Pike (1947:128) points out that suspect sequences should be analyzed in light of the nonsuspect patterns that occur in the language. Since the following nonsuspect vowel sequences do occur, the ambivalent vowel sequences can be analyzed as separate vowels filling separate slots.

(51) [laˈɛṭi]   /laeṭi/   'went'
      [haˈɛnhi]   /haenhi/   'also'
      [paˈeku]   /paeku/   'job'
      [hoˈɛṭi]   /hoeṭi/   'married'
      [maeˈkana]   /maekana/   'little girl'

Stress. As mentioned in §1, stress is predictable and occurs on the penultimate syllable of the word. Notice that stress falls on the penultimate syllable whether that syllable is in the root or is in the prefix.

(52) [na-.ˈʔa.han] /naʔahan/ 'he is angry'
      [ˈna-.ʔak]   /naʔak/   'he eats'
      [ˈna-.hur]   /nahur/   'he carries'
      [ˈra.ʔu]   /raʔu/   'dish'
      [no.u-.ˈna.ku] /nounaku/ 'to advise'

Stress placement on the following words indicates that the vowel sequences are separate fillers of peak slots of two syllables.

(53) [na.ʔa-.ˈmo.u]   /naʔamou/   'he cleans'
      [na.ʔa.ˈpe.i]   /naʔapei/   'he tricks'
      [na.ʔi-.ˈna.u]   /naʔinau/   'he peers'
      [na-.ˈla.u]   /nalau/   'he laughs'
      [ʔarˈpa.u]   /arpau/   'buffalo'
      [na-.ˈno.in]   /nanoin/   'he looks'
      [ʔinˈho.i]   /inhoi/   'who'
      [koˈno.in]   /konoin/   'stomach'
      [niˈko.in]   /nikoin/   'yard'
      [ʔo.roˈka.i]   /orokai/   'leader'
      [ʔoˈwa.i]   /owai/   'bamboo pipe'
      [poˈla.i]   /polai/   'wire'
      [pu.iˈla.i]   /puilai/   'proud'
      [ru.ruˈwa.i]   /ruruwai/   'earthquake'
      [ʔa.haˈwa.ir]   /ahawair/   'tree leaves'
      [ʔiˈna.i]   /inai/   'girl'

If these vowel sequences were to be analyzed as units in single syllables, a widespread exception would have to be made to the stress rule. In Kisar, stress is almost uniformly penultimate in nature; when suffixes are added the stress remains penultimate or shifts to antepenultimate; in no instance (except monosyllabic words) does the stress fall on the ultimate syllable.

Stress within vowel sequences. In the following words stress falls on the second vowel in the vowel sequence further showing that these sequences are individual peaks of two syllables. If these vowel sequences were diphthongs then stress would not be able to divide the diphthong.

(54) [naˈi.se]   /naise/   'like'
      [paˈe.ku]   /paeku/   'job'
      [pa.na.liˈon.ne]   /panalionne/   'port'
      [na.ʈiˈa.ur]   /naʈiaur/   'fall'
      [woˈi.ra]   /woira/   'how many'[12]

---

[12]Some of these words occur in free variation with /ʔ/ occurring between the two vowels.

  [naˈise] ~ [naˈʔise]
  [paˈeku] ~ [paˈʔeku]
  [woˈira] ~ [woˈʔira]

Reverse sequence rule (see Robinson 1970). This rule states that when the reverse sequence of an ambivalent sequence occurs in similar positions, the constituents of the ambivalent sequence are filling two peak slots.

(55) ['ri.uk]   /riuk/   'hour'
      ['hu.ik]   /huik/   'pick out'

      ['ka.un]   /kaun/   'not yet'
      ['su.ar]   /suar/   'hide'

      [po'la.i]   /polai/   'wire'
      ['pɛ.ni.a]   /penia/   'therefore'[13]

Syllabicity. The vowel sequences are of a longer duration than a single vowel. There are some words where the two vowels very definitely SOUND LIKE two syllables, as in the following examples.

(56) /ṭe.ul/   'short'
      /le.u/   'bed'
      /mu.i.ṭa.u/ 'name'

Other words with vowel sequences filling the peak slots are not so distinct, but their timing is closer to two moras as compared to words with a single vowel as the peak slot filler, which are closer to one mora.

(57) One mora   Two moras
      /min/   'stay'   /mai/   'come'
      /kan/   'he did not'   /kaun/   'not yet'
      /la/   'go'   /lour/   'ocean'
      /nahur/   'he carries'   /nanoin/ 'he looks'

Reduplication. The reduplication process (see §5.3) allows the vowel sequences to be divided, which also shows that these sequences are not units.

---

[13]This word is an exception to the penultimate stress rule. See footnote 4.

(58) /ṭeul/   'short'
     /ṭeṭeul/   'very short'

     /naʔamou/   'clean'
     /naʔamomou/   'really clean'

     /mai/   'come'
     /mamai/   'coming'

Syllable patterns. CV, CVC, V, and VC are the univalent syllable patterns.

(59) CV   /ka/   'not'
            /la/   'go'

      CVC   /min/   'stay'
            /hap/   'plant'

      V   /e.ni/   'this'
            /pa.e.ku/ 'job'

      VC   /es.ne/   'pineapple'
            /in.ho.i/ 'who'

The univalent syllable patterns allow for each vowel in a vowel sequence to be realized as a separate filler of a peak slot in a syllable.

(60) ['mai]   /ma.i/   CV.V
      ['aim]   /a.im/   V.VC
      ['lour]   /lo.ur/   CV.VC
      [in'hoi] /in.ho.i/ VC.CV.V

There are no univalent consonant clusters within syllables. Therefore the second vowel in a vowel sequence cannot be interpreted as a consonant when immediately followed by a consonant within the same syllable.

Kisar Phonology

(61) /lour/ 'ocean' */lowr/
　　　/nanoin/ 'he looks' */nanoyn/
　　　/aim/ 'us' */aym/
　　　/ein/ 'foot' */eyn/[14]

Hyman (1975:93) mentions that the phonemic analysis which posits the fewest phonemes is judged to be the most economical. If the vowel sequences were to be realized as diphthongs, more vowel phonemes would be required. If the vowel sequences were considered as vowel clusters within a syllable, more syllable types would be required. Realizing these vowel sequences as separate fillers for peak slots of syllables provides the most economical analysis. As shown above, this is also the analysis which finds greatest support in terms of the overall patterns of the language.

3.3. Geminate sequences

Geminate consonant sequences. The phonological sequences [nn], [ll], and [rr] contrast with [n], [l], and [r] respectively word medially. Because of this contrast and the fact that the sequences extend across syllable boundaries, these sequences are analyzed as geminate phonemes (sequences of two phonemes) rather than as single phonemes.

(62) /nn/ ['ʔan.na] /anna/ 'year'
　　　/n/ ['ʔan.a] /ana/ 'child'
　　　/ll/ ['kal.le] /kalle/ 'the road'
　　　/l/ ['ka.le] /kale/ 'gone'
　　　/rr/ ['hɛr.re] /herre/ 'change'
　　　/r/ ['hɛ.re] /here/ 'do it now'

Geminate vowel sequences. The phonological sequences [oo], [aa], and [ii] also occur. To date only one minimal pair has been found contrasting [ii] with [i]. Because of such minimal pairs, plus syllable patterns that allow for two vowels together, and the rule for penultimate stress placement in

---

[14]Historically, we can see these vowel sequences came from distinct syllables (from Wurm and Wilson 1975; the abbreviations for the source refer to the proto language, author, reference).

Source	PAN	Kisar	Gloss
PAMS	apu(y)	ai	'fire'
PAMS	kayu	au	'wood'
PANB	taruq	kau	'put'
PANPAWS	mari	mai	'come'
PANDLO	bayaᴅ	pair	'pay'

reduplicated forms, these sequences are analyzed as geminate phoneme sequences rather than separate unit phonemes. Following the analyzed vowel sequences above, each member of the geminate is interpreted as filling the nucleus of a separate syllable.

(63) Minimal pair   ['wo.hi]   /wohi/   'paddle'
                    [wo'hi.i] /wohii/ 'nine'

(64) Syllable patterns VC.CV.V
                    [ar'pa.u] /arpau/ 'buffalo'
                    [wo'ʔa.a] /woʔaa/ 'eight'

(65) Stress in reduplication
                    ['ho.o]   /hoo/   'marry'
                    [ho'ho.o] /hohoo/ 'wedding'

Note that in this final example, if this were a nongeminate [o], ['ho] instead of ['hoo], then the stress in the reduplicated form would be on the penultimate, as in *['hoho], which does not occur. Instead the stress occurs on the penultimate syllable of the reduplicated form as seen above, confirming the disyllabic geminate analysis.

4. Distribution of phonemes

4.1. Syllables

The syllable in Kisar consists of a vowel peak with an optional consonant onset and an optional consonant coda. The four syllable types are listed in order of frequency of occurrence: CV, CVC, V and VC. All syllable types may form monosyllabic words.

Kisar Phonology

(66) CV   /la/   'to'
           /pi/   'sago'
      CVC   /min/   'live'
           /hap/   'plant'
      V   /e/   'or'
           /o/   (2s)
      VC   /ik/   (1p INCL)
           /an/   (3s)

These syllable types join together freely to form words with the following restrictions: CV, CVC, and V occur in all positions; VC occurs only word initially and finally.

4.2. Consonants

Consonant distribution can be seen in the following chart where the vertical column shows the first consonant and the horizontal line shows the second consonant in the consonant clusters. These occur across syllable boundaries. The consonants are organized by point of articulation. /m/, /n/, /r/, and /l/ seem to occur most often as first members of these clusters. The second members that occur most often are /p/, /n/, /l/, and /k/.

(67)

C1\C2	p	m	w	t	s	n	r	l	ṭ	y	k	ʔ	h
m	mp	—	mw	mt	—	mn	mr	ml	—	my	mk	mʔ	mh
s	sp	—	—	st	—	sn	—	sl	—	—	sk	—	—
n	np	nm	nw	nt	—	nn	—	nl	nṭ	ny	nk	nʔ	nh
r	rp	rm	rw	—	rs	rn	rr	rl	—	ry	rk	—	rh
l	—	lm	lw	—	—	—	—	ll	—	—	lk	—	lh
k	kp	km	—	—	ks	kn	kr	kl	—	ky	—	kʔ	kh
h	—	hm	—	—	—	—	—	—	—	—	—	—	—

4.3. Vowels

Most vowels occur in all syllable types in all positions in the word with the following exceptions: in the v syllable type /o/ does not occur word medially; in the vc syllable type /a e o/ do not occur word finally and /i a u/ do not occur word medially.

(68)

		/i/	/e/	/a/	/o/	/u/
CV						
	initial	hi.ʔi	he.he	ha.ra	to.ro	ʈu.ʔu
	medial	o.u.ki.ʈa	am.he.ni	or.ka.ru	a.po.lu	u.lu.wa.kun
	final	e.wi	es.ne	an.na	on.no	a.hu
CVC						
	initial	kir.na	ker.re	kal.le	los.ne	hun.hu.ni
	medial	a.pin.ha	al.wer.he	a.ʔa.lar.na	o.hor.ne	wa.kun.ku.nu
	final	e.lik	e.rek	o.ras	o.kon	o.mun
V						
	initial	i.ʈa	e.wi	a.nan	o.mun	u.lu.wa.kun
	medial	o.i.ra.wi	pa.e.ku	tu.ri.a.na	———	a.u.ka.ni
	final	i.na.i	ri.e	en.pe.ni.a	ki.o	a.u
VC						
	initial	in.ho.i	es.ne	ar.pa.u	or.na.na	um.ʔu.mu
	medial	———	ha.en.hi	———	pa.na.li.on.ne	———
	final	o.ir	———	———	———	a.ur

In the following chart, the vertical column contains the first vowel and the horizontal line contains the second vowel in the clusters that occur across syllable boundaries.

(69)

	/i/	/e/	/a/	/o/	/u/
/i/	wo.hi.i	ri.e	la.ri.a.la	ki.o	ri.uk
/e/	me.i	———	———	———	ʈe.ul
/a/	ma.i	pa.e.ku	wo.ʔa.a	———	ka.un
/o/	po.ir	ho.e.ʈi	———	ho.o	mo.u
/u/	mu.i.ʈa.u	ho.ru.e.ʈi	pa.ku.a.la	———	———

It can be seen that the mid vowels are restricted; /e/ rarely occurs as the first member of a cluster, /o/ rarely occurs as the second member.

5. Morphophonemics

Two main processes occur in the morphophonemic changes in this language: vowel reduplication and final vowel elision. First, examples are shown of how these work. Next, reduplication is discussed briefly. Then, the various processes which affect the first-person-singular pronoun and the corresponding negative pronoun are shown. Finally, examples are given of how the morphophonemic processes show whether a V-initial word has an initial phonetic or phonemic glottal.

5.1. Vowel reduplication in the nominalizing infix

The nominalizing infix -nV- reduplicates the vowel in the first syllable of the root verb.

(70)   [wa'kunu]   /wakunu/   'to talk (verb)'
        [wana'kunu]   /wanakunu/   'talk (noun)'

        ['tori]   /tori/   'to cut'
        [to'nori]   /tonori/   'scissors'

        ['hɛlɛm]   /helem/   'to go down'
        [hɛ'nɛlɛm]   /henelem/   'sunset, setting (noun)'

5.2. Final vowel elision on nouns and verbs

When a morpheme ending in /e/, /o/, or /a/ is joined morphophonemically to a vowel-initial morpheme, the /e/, /o/, or /a/ elides. The vowels /i/ and /u/ do not elide unless the initial vowel is an /i/ or /u/ respectively. Resyllabification occurs after elision causing the onset of the final syllable in the stem to become the onset of the syllable containing the clitic or suffix.

Following are examples of where the /e/, /o/ and /a/ elide.

(71)   [lere -eni]   /le'reni/   'this day'
        day   this

        [maweke -onne]   /mawe'konne/   'that girl'
        girl   that

        [papa -eni]   /pa'peni/   'this father'
        father this

        [ornoho -iṭa]   /orno'hiṭa/   'one mouse'
        mouse   one

        [naroho -eṭi]   /naro'heṭi/   'he bathed'
        he bathes TNS

There are no morphemes with an initial /u/ to show that a final /u/ will elide before an initial /u/. Resyllabification does not occur with a final /i/ and /u/ followed by a nonsimilar vowel.

Following are examples of where /i/ and /u/ do and do not elide.

(72) [moʔoni -iṭa]   /moʔo'niṭa/   'one boy'
      boy   one

      [muʔu -eni]   /muʔu'eni/   'this banana'
      banana this

      [pipi -onne]   /pipi'onne/   'that goat'
      goat that

5.3. Reduplication

A full description of reduplication in Kisar is beyond the scope of this paper. Simply stated, a certain number of segments from the word can be reduplicated, usually beginning at the stressed syllable. The two most typical patterns of reduplication are reduplication of the stressed CV or CVC of the stem, and full reduplication.

(73) nam'kuru   'sleeps'
      namku'kuru   'sleeping'

      'deul   'short'
      de'deul   'really short'

      'huni   'boil'
      hun'huni   'boiling'

      'mori   'alive'
      mori'mori   'living'

      maʔa'nana   'when'
      maʔananmaʔa'nana   'whenever'

5.4. Pronouns

First-person-singular pronoun, *yaʔu*. In Kisar there are verbs which are vowel initial and verbs which are consonant initial. When *yaʔu*

Kisar Phonology

precedes a C-initial verb no change takes place; however, when *yaʔu* precedes a V-initial verb the following changes occur:[15]

/yaʔu/ + C-initial verbs:

(74) yaʔu ṭerne 'I hear'
 yaʔu hiʔi 'I make'
 yaʔu leʔu 'I carry'
 yaʔu moko 'I vomit'

/yaʔu/ + V-initial verbs:

(75) yaʔu alaʔa 'I go'
 yaʔ alaʔa v-deletion; the final /u/ of /yaʔu/ is deleted[16]
 ya alaʔa c-deletion; the glottal of /yaʔ/ is deleted[17]
 ya alaʔa v-assimilation; the final vowel of the prefix assimilates to initial vowel of verb
 ya ʔalaʔa glottal insertion rule inserts a phonetic glottal on all free-standing v-initial words after the morphophonemic processes are completed.

(76) yaʔu omun 'I drink'
 yaʔ omun v-deletion
 ya omun c-deletion
 yo omun v-assimilation
 yo ʔomun glottal insertion rule

(77) yaʔu iʔik 'I pick up'
 yaʔ iʔik v-deletion
 ya iʔik c-deletion
 yi iʔik v-assimilation
 yi ʔiʔik glottal insertion rule

First-person-singular-negative pronoun, *kaʔu*. The same types of processes occur on the negative pronoun *kaʔu*, with the exception of

---

[15]These sets of changes occur only on the pronoun /yaʔu/ and the corresponding negative pronoun. Evidence for analyzing this morpheme as a pronoun rather than a prefix lies in the fact that the negative as well as various auxiliary verbs can come between the pronoun and the main verb. (Pike and Pike 1977:112) For a fuller treatment of subject verb agreement see Blood, to appear.

[16]This vowel deletion rule is different from the vowel elision described in §5.2 since /i/ and /u/ do not normally elide. This vowel deletion occurs only in this specific process.

[17]One might ask why the glottal deletion rule is necessary. The glottal must be deleted at this point because vowel assimilation occurs.

V-assimilation.[18] This negative pronoun occurs between the pronoun and the verb. The pronoun *ya?u* does not change in this construction because it no longer precedes a vowel-initial morpheme.

(78)   *ya?u ka?u*   *aroho*   'I did not bathe'
        ya?u ka?   *aroho*   v-deletion
        ya?u ka   *aroho*   c-deletion
        ya?u ka   *?aroho*   glottal insertion rule

(79)   *ya?u ka?u*   *omun*   'I did not drink'
        ya?u ka?   *omun*   v-deletion
        ya?u ka   *omun*   c-deletion
        ya?u ka   *?omun*   glottal insertion rule

(80)   *ya?u ka?u*   *eku*   'I did not pick'
        ya?u ka?   *eku*   v-deletion
        ya?u ka   *eku*   c-deletion
        ya?u ka   *?eku*   glottal insertion rule

5.5. Initial glottal stop

As mentioned in §2.1, glottal stop occurs phonemically word initially and medially. It also occurs phonetically word initially on all V-initial words. The initial phonemic glottal can be distinguished from the initial phonetic glottal only by observing morphophonemic processes. During application of morphophonemic processes, the phonemic initial glottal surfaces as a member of the consonant class. The phonetic initial glottal does not surface until the morphophonemic processes are completed, then a phonetic glottal is assigned to all V-initial words by a late glottal insertion rule.

(81)   Glottal insertion rule
        $\emptyset \rightarrow \text{?}/\#\_\_v$

The following discussion shows just why this differentiation is made.

***ya?u* and initial glottal stop on V-initial verbs.** As mentioned in the preceding section, *ya?u* does not change when followed by a C-initial verb and does change when followed by a V-initial verb. In the following

---

[18]Because V-assimilation does not occur, an alternative analysis could have only V-deletion applying in these derivations. In either case, the same surface form results. More research is needed to resolve this question.

examples notice that certain V-initial verbs pattern as C-initial verbs; it is these which are interpreted as having the phonemic initial glottal. Other V-initial verbs do not pattern as C-initial verbs; these are interpreted as having only a phonetic initial glottal.

(82) Pronoun + c-initial verbs

    yaʔu ṭerne   'I hear'
    yaʔu hiʔi   'I do'
    yaʔu karu   'I bury'

(83) Pronoun + v-initial verbs with an initial phonemic glottal

    yaʔu ʔapun   'I am pregnant'
    yaʔu ʔomhe   'I wash'
    yaʔu ʔelek   'I close'

(84) Pronoun + v-initial verbs with an initial phonetic glottal

    ya ʔamkuru   'I sleep'
    ye ʔesne   'I kill'
    yo ʔomun   'I drink'

Until this morphophonemic process is applied it is impossible to differentiate between the initial glottal in the examples above; they are identical phonetically. After observing this process, however, it is clear that the examples in (83) have an initial phonemic glottal and those in (84) have an initial phonetic glottal.

Reduplication and v-initial words. In addition to the allomorphy discussed above, the distinction between initial phonemic glottal stop and initial phonetic glottal stop is seen also in reduplication. The following examples of reduplication show that an initial phonemic glottal surfaces in the process of reduplication.

(85) /ʔumu/   'dense'
      /ʔumʔumu/   'very dense'
      *umumu

(86) /ʔalam/   'night'
      /ʔalʔalam/   'early morning'
      *alalam

(87) /ʔapun/ 'pregnant'
/ʔapʔapun/ 'to be pregnant'
*apapun

The following example shows the reduplication of an initial phonetic glottal. This phonetic glottal does not surface in reduplication.

(88) [ʔeni] /eni/ 'this'
[ʔenieni] /enieni/ 'this one here'
*eniʔeni

Nouns and verbs + V-initial clitics and suffixes. The following examples show that V-initial clitics and suffixes have only a phonetic initial glottal stop, not a phonemic glottal stop. Notice the final vowel ELIDES (see §5.2) and no initial glottal surfaces.

(89) Nouns + v-initial clitic

[lere -eni] /lereni/ 'this day'
day this

[maweke -onne] /mawekonne/ 'that girl'
girl that

[ornoho -iṭa] /ornohiṭa/ 'one mouse'
mouse one

(90) Verbs + v-initial suffix

[namaka -eṭi] /namakeṭi/ 'he awoke'
he awakens TNS

[herre -eṭi] /herreṭi/ 'already changed'
change TNS

[moko -e] /moke/ 'her vomit'
vomit POSS

The initial phonetic glottal on the clitics *eni* and *onno* does not surface until all morphophonemic processes are finished and they are free standing, as in (91); the suffixes *-eṭi* and *-e* never occur by themselves.

(91) [ʔonno inhawa] 'What is that?'
    [ʔəni inhoi] 'Who is this?'

6. Conclusion

The Kisar phonological system is particularly interesting because of its stop inventory (with five voiceless stops and no voiced stops), and the variable status of glottal stop. As we have shown, both of these relatively unusual characteristics are clearly evidenced in the data.

Nevertheless, this preliminary study of Kisar phonology has left unanswered several questions requiring further research, and the discussion of morphophonemic alternations is especially introductory. In spite of such limitations, however, we hope that even this brief description of this little known language will be of benefit to other scholars in the field.

References

Blust, Robert. 1977. The Soboyo reflexes of Proto-Austronesian *S. In Robert Blust (ed.), Historical linguistics in Indonesia, Part I. NUSA 10:21–30.

Blood, Cynthia. To appear. Subject-verb agreement in Kisar. Studies in Maluku Languages, Part I. NUSA.

Hogg, R. and C. B. McCully. 1987. Metrical phonology. Cambridge: Cambridge University Press.

Hyman, Larry. 1975. Phonology: Theory and analysis. New York: Holt, Rinehart and Winston.

Pike, Kenneth. 1947. Phonemics. Ann Arbor: The University of Michigan Press.

―――― and Evelyn Pike. 1977. Grammatical analysis. Dallas: Summer Institute of Linguistics.

Robinson, Dow. 1970. Manual for analytical procedures in phonology. Santa Ana: Summer Institute of Linguistics.

Taber, Mark. 1990. Towards a better understanding of the indigenous languages of Southwestern Maluku. Paper presented at the Conference on Maluku Research, University of Hawaii at Manoa, 16–18 March 1990.

Wurm, Stephen and B. Wilson. 1975. English finderlist of reconstructions in Austronesian languages. Pacific Linguistics C-33.

Segments, Syllables, and Stress in Larike

Carol J. Laidig
Pattimura University and The Summer Institute of Linguistics

Larike is an Austronesian language spoken on the western edge of the northern peninsula of Ambon Island in the province of Maluku, Indonesia. There are about 8,000 speakers of Larike, including the inhabitants of the village of Larike and the two neighboring villages of Wakasihu and Allang, where a dialect of Larike is spoken. The largest concentration of speakers is by far in the two villages of Larike and Wakasihu. Other small concentrations of speakers exist on other islands of this area, but these groups are the result of recent migrations from Larike or Wakasihu. The map shown in (1) indicates village locations and approximate language boundaries for Larike as well as neighboring indigenous languages spoken on the island of Ambon.

Historically, the inhabitants of Allang spoke Larike, but today the only remaining speakers from that village are of the oldest generation, consisting primarily of those over the age of 60. The younger generations do not use the language in daily activities and can generally only recall words or simple phrases. In conversing with the older people, it is evident that even they no longer use Larike in everyday communication.

(1) Larike and surrounding area

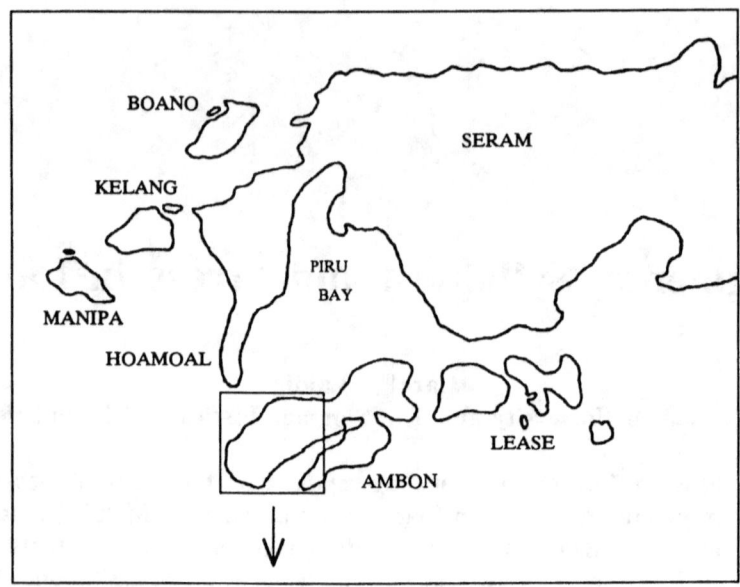

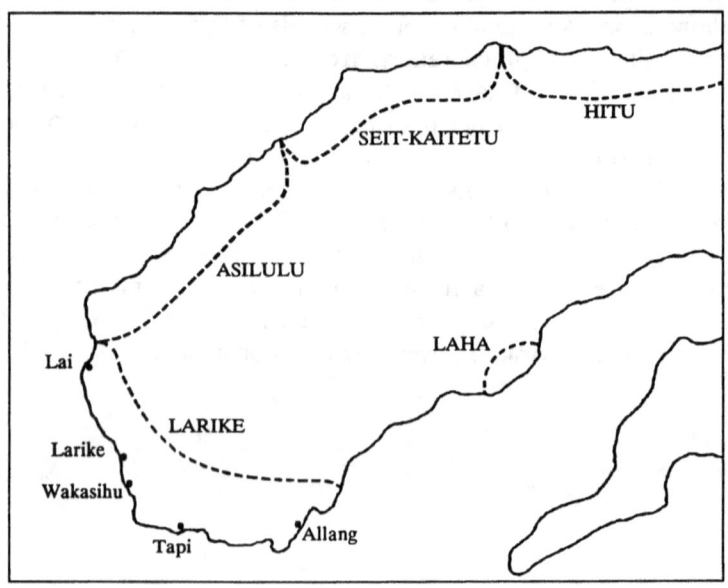

The trend in Allang is toward total language loss, or more accurately, replacement by Ambonese Malay.[1] This may be attributed at least in part to the fact that Allang has been a Christian village for several centuries. In this village, as in other Christian villages on Ambon, the inhabitants were formerly closely tied to the Dutch. The Dutch provided schools and jobs where the native languages were not used. Even the Bible and worship services were in Malay, which meant that people had to use a language other than their mother tongue. This resulted in the decline of the vernacular language among many Christian villages in Central Maluku. Allang is the only 100 percent Christian village remaining on Ambon which still has speakers of its indigenous language.

Larike is a religiously mixed village with its population of 4,000 consisting of approximately 95 percent Muslim and 5 percent Christian. According to tradition, the Christians are descendants of slaves from Saparua brought by the Portuguese during the sixteenth century to defend the fort in Larike. Even though the Christian inhabitants say they can speak the language, they do so only on a very limited basis when conversing with Muslim neighbors, and even then, only concerning the most common everyday activities. They do not claim that Larike is *their language* as the Muslim population does. Among the Muslims, Ambonese Malay and Larike are used with about the same overall frequency, although this depends on the particular domains of language usage. The same is true in Wakasihu, a 100 percent Muslim village.

It may be worth noting that even though there are no roads to any of these villages (Larike, Wakasihu, or Allang), there is an extensive network of foot trails to other villages. Also, there are boats that go to the city of Ambon every day where the people have quite a bit of outside contact with Indonesian speakers.

Historically, Larike was a fortress village during Portuguese and later Dutch occupation, ending with the Japanese invasion during World War II. The village of Larike was often called New Rotterdam by the Dutch. The fort is now in ruins, but the language abounds with borrowed words which serve as a reminder of past occupation. All of these influences should be kept in mind when understanding Larike, for these are not an

---

[1] One *lingua franca* in the Maluku province is Ambonese Malay. It developed as a trade language which was probably brought to Maluku centuries ago by Malay-speaking traders from Asia. Ambonese Malay is a creole, using the local languages of Central Maluku as its base. Therefore, structurally Ambonese Malay bears resemblance to Central Moluccan languages. Although its vocabulary consists largely of words which are very similar to those of Standard Malay, Ambonese Malay is actually quite distinct from Standard Malay, and is sometimes nearly unintelligible to Standard Malay speakers (Grimes 1988).

isolated and static people. The people as well as their language are continually changing and adapting to their circumstances.

Today there are primary schools in the villages of Larike and Wakasihu which have greatly influenced the use of language. Only Bahasa Indonesia[2] is spoken in the classroom by the school teachers and all of the textbooks are printed in Bahasa Indonesia. So that the children are prepared for this school experience, the parents start to teach their children Ambonese Malay (or Bahasa Indonesia, if the parents are capable) from infancy so that they can succeed in the school system. Therefore, all of the children can speak at least Ambonese Malay from the time they start to speak. It has been observed that mothers will sing songs, count, or point out body parts to the child in Bahasa Indonesia or Ambonese Malay even before the child can speak. In mixed groups of adults and children, many adults will speak to their children using Ambonese Malay, but speak to their peers using Larike.

It is evident though, that most of the Muslim children and young people use Larike as the language of choice in casual conversation or in their play. Often they also use a mixture of Larike and Ambonese Malay. The Christian children, in Larike, use Ambonese Malay exclusively.

In addition to these factors, there are also many borrowings from Bahasa Indonesia, Dutch, Ambonese Malay, and Arabic which have a substantial impact on the overall sound system of the language. In effect, this makes the task of unraveling and discovering the true characteristics of Larike a little more difficult.

Until recently, there have been limited data available on the language of Larike except for several wordlists taken during the nineteenth century. Van der Crab (1862) compiled a wordlist with over 400 entries. Both Ludeking (1868) and Wallace (1869) have collected wordlists for comparison studies with other Moluccan languages of the area. Ludeking provides a wordlist of several hundred words while the Wallace wordlist contains only about 100 entries. More recently, Collins (1980, 1982, 1983) collected wordlists for genetic classification and Travis (1989) gathered wordlists for lexicostatistical studies.

Genetically, Larike is a member of the Austronesian language family. Chlenov (1976) and Blust (1978) classified Larike as a member of the Malayo-Polynesian primary subgroup of Austronesian. Collins (1980, 1982, 1983), who has done extensive research in this geographical area, further

---

[2]Bahasa Indonesia (or Indonesian) became the official language of Indonesia after its independence in 1945. It is a dialect of the Standard Malay used in Malaysia, Singapore and Brunei. The Indonesian spoken in many of the schools in Central Maluku is actually a combination of Indonesian mixed with Ambonese Malay.

Segments, Syllables, and Stress in Larike   71

classifies Larike as a member of the Proto-East Central Maluku subgroup of Proto-Central Maluku. More specifically, he proposes that Larike is a member of the Proto-West Piru Bay branch, a subgroup of Piru Bay which in turn is a subgroup of Nunusaku. It is proposed that Larike's closest linguistic neighbor is Boano (on an island northeast of Seram), both having descended from East Hoamoal subgroup of Hoamoal. This genetic classification of Larike following Collins' proposals is summarized in the diagram of (2).

(2)   Genetic classification of Larike

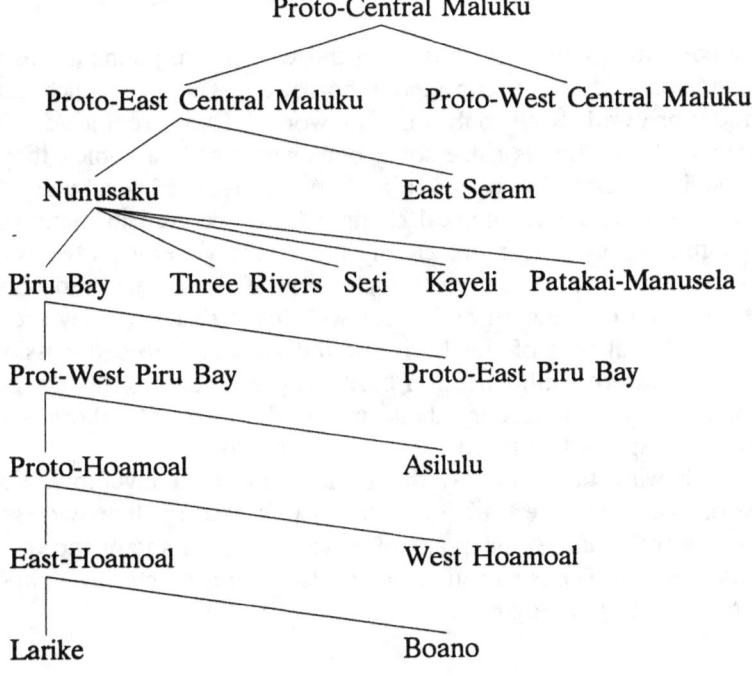

Prior to the author's field work,[3] there has been no linguistic study focussed on Larike. Apart from the wordlists mentioned above and one previous report by the author (Laidig and Laidig 1990), there has been no documentation of either the phonology or grammar of the language. The purpose of this paper is to provide an initial description of the phonology of Larike.

1. Segments

1.1. Consonants

The consonant inventory consists of thirteen Larike phonemes as well as five phonemes that are considered borrowed. The five which are considered borrowed occur only in loan words. They are included in the inventory of consonants since some borrowed words in which they occur are now incorporated into Larike as common items of vocabulary. Necessary affixation and phonological changes have occurred in many of these borrowings, in order to more closely follow the general pattern of other Larike words. Therefore, even though some of these borrowed phonemes have a limited distribution and occur with low frequency, they are at this time an integral part of the Larike sound system. (More discussion concerning the external influences on Larike is presented in §1.3.) Throughout this paper, parenthesized symbols are used to indicate those segments which are suspected to be the result of borrowing.

The following tables display the Larike consonant inventory. For purposes of discussion, the traditional chart (3) is used to show each segment as well as the manner and point of articulation; (4) shows the distinctive feature matrix, which is sometimes more useful in characterizing phonological processes in the language.

---

[3]Research for this paper was carried out in the village of Larike between July 1988–May 1990. It was done under the auspices of Pattimura University and the Summer Institute of Linguistics. During this time a lexicon of approximately 2,000 entries was collected which has been used in this research. Along with the many neighbors and friends which contributed to my understanding of the language, I would like to thank my principal language consultants, Tete Hasan Latuapo and Pak Ahmad Hukul, for the many hours of talking, listening, and story telling that made this paper possible. I am also grateful to Don Burquest and to my husband, Wyn Laidig, for their helpful suggestions during the preparation of this manuscript.

Segments, Syllables, and Stress in Larike

(3)

	labial	alveolar	palatal	velar	glottal
voiceless stops	p	t	(c)	k	ʔ
voiced stops	(b)	d	(j)	(g)	
fricatives		s			h
nasals	m	n		(ŋ)	
lateral		l			
flap		r			
semivowel	w		y		

(4)

	(b)	d	(j)	(g)	ʔ	p	t	(c)	k	s	h
sonorant	−	−	−	−	−	−	−	−	−	−	−
consonantal	+	+	+	+	−	+	+	+	+	+	+
coronal	−	+	+	−	−	−	+	+	−	+	−
continuant	−	−	−	−	−	−	−	−	−	+	+
voice	+	+	+	+	−	−	−	−	−	−	−
anterior	+	+	−	−	−	+	+	−	−	+	−

	m	n	(ŋ)	l	r	w	y
sonorant	+	+	+	+	+	+	+
consonantal	+	+	+	+	+	−	−
coronal	−	+	−	+	+	−	−
nasal	+	+	+	−	−	−	−
lateral	−	−	−	+	−	−	−
round	−	−	−	−	−	+	−
anterior	+	+	−	+	+	−	−

Formational statements for each of the consonants are presented below.

(/b/) [b] voiced labial stop. This phoneme occurs with very low frequency and is found in words that have been clearly borrowed from Malay or other sources. Even though these words have been borrowed, they have been assimilated into Larike, taking many affixes typical in Larike as well as undergoing vowel changes.

(5)
/baruba/   [ba'ruba]   'to medicate'
/bebek-u/ ['bɛbeku]   'duck'
/kubur-u/ ['kuburu]   'cemetery'

The verb /baruba/, borrowed from Ambonese Malay *baruba* (Indonesian *berobat*), takes the appropriate pronoun markers that are required on verbs in Larike such as, /aubarubama/ 'I medicate him'. In the case of the nouns /bebeku/ and /kuburu/, borrowed from Malay *bebek* and *kubur*, an epenthetic /u/ has been added, typical of borrowed nouns ending with a final consonant (see §3.4). These nouns can be pluralized by the suffix /i/; for example /bebek-u/ 'duck' becomes /bebekui/ 'ducks'.

/d/   [d] voiced alveolar stop

(6)   /dide/   ['dide]   'post, pole'
     /sudi/   ['sudi]   'to wear'

(/ɉ/)   [dʒ] voiced alveopalatal affricate. It occurs with low frequency and mainly in obvious Malay borrowings. Words with [dʒ] have undergone assimilation into Larike as evidenced by the fact that they undergo normal affixation.

(7)   /jaji/   ['dʒadʒi]   'to be born'
     /ajar/   ['ʔadʒar]   'to teach, study'
     /pajawe/   [pa'dʒawe]   'to watch'

The first two words are direct borrowings from Malay (Indonesian *jaji* and *ajar*). The last word, /pajawe/, is the only known Larike word containing the segment /ɉ/ where the source of the borrowing is not clear.

(/g/)   [g] voiced velar stop which occurs in obvious Malay borrowings. In the examples below (from Malay *garis, dagang, jagung*) the words display either affixation or the addition of an epenthetic vowel as evidence of their assimilation.

(8)   /garis-e/   ['garise]   'match'
     /daga-ri/   ['dagari]   'merchants'
     /jagun-u/   ['dʒagunu]   'corn'

/ʔ/   [ʔ] voiceless glottal stop

(9)   /duʔi/   ['duʔi]   'to crawl'
     /saʔo/   ['saʔo]   'to chop sago'

It is important to note that [ʔ] is not only a manifestation of the underlying phoneme /ʔ/, but also a result of a rule which inserts a surface glottal before a word initial vowel and also between geminate vowels. It is assumed that glottal stop in these situations is not a real phoneme, but a manifestation of the phonological rule represented in (10).

Segments, Syllables, and Stress in Larike

(10) Rule 1. $\emptyset \rightarrow \begin{bmatrix} -\text{son} \\ -\text{cons} \end{bmatrix} / \left\{ \begin{matrix} \# \underline{\quad} [+\text{syl}] \\ \begin{bmatrix} +\text{syl} \\ \alpha F \end{bmatrix} \underline{\quad} \begin{bmatrix} +\text{syl} \\ \alpha F \end{bmatrix} \end{matrix} \right\}$

The following examples illustrate Rule 1.

(11) /ina/ ['ʔina] 'woman'
/ana/ ['ʔana] 'child'
/ute/ ['ʔute] 'penis'

(12) /waa/ ['waʔa] 'root'
/kii/ ['kiʔi] 'to bite'
/ee/ ['ʔɛʔe] 'affirmative'

/p/ [p] voiceless labial stop

(13) /panau/ [pa'nau] 'to cook'
/lepa/ ['lepa] 'to speak'

/t/ [t] voiceless alveolar stop

(14) /taʔo/ ['taʔo] 'clay bowl'
/hato/ ['hato] 'rock'

(/c/) [tʃ] voiceless grooved alveopalatal affricate. It occurs with low frequency and only in borrowed words, as illustrated by the following two examples (Indonesian *cerai* and *baca*).

(15) /cere/ ['tʃɛre] 'to divorce'
/baca/ ['batʃa] 'to read'

/k/ [k] voiceless velar stop

(16) /kanu/ ['kanu] 'to eat'
/niko/ ['niko] 'earlier'

/s/ [s] voiceless grooved alveolar fricative

(17) /siwa/ ['siwa] 'nine'
/miso/ ['miso] 'earthquake'

/h/ [h] voiceless glottal fricative

(18) /hina/ ['hina] 'village'
    /puhu/ ['puhu] 'to cough'

/m/ [m] voiced bilabial nasal

(19) /molo/ ['molo] 'to sink'
    /ume/ ['ʔume] 'earth, dirt'

/n/ [ŋ] voiced velar nasal found only before velar stops

(20) /man-keu/ [maŋ'keu] 'he will go'
    /i-n-kan/ [iŋkana] 'it's strong'

The distribution can be described by the following rule, which assimilates an alveolar nasal to the point of articulation of the following velar stop.

(21) Rule 2. $\begin{bmatrix} +\text{nas} \\ +\text{cor} \end{bmatrix} \rightarrow \begin{bmatrix} -\text{cor} \\ -\text{ant} \end{bmatrix} / \underline{\quad} \begin{bmatrix} +\text{cons} \\ -\text{cor} \\ -\text{ant} \end{bmatrix}$

[n] voiced alveolar nasal

(22) /nasu/ ['nasu] 'sugar'
    /hunu/ ['hunu] 'to hit'

(/ŋ/) [ŋ] voiced velar nasal occurring with low frequency and only in borrowed words

(23) /ŋaji/ ['ŋaji] 'to recite the Koran'
    /manjaŋane/ [man'jaŋane] 'deer'

/l/ [l] voiced alveolar lateral

(24) /lena/ ['lena] 'to travel by foot'
    /molo/ ['molo] 'to sink'

/r/ [r] voiced alveolar flapped vibrant

(25) /rene/ ['rɛne] 'sick'
    /hiru/ ['hiru] 'to throw, toss'

/w/ [w] voiced rounded labiovelar semivowel

(26) /waʔa/ ['waʔa] 'root'
     /lawa/ ['lawa] 'garden'

/y/ [y] voiced unrounded palatal semivowel

(27) /yaka/ ['yaka] 'don't'
     /taiya/ ['taiya] 'ugly'

The following data show contrasts for various sets of segments in similar phonological environments.

/p/–(/b/)–/w/

(28) /pise/ ['pise] 'money'
     /bisa/ ['bisa] 'to be able'
     /wiwo/ ['wiwo] 'shark'

(29) /rapa/ ['rapa] 'to be tangled'
     /baba/ ['baba] 'grandfather'
     /nawa/ ['nawa] 'palm fiber'

/t/–/d/–/r/

(30) /titu/ ['titu] 'peak, summit'
     /ditu/ ['ditu] 'to slice'
     /riti/ ['riti] 'to flow'

(31) /ute/ ['ʔute] 'penis'
     /ude/ ['ʔude] 'caterpillar'
     /ure/ ['ʔure] 'banana'

/t/–(/c/)–(/j/)–/s/–/d/

Due to the fact that (/c/) and (/j/) occur infrequently and only in borrowed words, the contrasts are not always ideal, but below are the best examples available.

(32) /tupa/   ['tupa]   'spear'
      /cupa/   ['tʃupa]   'cup'
      /juŋku/   ['dʒuŋku]   'large boat'
      /suso/   ['suso]   'breast'
      /dupu/   ['dupu]   'to gather'

(33) /ata/   ['ʔata]   'tall'
      /baca/   ['batʃa]   'to read'
      /ajar/   ['ʔadʒar]   'to teach, study'
      /hasa/   ['hasa]   'to rub'
      /ida/   ['ʔida]   'big'

/d/–/r/–/l/–/n/[4]

(34) /daga/   ['daga]   'merchant'
      /rapa/   ['rapa]   'to tangle'
      /lawa/   ['lawa]   'to run'
      /nala/   ['nala]   'to be named'

There is not a four-way contrast for /d r l n/ medially, but the following two sets of words demonstrate that these consonants are contrastive.

(35) /ida/   ['ʔida]   'big'
      /sira/   ['sira]   'to comb'
      /rina/   ['rina]   'to light'

(36) /were/   ['wɛre]   'barracuda'
      /sele/   ['sɛle]   'throat'
      /rene/   ['rɛne]   'sick'

/k/–(/g/)

Because (/g/) has been borrowed into Larike, words containing this phoneme are limited. It is clear nevertheless, that (/g/) and /k/ are separate phonemes, as suggested by the following data.

---

[4]All of the examples occur with an /a/ following the /l/. The reason for this limited distribution seems to be due to the following historical rule (Collins 1983):

$$\text{Rule 8.} \quad l \;>\; d \;/\; \underline{\quad} \quad \begin{bmatrix} +\text{syl} \\ +\text{high} \end{bmatrix}$$

(37)	/koro/	['koro]	'smooth'
	/goreŋ/	['goreŋ]	'to fry'
(38)	/haka/	['haka]	'canoe'
	/daga/	['daga]	'merchant'
(39)	/dikata/	['dikata]	'wood'
	/tigaru/	['tigaru]	'busy'

/ʔ/–/h/

(40)	/siʔu/	['siʔu]	'also'
	/sihu/	['sihu]	'drizzle'
(41)	/puʔu/	['puʔu]	'mushroom'
	/puhu/	['puhu]	'to cough'

The presence of /ʔ/ is not contrastive with its absence initially nor between geminate vowels. (See formational statement for /ʔ/ in §1.1.) However, glottal stop is contrastive with its absence intervocalically, between nongeminate vowels, as shown below.

(42)	/au-peʔu/	['ʔauʔeʔu]	'I put'
	/au-keu/	['ʔauʔeu]	'I go'
(43)	/keʔi/	['kɛʔi]	'fast'
	/tei/	['tei]	'waste'
(44)	/huapaʔo/	[hua'paʔo]	'butterfly'
	/papao/	[pa'pao]	'sago bricks'

/n/–(/ŋ/)

The examples of contrasts are limited for these phonemes since (/ŋ/) mainly occurs in borrowed words.

(45) /nala/ ['nala] 'to be named'
    /ŋaji/ ['ŋadʒi] 'to recite the Koran'

(46) /anana/ ['ʔanana] 'CLASS fish'[5]
    /aɲate/ ['ʔaɲate] 'lukewarm'

(/g/)–(/ŋ/)

Data for these segments, both of which are considered borrowed, is limited, but both are presently used in Larike. The following pair of words, however, provides evidence that these segments do contrast with one another.

(47) /jaga/ ['dʒaga] 'to watch over'
    /ilaŋa/ [ʔi'laŋa] 'to lose'

1.2. Vowels

In Larike, there are five underlying vowels, /i e a o u/, with three additional vowels, [ɪ ɛ ə], appearing on the surface. The following two tables display both the traditional vowel chart as well as the feature matrix.

(48)

	front	central	back
high	i		u
mid	e		o
low		a	

---

[5]Abbreviations used in the examples in this paper: 1s first-person singular, 1de first person dual exclusive, 1pi first person plural inclusive, 1pe first person plural exclusive, 2s second person singular informal, 2p second person plural (and second person singular formal), 3s third person singular human, 3sn third person singular nonhuman, 3n third person nonhuman (singular and plural), 3p third person plural human, 3pn third person plural nonhuman, CA causative, CLASS classifier, COM completive marker, DET determiner, IMM immediacy marker and yes/no question marker, IR irrealis marker, RECIP reciprocal, RL realis marker, NEG negative marker, NOM nominalization marker, O object marker, p primary stress, P possessive marker, PL plural, TQM tag question marker, s secondary stress, S subject, sp species, ST stative marker, u unstressed, ' primary stress, and '' secondary stress.

Segments, Syllables, and Stress in Larike

(49)

	i	e	a	o	u
high	+	−	−	−	+
back	−	−	+	+	+
round	−	−	−	+	+
ATR	+	+	+	+	+

Note that all five underlying vowels are redundantly [+ATR]. This feature is explicitly listed since it is important to the rules which result in the three additional surface vowels. The surface vowels [ɪ ɛ ə] differ from [i e a] respectively in that the former display the feature [−ATR].

The following formational statements describe the five vowels and their surface alternations.

/i/   [ɪ] voiced high open front unrounded vocoid. This vocoid is found in closed syllables, which are relatively rare in Larike. The distribution of [ɪ] can be characterized by the following rule, where $ represents the syllable boundary.

(50)   Rule 3. $\begin{bmatrix} +\text{syl} \\ +\text{high} \\ -\text{back} \end{bmatrix} \rightarrow [-\text{ATR}] / \text{\_\_\_\_} [-\text{syl}] \, \$$

(51)
/parinta/	[paˈrɪnta]	'government'
/senin/	[sɛˈnɪn]	'Monday'
/tahalil/	[tahaˈlɪl]	'funeral service'
/imi-r-ure/	[ʔimɪrˈʔure]	'2p-P-banana'

[i] voiced high close front unrounded vocoid

(52)
/ise/	[ˈʔise]	'tree sap'
/hina/	[ˈhina]	'village'
/kahi/	[ˈkahi]	'crooked'

/e/   [ɛ] voiced mid front open unrounded vocoid occurring when directly preceding a syllable containing a front vowel. In all other circumstances the vowel is realized as [e]. This can be summarized by the following rule:

(53)   Rule 4. $\begin{bmatrix} +\text{syl} \\ -\text{high} \\ -\text{back} \end{bmatrix} \rightarrow [-\text{ATR}] / \text{\_\_\_\_} [-\text{syl}] \begin{bmatrix} +\text{syl} \\ -\text{back} \end{bmatrix}$

This rule is demonstrated in the following words.

(54) /paledi/ [paˈlɛdi] 'to sell'
/sele/ [ˈsɛle] 'throat'
/hened-u/ [ˈhɛnedu] 'flood'
/heke-ta/ [ˈhɛketa] 'CLASS bundle'
/heti-ke/ [ˈhɛtike] 'to snap'

The following set of words demonstrates the process of raising when a word contains a series of /e/ phonemes.

(55) /pese-ne/ [ˈpɛsɛne] 'to hold-2s o'
/mete-te/ [ˈmɛtɛte] 'black'
/tehe-te/ [ˈtɛhɛte] 'forbidden'

The set of words in (56) demonstrates how the raising process is interrupted when the /e/ phoneme is separated from the front vowel by a syllable containing a back vowel.

(56) /pakedu-ke/ [paˈkeduke] 'again'
/pedu-ke/ [ˈpeduke] 'again'
/sele-mudi/ [sɛleˈmudi] 'nape'
/hale-mudi/ [haleˈmudi] 'behind'

[e] voiced mid front close unrounded vocoid occurring in all circumstances where [e] does not precede a front vowel

(57) /ela-u/ [ˈʔelau] 'many'
/aʔera/ [ʔaˈʔera] 'sacklunch'
/leu/ [ˈleu] 'to crawl'
/ure/ [ˈʔure] 'banana'
/metoʔo-ku/ [meˈtoʔoku] 'dark'

/a/ [ə] voiced mid central unrounded vocoid occurring in unstressed position directly following a front vowel. This can be summarized by the following rule:

(58) Rule 5. $\begin{bmatrix} +\text{syl} \\ +\text{low} \\ -\text{stress} \end{bmatrix} \rightarrow [-\text{ATR}] / \begin{bmatrix} +\text{syl} \\ -\text{back} \end{bmatrix}$ ___

(59) /pakiniaku/   [paki'niəku]   'to ask'
     /diamata/   [diə'mata]   'sun'
     /tudia/   ['tudiə]   'machete'
     /itia/   ['ʔitiə]   'lightning'
     /marea/   [ma'reə]   'cousin'
     /alea/   ['ʔaleə]   'door'

[a] voiced open central unrounded vocoid occurs in circumstances where [a] is not in final, unstressed position directly following a front vowel

(60) /aso/   ['ʔaso]   'dog'
     /kaki/   ['kaki]   'to scratch'
     /ina/   ['ʔina]   'mother'

/u/ [u] voiced back rounded vocoid

(61) /ume/   ['ʔume]   'dirt, earth'
     /puhoi/   [pu'hoi]   'to bathe'
     /kamu/   ['kamu]   'betel nut'

/o/ [o] voiced mid back rounded vocoid

(62) /oso/   ['ʔoso]   'heart'
     /hola/   ['hola]   'gun, weapon'
     /duto/   ['duto]   'to press'

The following data show vowel contrasts in similar phonological environments.

Vowels /i e a u o/ contrast initially as in:

(63) /ite/   ['ʔite]   (1pi)
     /eta/   ['ʔeta]   'needle'
     /ata/   ['ʔata]   'above'
     /ute/   ['ʔute]   'penis'
     /oto/   ['ʔoto]   'car'

Vowels /i e a u o/ contrast interconsonantally as in:

(64) /hiha/ ['hiha] 'to call'
 /hehe/ ['hɛhe] 'below'
 /haha/ ['haha] 'above'
 /huho/ ['huho] 'fish trap'
 /hoka/ ['hoka] 'to laugh'

Vowels /i e a u o/ contrast in final position as in:

(65) /tahi/ ['tahi] 'does not exist'
 /hehe/ ['hɛhe] 'below'
 /haha/ ['haha] 'above'
 /dihu/ ['dihu] 'beneath'
 /haho/ ['haho] 'pig'

The following are sets of vowel contrasts.

/i/–/e/

(66) /ite/ ['ʔite] (1pi)
 /eta/ ['ʔeta] 'needle'

(67) /tipa/ ['tipa] 'to carry'
 /tepa/ ['tepa] 'chop down'

(68) /pise/ ['pise] 'money'
 /pese/ ['pɛse] 'to work'

(69) /koli/ ['koli] 'to sprain'
 /kole/ ['kole] 'lower back'

/e/–/a/–/o/

(70) /ei-na/ ['ʔeina] 'CLASS tree-one'
 /ai-ka/ ['ʔaika] '2s RL-eat'
 /oi-na/ ['ʔoina] 'CLASS nut-one'

(71) /heka/ ['heka] 'to accompany'
 /haka/ ['haka] 'boat, canoe'
 /hoka/ ['hoka] 'to laugh'

(72) /keʔi/   ['kɛʔi]   'fast'
     /kaʔi/   ['kaʔi]   'to bring'
     /koʔi/   ['koʔi]   'little'

(73) /nise/   ['nise]   'to move'
     /nisa/   ['nisa]   'to wipe'
     /miso/   ['miso]   'earthquake'

(74) /kuse/   ['kuse]   'to snap'
     /husa/   ['husa]   'to go outside'
     /suso/   ['suso]   'breast'

/o/–/u/

(75) /opo/   ['ʔopo]   'unripe'
     /upo/   ['ʔupo]   'grandfather'

(76) /hotu/   ['hotu]   'to climb'
     /hutu/   ['hutu]   'to cut'

(77) /taʔo/   ['taʔo]   'clay pot'
     /taʔu/   ['taʔu]   'afraid'

(78) /tito/   ['tito]   'to throw'
     /titu/   ['titu]   'peak, summit'

1.3. External influences

It is evident that Larike, as it is spoken today, contains several phonemes as well as many words borrowed from languages such as Malay, Dutch, Arabic, and Portuguese. Malay seems to be the main source of borrowings. This is only logical since a dialect of Malay has been used as a trade language in Central Maluku for many centuries. Today, there is a high degree of bilingualism in Ambonese Malay. Most children now learn Ambonese Malay as their first language, acquiring Larike some years later.

As a result of centuries of close contact with other languages, and the increasing degree of bilingualism in Malay, a significant number of borrowings have become an integral part of Larike's phonological system. An adequate synchronic analysis must take these borrowings into account.

Note, however, that if the borrowed phonemes were removed from the inventory presented in §1.1, the remainder would more likely approximate the original inventory of phonemes in Larike. Investigation of related languages gives evidence of a much smaller inventory of consonant phonemes than Larike currently presents.

For example, on the island of Seram there is a more isolated language group where bilingualism and literacy are much lower than in Larike. This is the Nuaulu language, which like Larike is a member of the Nunusaku Subgroup (see (2)). The phonology of Nuaulu (Bolton 1989) presents a much simpler repertoire of phonemes. Although the vowels in Nuaulu are identical to those of Larike, the consonant inventory is much smaller. However, if the borrowed phonemes are not included in the Larike inventory, it becomes nearly identical to that of Nuaulu.[6] This can be seen by comparing the Nuaulu consonant inventory in (79) with that of Larike in (3).

(79)

	labial	alveolar	velar	glottal
stops	p	t	k	ʔ
fricatives		s		h
nasals	m	n		
flaps		r		
laterals		l		
semivowels	w	y		

In effect, external influences of borrowings from other languages have added substantially to the number of phonemes in the Larike inventory. Ignoring borrowings, the inventory is almost the same as that of other Central Moluccan languages in which external influences have had less impact.

1.4. Morphophonemic alternations

Verb stems: k/ʔ and p/ʔ. In Larike, there is an alternation which occurs in verbal stems with underlying initial /k p/. When conjugating transitive or intransitive verbs, all initial /k p/ alternate with /ʔ/ except in the 2s, 3s, and 3n (singular and plural) forms, as indicated by the minus sign preceding the

---

[6]The only difference between these inventories is the presence of /d/ in Larike, which is the result of a historical sound change.

curly brackets in the rule below.[7] The rule, which states that the initial /k p/ of a verbal stem alternates with /ʔ/ in 2s, 3s, and 3n forms, does not apply to unaccusative verbs. With unaccusative verbs the personal pronoun is not a prefix that would affect the conjugation of the verb, but rather a suffix. It has no effect on the initial consonant of the verbal stem. The process of /k p/ alternating with /ʔ/ can be characterized by the following rule.

(80) Rule 6. $\begin{bmatrix} +\text{cons} \\ -\text{vce} \\ -\text{cor} \end{bmatrix} \rightarrow \begin{bmatrix} -\text{cons} \\ -\text{ant} \end{bmatrix} / - \begin{Bmatrix} 2s \\ 3s \\ 3n \end{Bmatrix}$ (prefix) $\begin{bmatrix} \underline{\qquad} \\ \text{verb stem} \end{bmatrix}$

---

[7]Historically there were obligatory subject agreement prefixes on verbs which led to the alternations observed today. Collins (1983) proposes that a series of historical changes led to these obligatory person markers reducing to a single consonant and fusing to the verbal root. In the case of the 2s and 3s forms, the consonant was a nasal that preceded the initial consonant of the verb stem. It was this nasal that preserved the initial consonant of the verb stem, now reflected in Larike /k p/. The other conjugated forms which did not have a nasal preceding the initial consonant of the verb stem underwent subsequent sound changes resulting in the consonants /k p/ becoming glottal.

Similarly, a historical sound change occurred where the initial consonant of the verb stem was /t s/. The 2s and 3s forms then became prenasalized, undergoing a subsequent change to /r/. The nonprenasalized /t s/ in the remaining conjugated forms were preserved from this sound change to /r/, and remained unchanged as /t s/. Larike later added another layer of subject agreement prefixes to develop the verbal conjugational system observed today.

Stresemann (1927:119–125) shows that there are six different conjugations of verbs observable in languages of Central Maluku. Larike exhibits only two of these conjugation patterns: those verbs with verb initial /p/ or /k/ and those with verb initial /t/ or /s/, referred to as the *p/k* and *t/s* conjugations, respectively. The following examples show Larike's conjugation patterns from each group.

	p 'work'	k 'bite'	t 'know'	s 'climb'
1s	*au-ʔese*	*au-ʔiʔi*	*au-tiwa*	*au-saʔa*
2s	*ai-pese*	*ai-kiʔi*	*ai-riwa*	*ai-raʔa*
3s	*mei-pese*	*mei-kiʔi*	*mei-riwa*	*mei-raʔa*
3n	*i-pese*	*i-kiʔi*	*i-riwa*	*i-raʔa*
1pi	*ite-ʔese*	*ite-ʔiʔi*	*ite-tiwa*	*ite-saʔa*
1pe	*ami-ʔese*	*ami-ʔiʔi*	*ami-tiwa*	*ami-saʔa*
2p	*imi-ʔese*	*imi-ʔiʔi*	*imi-tiwa*	*imi-saʔa*
3p	*mati-ʔese*	*mati-ʔiʔi*	*mati-tiwa*	*mati-saʔa*
3pn	*iri-pese*	*iri-kiʔi*	*iri-riwa*	*iri-raʔa*

Some examples that demonstrate this process are shown below.

(81) /au-kanu/   [ʔauˈʔanu]   '1s-eat'
     /i-kanu/   [ʔiˈkanu]   '3sn-eats'

(82) /imi-kolo/   [ʔimiˈʔolo]   '2p-cry'
     /iri-kolo/   [ʔiriˈkolo]   '3pn-cry'

(83) /ami-padime/ [ʔamiʔaˈdime] '1p-play'
     /a-i-padime/ [ʔaipaˈdime]   '2s-RL-play'

(84) /mati-pajawe/ [matiʔaˈdʒawe] '3p-watch'
     /mei-pajawe/ [meipaˈdʒawe] '3s RL-watch'

There are two prefixes that are commonly inserted between the person marker and the verbal stem identified by the label PREFIX in the above rule: the negative marker *ta-* and the irrealis marker *na-*. These prefixes do not interrupt the alternation between /k p/ and /ʔ/ as shown in the following examples.[8]

(85) /ami-ta-kanu/ [ʔamitaˈʔanu]   '1pe-NEG-eat'
     /imi-ta-keu/   [ʔimitaˈʔeu]   '2p-NEG-put'

(86) /au-na-padime/ [ʔaunaʔaˈdime] '1s-IR-play'
     /imi-na-pese/ [ʔiminaˈʔɛse]   '2p-IR-work'

---

[8]There is an interesting conjugational variation where /k/ alternates with /ʔ/. In this instance, when the prefix *ka-* is affixed to the word *kele* 'stand' the /k/ alternates with /ʔ/ in the prefix as well as in the root, just as it does without the prefix. It is conjugated in the following way:

/au-ka-kele/   [ʔauʔaˈʔele]   '1s-stand up'
/mei-ka-kele/ [meikaˈkele]   '3s RL-stands up'

There are only a few exceptions to this rule where initial /k p/ on verbal stems are not altered. For the most part, these occur in words borrowed from Ambonese Malay or other languages.[9] Some examples are listed below.

(87) /ami-kawin-u/ [ʔami'kawinu] '1pe-marry'
/imi-kipas/ [ʔimi'kipas] '2p-fan'

(88) /ami-paru/ [ʔami'paru] '1pe-grate'
/imi-pikir-e/ [ʔimi'pikire] '2p-think'

Verb roots: t/r and s/r. When conjugating transitive and intransitive verbs with an underlying initial /t s/, every initial /t s/ has an alternate of /r/ in the 2s, 3s, and 3n (singular and plural) forms.[10] In all other positions /t s/ are evident in the surface form (see footnote 7). This is a complementary process to that which occurs in verb roots with initial /p k/ alternating with /ʔ/ (see §1.4 verb stems). The process of /t s/ alternating with /r/ can be specified by the following rule.

(89) Rule 7. $\begin{bmatrix} +\text{cons} \\ -\text{vce} \\ +\text{cor} \\ +\text{ant} \end{bmatrix} \rightarrow \begin{bmatrix} +\text{son} \\ +\text{vce} \\ -\text{nas} \end{bmatrix} / \begin{Bmatrix} 2s \\ 3s \\ 3n \end{Bmatrix} (\text{prefix}) [\underline{\quad\quad}_{\text{verb stem}}$

Some examples of the verb conjugations with initial /t s/ are listed below.

(90) /au-sei/ [ʔau'sei] '1s-paddle'
/iri-sei/ [ʔiri'rei] '3pn-paddle'

---

[9] The exceptions in Larike that do not follow the conjugational pattern for verbal stems with initial /k p/ alternating with glottal could be either words borrowed into the language at a time after this innovation took place or words which may have been derived from proto-forms which did not undergo this innovation (perhaps words which were originally nouns but at a later time began to function as verbs). There are only a few words from the latter category:

/au-kaki/ [ʔau'kaki] '1s-scratch'
/ami-puka/ [ʔami'puka] '1pe-break fast'
/imi-puhoi/ [ʔimi'puhoi] '2p-bathe'

[10] The rule which states that the initial /t s/ → /r/ on verb stems (2s, 3s, and 3n forms) does not apply to unaccusative verbs, for the same reason discussed that the /k p/ and glottal alternation did not apply to unaccusative verbs.

(91) /imi-sahe/ [ʔimi'sahe] '2p-buy'
    /a-i-sahe/ [ʔai'rahe] '2s-RL-buy'

(92) /ami-tehe/ [ʔami'tɛhe] '1pe-break open'
    /mei-tehe/ [mei'rɛhe] '3s RL-break open'

(93) /mati-tihu/ [mati'tihu] '3s-fly'
    /i-tihu/ [ʔi'rihu] '3sn-fly'

There are three affixes which can be inserted between the pronoun and the verbal root which do not interrupt the alternation of /t s/ with /r/.[11] These affixes are the irrealis marker *na-*, the negative marker *ta-*, and the realis marker *i-*. These markers function in exactly the same way in verbs with initial /p k/. This can be seen in the following examples.

(94) /ma-ta-sahe/ [mata'rahe] '3s-NEG-buy'
    /a-ta-tiwa/ [ʔata'riwa] '2s-NEG-know'

(95) /i-ri-na-siha/ [ʔirina'riha] '3pn-IR-dig out'
    /i-na-tihu/ [ʔina'rihu] '3sn-IR-fly'

(96) /a-i-soha/ [ʔai'roha] '2s-RL-pour'
    /mei-tito/[12] [mei'rito] '3s RL-throw'

---

[11]There is an interesting variation which occurs with a verbal root beginning with initial /t s/. In the first pair below, the root has undergone the typical /s/ → /r/ alternation. The last two pairs of words show that a new verb root is created by adding the prefix *pa-* (causative) to the root *saʔa* which now undergoes the /k p/ → /ʔ/ alternation. In both of these cases the verbal root is in a fixed form not affected anymore by the pronoun.

/au-saʔa/ [ʔau'saʔa] '1s-ride'
/mei-saʔa/ [mei'raʔa] '3s RL-ride'
/au-paka-saʔa/ [ʔauʔaka'saʔa] '1s-mounted'
/mei-paka-saʔa/ [meipaka'saʔa] '3s RL-mounted'
/au-paraʔa-ku/ [ʔauʔa'raʔaku] '1s-load a thing'
/mei-paraʔa-ku/ [meipa'raʔaku] '3s RL-load a thing'

[12]For the purposes of this paper the 3s subject agreement marker and the realis marker will be treated as a fused form. Historically, there may have been a vowel raising which altered the form of the third-person-singular pronoun. Presently, the usual

There is one instance of a verbal root with an initial /t/ that does not alternate with /r/ which appears at first to be an exception to the rule. Upon closer inspection, however, the form in question is really a fused contracted form of *ta-* (negative) and the verbal root (see discussion in §4.5). In this particular root, the initial /t/ of the contracted form is not affected by the alternation rule, just as /t/ in the negative prefix *ta-* is never affected. The set of examples in (97) shows the negative prefix attached to the verb root, while those in (98) show the contracted form of the negative prefix and the verb root.

(97) /ma-ta-ʔiya/ [mata'ʔiya] '3s-NEG-good'
     /i-ta-ʔiya/ [ʔita'ʔiya] '3sn-NEG-good'

(98) /mei-taiya/ [mei'taiya] '3s RL-ugly (no good)'
     /i-taiya/ [ʔi'taiya] '3sn-broken (no good)'

Rule 7 does not apply to some borrowed words from Ambonese Malay or from other languages, as seen in the examples below (from Ambonese Malay *samboŋ, suka, tawar, tarima*).

(99) /a-i-samboŋ/ [ʔai'samboŋ] '2s-RL-add'
     /mei-suka/ [ʔmei'suka] '3s RL-like'

(100) /a-i-tawar/ [ʔai'tawar] '2s-RL-bargain'
      /mei-tarima/ [meita'rima] '3s RL-receive'

---

form of the morpheme is *ma-*, but when the realis marker *i-* is immediately following, the pronoun takes the form *mei-*. The vowel raising could be denoted by:

    ma- + i- → mei-
    3s   RL   '3s RL'

Today at least one older person still pronounces the sequence as *mai-*, but everyone is not in agreement with this. This may indicate that this raising has been the result of a recently introduced rule; however, there are many instances of words which do not undergo this change.

Note that this same vowel raising also occurs in several contracted words as shown by the examples below:

    hu'sa + 'ida + tidu → hu"seida'tidu
    ten   big   three   'thirteen'
    mana- + ina → ma'neina
    3s P   mother 'his mother'

2. Syllables

2.1. Syllable structure

In Larike, there are four basic syllable types: V, CV, VC, and CVC. These four syllable types do not have equal distribution. When looking at monomorphemic roots, the most common syllable type is CV, with V also occurring quite frequently. The remaining two syllable types, VC and CVC, are quite limited in their distribution, occurring only in multimorphemic words or in borrowings. Although there are some apparent exceptions, in the final analysis most can be attributed to either borrowings or to a fusion of multimorphemic words, as in the words /undana/ 'man' and /undaha/ 'mouse'.[13]

According to Clements and Keyser (1983), a language such as Larike is a Type 4 language since it includes all of the basic syllable patterns; V, CV, VC, and CVC.

Below are examples of all four syllable patterns. The sets of examples in (101)–(102) show V and CV syllable patterns in monomorphemic words.[14] The last sets in (103)–(104) show the remaining syllable types, VC and CVC, which (except for borrowings) occur only in multimorphemic words. Syllable breaks are designated by a period or by the stress mark if the following syllable has primary word stress.

(101) v /aso/   ['ʔa.so]   'dog'
         /diamata/   [di.ə'ma.ta]   'sun'
         /unduo/   [ʔun'du.o]   'eel'
         /roa/   ['ro.a]   'to whistle'
         /hantoata/ [han'toata]   'morning'
         /dupia/   [du'pi.ə]   'sago paste'

(102) cv /duma/   ['du.ma]   'house'
         /pipe/   ['pi.pe]   'goat'
         /nehe/   ['nɛ.he]   'downward'
         /hise/   ['hi.se]   'exist'

---

[13]There is evidence from historical data indicating that these apparent exceptions are really multimorphemic. Collins (1983:84) suggests that /undana/ 'male' is derived from PAN *ma-Ruqanay. The PAN *ma- morpheme developed through various changes into Larike /un/ in the above example. Similar changes also occurred in Larike /undaha/ 'mouse'.

[14]Note that unambiguous occurrences of V and VC syllables are not found word initially because of Rule 1 (see §1.1), which inserts a glottal before vowels in word initial position.

(103)	vc	/arua-r-sika/	[ʔa.ru.arˈsi.ka]	'1de-P-cat'
		/hua-r-dua/	[hu.arˈdu.a]	'CLASS^pieces-two'
		/i-n-tudo/	[ʔɪnˈtu.do]	'3sn-ST-sleep'

(104)	cvc	/ami-n-taʔu/	[ʔa.mɪnˈta.ʔu]	'1pe-ST-scared'
		/ite-r-pise/	[ʔi.tɛrˈpi.se]	'1pi-P-money'
		/ma-ta-n-susu/	[ma.tanˈsu.su]	'3s-NEG-ST-sweet'

2.2. Consonant sequences

Consonant sequences are rare in Larike. This is a direct result of the fact that V and CV are by far the dominant syllable types in the language. Although there are several situations where CC's are found, these are clearly the exception rather than the rule. When they do exist, they occur in syllable-onset position and never syllable-coda position. Although CC's are most often found in borrowed words, they occasionally occur in multimorphemic words and in contractions across morpheme boundaries. In the discussion that follows, each of these exceptions to the usual syllable construction in Larike will be briefly examined. It should be emphasized here that consonant clusters are not the norm and occur with low frequency.

The most common source of consonant clusters in nonborrowed Larike words is the possessive marker -r or the stative marker -n. Thus, the resulting CC's necessarily cross morpheme boundaries. Examples are shown below.

(105)	/imi-r-duma/	[ʔi.mɪrˈdu.ma]	'2p-P-house'
	/mati-r-haho/	[ma.tɪrˈhaho]	'3p-P-pig'

(106)	/ma-n-tola/	[manˈto.la]	'3s-S-pretty'
	/i-n-susu/	[ʔɪnˈsu.su]	'3sn-S-sweet'

Another instance where consonant sequences occur across morpheme boundaries is in Larike words which have undergone contraction. Although it is not predictable which words can undergo contraction, it is always the unstressed vowel which is elided as in the following words.

(107)	/hunduma/	[hunˈduma]	'to fight each other'
	from /hunu-duma/		'fight-RECIP'

(108) /mastidu/ [mas'tidu] 'three people'
from /masi-tidu/ 'CLASS people-three'

(109) /lohansa/ ['lo'hansa] 'little'
from /lohana-sa/ 'little-one'

The above contractions are optional in that either the contracted form or the full form may be used. However, the following examples show contracted forms which appear to be permanently fused. In other words, uncontracted forms do not currently exist in the language.

(110) /mantido/ [man'tido] 'egg'
from /manua + tido/ 'chicken + CLASS egg'

(111) /panosta/ [pa'nosta] 'dirt'
from /panoso + -ta/ 'dirty + nominalizer'

(112) /kudanto/ [kudan'to] 'swell, wave'
possibly from /kududanu + tou/ 'wave + gather'

Borrowed words, usually originating from Dutch, Arabic, or Malay, also exhibit consonant clusters. Usually these occur across syllable boundaries, but occasionally they are also found in syllable onset position. Examples of borrowings with cc's are shown below.

(113) /beŋko/ ['beŋ.ko] 'to fall forward'
/kwar/ ['kwar] 'quarter'
/lesta/ ['les.ta] 'wall'
/manjaŋane/ [man'jaŋ.a.ne] 'deer'
/margrib/ ['mar.grɪb] 'evening prayer'
/ronta/ ['ron.ta] 'walk around'
/skosteŋ/ ['skos.teŋ] 'chimney'

2.3. Vowel sequences

In Larike, vowel sequences are very common, occurring with greatest frequency in word-medial or word-final position. Even though there are several ambiguous vowel sequences realized as diphthongs in the surface representation, all VV sequences are best analyzed in the underlying representation as two separate segments, with each vowel considered to be a separate underlying syllable. No vowel sequences are treated as diphthongs in the underlying representation, even though they are pronounced as such on the surface. The following discussion will attempt to give evidence and justification for this analysis of vowel sequences.

There seem to be four major reasons for analyzing the ambiguous VV sequences as sequences of segments and not diphthongs. First, all combinations of vowels except geminate vowels can occur in a sequence; either in a root[15] or in multimorphemic words. Except for the fact that geminate vowels do not occur,[16] there seem to be no restrictions on which vowels may occur in sequence, as seen in the following examples.

(114) iv /au-panedi-e/ [ʔau'ʔanɛdie] '1s-weed-COM'
         /dupia/   [du'piə]   'sago paste'
         /ati-u/   ['ʔatiu]   'four-PL'
         /a-puhoi-o/   [ʔapu'hoio]   '2s-bathe-IMM'

(115) ev /nei/   ['nei]   'here'
         /marea/   [ma'reə]   'cousin'
         /keu/   ['keu]   'to go'
         /au-pese-o/   [ʔau'ʔɛseo]   '1s-work-IMM'

(116) av /lai/   ['lai]   'here'
         /rupae/   [ru'pae]   'woman'
         /tau/   ['tau]   'not yet'
         /ao/   ['ʔao]   'fire'

---

[15]Except for geminate vowels, almost all combinations of vowel sequences are present in roots. Those nongeminate combinations of vowels which are not found in roots (namely eo, oe, ui, iu, ie and io) do occur in multimorphemic words.

[16]Although there is clear evidence of situations where an underlying glottal must be recognized, there are also situations where a glottal is inserted at the surface (see Rule 1). In Larike words which contain identical vowels separated by glottal, there is no way of knowing whether that glottal is present in the underlying representation, or whether it was the result of the glottal insertion rule. For economy's sake, it will be assumed that these glottals are the result of the insertion rule, and that there is no need to recognize them in the underlying representation. Examples are:

/kii/   ['kiʔi]   'to bite'
/saa/   ['saʔa]   'to ride'
/puu/   ['puʔu]   'mushroom'
/soo/   ['soʔo]   'hut'
/hee/   [heʔe]   'yes'

(117) uv /tidu-i/   ['tidui]   'three-PL'
         /tue/   ['tue]   'to live'
         /hua/   ['hua]   'fruit'
         /unduo/   [ʔun'duo]   'eel'

(118) ov /puhoi/   [pu'hoi]   'to bathe'
         /imi-loko-e/ [ʔimi'lokoe]   '2p-sit-COM'
         /soa/   ['soa]   'to whistle'
         /lou/   ['lou]   'far'

The second major reason for viewing vowel sequences as two segments and not diphthongs is that this interpretation fits with the stress rule. This rule simply states that primary stress is on the underlying penultimate syllable of the root. Therefore, if the ambiguous VV sequences in words such as /pa'nau/ 'to cook' and /pu'hoi/ 'bathe' are analyzed as two vowel segments, the stress falls on the underlying penultimate syllable (see §3.3). If such sequences are treated as monosyllabic diphthongs, each instance would be an exception to the otherwise general stress rule.

Although several of the VV sequences could be viewed as vowel plus a semi-vowel on the surface, this treatment is not general enough to accommodate the other VV sequences. If the only ambiguous sequences were V*i* and V*u*, then there would be some motivation to view /i u/ as /w y/, but there are two other vowel sequences, /ae/ and /ao/, which act in the same way as V*i* and V*u*. When the sequences /ae/, /ao/, V*i* or V*u* are spoken, they are spoken with the timing of one syllable. It would not be expedient to postulate V*i* as V*y* and V*u* as V*w* when /ae/ and /ao/ also exist and are spoken with the same syllable timing as the former pair. Since a VV sequence can be represented by any vowels except geminate vowels, it would seem likely that the sequences V*i*, V*u*, /ao/, and /ae/ should be treated in an analogous manner. The following examples show this similarity.

(119) /papei/   [pa'pei]   'to wait'
      /panau/   [pa'nau]   'to cook'
      /rupae/   [ru'pae]   'woman'
      /papao/   [pa'pao]   'sago paste'

Another reason to view the surface diphthongs, V*i* and V*u*, as VV sequences rather than sequences involving glides is that they often occur in word-final position. If /i u/ were considered to be semi-vowels /y w/ in these cases, the result would be a consonant in word-final position. However, word-final consonants do not occur in Larike, except in borrowed words.

The fourth reason for analyzing the ambiguous vowels as sequences of segments and not as diphthongs is that most related languages in Central Maluku (Nuaulu and Alune for example) have inventories of only five vowels. If the ambiguous vowel segments were added to the Larike vowel inventory as diphthongs, this would greatly increase the number of vowels present.

Given the evidence above, it seems justifiable to uniformly treat VV sequences in Larike as separate vowel segments.

3. Stress and the phonological word

3.1. Word structure

As shown in §2.1, there are four syllable patterns in Larike words: V, CV, VC, and CVC. A word consists of one or more of these syllables in a string where one of the syllables carries the primary word stress. The most frequent of all syllable types is CV and the most frequent of all word patterns is CV.CV, as shown in the following examples.

(120) cv.cv /lamu/ ['la.mu] 'to lick'
/niwa/ ['ni.wa] 'thin'
/seko/ ['se.ko] 'high tide'
/tuhe/ ['tu.he] 'to cut'

Other common word patterns are CV.V and V.CV, but these are not so numerous as the CV.CV pattern. Examples of these words are shown below.

(121) cv.v /dua/ ['du.a] 'two'
/nia/ ['ni.a] 'snake'

(122) v.cv /ala/ ['ʔa.la] 'rice'
/itu/ ['ʔi.tu] 'seven'

There are some word-level constraints regarding the distribution of the VC and CVC syllable types. Specifically, Larike words do not end in consonants, therefore these two syllable types cannot occur in word-final position. VC and CVC syllable types can occur elsewhere in the word. It should be noted, however, that excluding borrowed words, the only consonants that can fill the final C slot are /n r/, from the stative morpheme *-n* and the possessive morpheme *-r*. Examples are shown below.

(123) /mana-n-tola-ta/ [ma.nan'to.la.ta] '3s P-ST-beauty-NOM'
/i-na-n-susu-ta/ [ʔi.nan'susu.ta] '3sn-P-ST-sweet-NOM'

(124) /mati-r-duma/ [ma.tɪr'duma] '3p-P-house'
/ite-r-ana-u/ [ʔi.ter'ʔa.nau] '1pi-P-children-PL'

In summary, the word pattern which is the most frequent is CVCV, followed by CVV and VCV. The VC and CVC syllable patterns have limited frequency and distribution. Except for borrowings, they never occur in word-final position.

3.2. Syllabification rules

It is assumed that in the underlying representation each vowel is associated with one syllable. However, in the surface representation this is no longer true. As discussed in §2.3, there are a number of VV sequences which on the surface are pronounced as a single unit. These VV sequences must be considered as one syllable in the surface representation.

To account for this, it is proposed that there must exist a set of syllabification rules. These rules derive the surface syllable structure from the underlying segments.[17] The following syllabification steps are found to correctly predict the syllable structure of Larike words.

(125) Syllabification rules:

Step 1. Assign C and V labels to segments in the normal manner.
Step 2. Assign σ to the first V in every sequence.
Step 3. Assign right V's to σ on the left as allowed by VV constraint.
Step 4. Repeat steps 2 and 3 treating any V's not yet associated with a σ as a new sequence.
Step 5. Assign left C's to σ on the right as allowed by CC constraint.
Step 6. Assign any remaining C's to the σ on the left.

cc constraint: No CC clusters are allowed within a syllable.
vv constraint: The only allowed vv clusters within a surface syllable are *a*V, V*i*, V*u*, denoted by:

$$\begin{bmatrix} +\text{syl} \\ +\text{low} \end{bmatrix} [+\text{syl}] \quad and \quad [+\text{syl}] \begin{bmatrix} +\text{syl} \\ +\text{high} \end{bmatrix}$$

---

[17] These syllabification rules assume an earlier application of the glottal insertion rule.

Segments, Syllables, and Stress in Larike

The application of these syllabification steps is demonstrated by the example in (126).

(126) Step 1. v c v c c v v v
              i t e r h u a e   'their crocodile'

Step 2.

Step 3. does not apply

Step 4. repeat steps 2 and 3 for unassociated v's

Step 2.

Step 3.

Step 5.

Step 6.

Examples (127)–(129) display the net result of the syllabification rules applied to several additional words. The details of each individual step have been omitted.

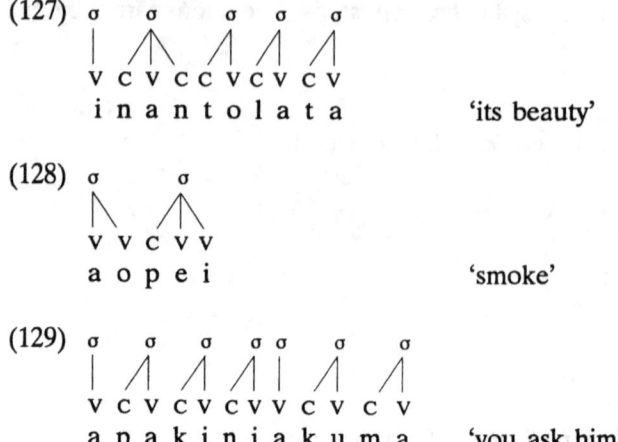

(127) inantolata 'its beauty'

(128) aopei 'smoke'

(129) apakiniakuma 'you ask him'

3.3. Stress assignment

In assigning stress in Larike, it is necessary to have access to the underlying root. Stress does not shift; it is always associated with the underlying penultimate syllable of the root. It should be emphasized that this is not always the same as the surface penultimate syllable of the root. There are several roots that contain a final VV sequence, such as [pa'tae] 'to leave' where the VV sequence is pronounced as a surface diphthong. Therefore, [pa'tae] is realized on the surface as a two-syllable word, apparently receiving stress on the ultimate syllable. In its underlying form, however, it is a three-syllable word, with primary word stress associated with the underlying penultimate syllable.

Once primary stress has been assigned, secondary stress is then assigned following an alternating pattern (such as s-u-p-u, where 'p' stands for primary stress, 's' is for secondary stress, and 'u' denotes unstressed). Secondary stress falls on the second (and fourth) surface syllable away from the primary stressed syllable. Since stress does not shift off of the underlying penultimate syllable of the root, secondary stress can occur either to the right or left of the primary stressed syllable. The examples below show primary and secondary stress assignment for several Larike words. In each case the root appears in bolded letters.

Segments, Syllables, and Stress in Larike

(131)

```
    s    u       p    u    s
    σ    σ       σ    σ    σ
    |   /\      /\   /\   /\
    V C V C    C V C V C V
    i n a n    t o l a t a     'its beauty'
```

If affixes are attached, stress does not shift, since stress is determined by the root.[18] The following examples will lend support to this statement. First, a list of unaffixed words is presented to show that stress is in fact on the underlying penultimate syllable of the root.

(132) /ure/   ['ʔu.re]   'banana'
       /ana/   ['ʔa.na]   'child'
       /paledi/   [pa'lɛ.di]   'to sell'
       /molo/   ['mo.lo]   'to sink'
       /ata/   ['ʔa.ta]   'tall'
       /nadu/   ['na.du]   'long'

When there are affixes added to the root, stress is not affected by the addition, but remains associated with the underlying penultimate syllable of the root. The following are examples with various types of affixes added to the root (bolded) showing no change in stress.

(133) transitivizer:
       /**loto**-ku/   ['**lo.to**''ku]   'to dry something'
       /**pakinia**-ku/   [pa.ki'**ni.ə**''ku]   'to ask something'

(134) nominalizer:
       /ra-**rene**-ta/   [ra'**rɛ.ne**''ta]   'sickness'
       /ta-**toti**-ta/   [ta'**to.ti**''ta]   'stairs'

---

[18] This differs from Collins (1983:82) who states that "stress in Hoamoal languages is always penultimate; if a suffix or particle is added to the word the stress shifts accordingly."

(135) possessives:
    /tida-na/   ['ti.da''na]   'blossom of something'
    /tida-ri/   ['ti.da''ri]   'blossoms of something'
    /rupae-ri/   [ru'pae.ri]   'women of someone'

(136) pluralizer:
    /ana-u/   ['ʔa.nau]   'children'
    /huta-u/   ['hu.tau]   'weeds'
    /disu-i/   ['di.sui]   'noses'
    /udo-i/   ['ʔu.doi]   'heads'

(137) multiple suffixes:
    /pa-loto-ku-ma/   [pa'lo.to''ku.ma]   'dry him'
    /pa-lae-ku-mati/   [pa'lae.ku''ma.ti]   'remember them'

Consider also, the following examples:

(138) /saʔa/   ['sa.ʔa]   'to ride'
    /aka-saʔa-ta/   [''ʔa.ka'sa.ʔa''ta]   'passenger'
    /maka-aka-saʔa-tu/   [''ma.ka''ʔa.ka'sa.ʔa''tu]   'ones who ride'

(139) /saʔo/   ['sa.ʔo]   'to chop sago'
    /sa-saʔo-du/   [sa'sa.ʔo''du]   'sago chopping tool'
    /maka-saʔo-ta/   [''ma.ka'sa.ʔo''ta]   'one who chops sago'

Stress could be considered contrastive in a technical sense, since there are several sets of minimal pairs distinguished only by which syllable is stressed. However, upon closer inspection, stress can be predicted in these words if only the root is known. For example, in the following sets of words stress seems to be contrastive until the morphological composition of the word is recognized. It is then clear that stress has not changed from the underlying penultimate syllable of the root, in accordance with the general stress rule.

(140) /ana-na/   ['ʔa.na.na]   'CLASS fish-one'
    /anana/   [ʔa'na.na]   'body'

(141) /ana-u/   ['ʔa.nau]   'children'
    /anau/   [ʔa'nau]   'to cook'

(142) /pa-kadi-ku/   [pa'ka.di''ku]   'to sun-dry'
      /paka-diku/   [''pa.ka'di.ku]   'to lean'

(143) /masa/   ['ma.sa]   'to cook'
      /ma-sa/   [ma'sa]   'one person'

(144) /apa/   ['a.pa]   'to cut'
      /a-pa/   [ʔa'pa]   'where'

Even though stress is very predictable in the great majority of words, there are some exceptions which do not appear to follow the pattern. Although the following words appear to be exceptions to the stress rule, there is evidence that they are actually multimorphemic words (or they were historically multimorphemic words). In these words the final morpheme is (or at one time was) the actual root; it is this morpheme (the final syllable of the compound) which carries word stress. Therefore, although at first glance these words seem to be exceptions to the stress placement rule, upon closer examination, they actually follow the rule, in that the root is recognized to be a monosyllabic morpheme occurring word finally. This analysis follows the general rules for contractions and compounds discussed in §4.1. In addition, the morphemes *ma, hi, a, se, me, pa, sa,* and *la* can all occur in isolation. This lends further weight to the hypothesis that the apparent exceptions to the stress rule are actually multimorphemic compounds. Examples of these words are given below.

(145) /masa/   [ma'sa]   'one person'
      /isa/   [ʔi'sa]   'one thing'
      /sasa/   [sa'sa]   'anything'
      /nahi/   [na'hi]   'like this'
      /nama/   [na'ma]   'like that'
      /hima/   [hi'ma]   'that there'
      /ama/   [ʔa'ma]   'there'
      /sase/   [sa'se]   'some'
      /seme/   [sɛ'me]   'what?'
      /apa/   [ʔa'pa]   'where?'
      /lapa/   [la'pa]   'from where?'
      /napa/   [na'pa]   'how?'
      /kudapa/   [ku.da'pa]   'why?'

Another exception to the stress rule is a final unstressed /ə/. This may have a historical basis, also.[19]

(146) /niria/ ['niriə] 'tooth'
/alea/ ['aleə] 'door'
/itia/ ['ʔitiə] 'lightning'
/tudia/ ['tudiə] 'machete'

The following set of exceptions to the stress rule is more difficult to explain. Each word is a noun, and has a final nonpeak /i/ or /u/, typically used to designate plural nouns in Larike. If these were in fact plural suffixes, they would not violate the stress rule. However, since the notion of plurality does not seem to fit these words, they are considered to be lexically marked for exceptional stress.

(147) /sinorai/ [si'norai] 'knuckle'
/tonai/ ['tonai] 'mud'
/pitui/ ['pitui] 'corpse'
/walau/ ['walau] 'place'
/lalau/ ['lalau] 'blood'

As shown by the above discussion, stress is predictable in the vast majority of Larike words. With few exceptions, stress is associated with the underlying penultimate syllable of the root.

3.4. Epenthetic vowels

There are two classes of words in Larike which appear with an epenthetic vowel. One appears with an epenthetic /e/ and the other with an epenthetic /u/. Both are suffixed directly to the root.

The class of words with an epenthetic /e/ includes nouns, verbs, and nominal modifiers. These words appear to be recent loan words with word-final consonants, mostly from Malay. Since Larike does not have word-final consonants, the epenthetic /e/ is used to assimilate these borrowings to the typical Larike structure. Since the epenthetic /e/ is not part of the underlying root, it does not affect penultimate syllable stress on the root (bolded) as shown in the following examples.

---

[19]Collins (1983:123) reconstructs Proto Central Maluku *-ə (singular noun marker) and *-a (plural noun marker). Since the words in question are all nouns, it is possible that the final /a/ in Larike words could be a remnant of one of these suffixed noun markers.

(148) /ator-e/ ['ʔatore] 'to arrange'
/batal-e/ ['batale] 'to break the fast'
/biaŋ-e/ ['biaŋe] 'midwife'
/kuat-e/ ['kuate] 'strong'

The second class of words, all nouns, ends with a final syllable /du/ or /nu/. Historically, it is clear that these nouns had a word-final consonant.[20] Since this structure does not fit the typical Larike word pattern, an epenthetic /u/ was added. Because this vowel is not considered a part of the underlying root, it is not considered when assigning stress to the words. Words in this class appear with stress on the penultimate syllable of the root (bolded), excluding the final epenthetic vowel.

(149) /iʔan-u/ ['ʔiʔanu] 'fish'
/hudan-u/ ['hudanu] 'rain'
/kapad-u/ ['kapadu] 'boat'
/apid-u/ ['ʔapidu] 'saliva'
/asad-u/ ['ʔasadu] 'market'

As this discussion has shown, certain classes of words, whether borrowed or historically based, have been altered to fit the syllable pattern of Larike. Once the underlying root is recognized, these words conform to the general stress rule stated previously.

4. Stress in contractions and compounds

4.1. General treatment

In Larike, contractions and compounds are fairly common. The most frequently occurring cases are those consisting of prepositions and oblique pronouns. Other cases occur when nouns or verbs are contracted or compounded with other nouns, modifiers, verbs, or prefixes.

Compounds and contractions in Larike can be treated as consisting of a series of ordered steps: first juxtaposition followed by possible deletion or assimilation, then resyllabification, and finally stress placement. While there is no way to predict which words will undergo contraction, virtually all contracted forms have met one requirement: contraction occurred when a syllable ending in a vowel preceded a stressed syllable beginning with a

---

[20]Historically, words such as /iʔanu/, /lalanu/, and /weidu/ originated from PAN *ikan, *jalan, and *wer respectively (Wurm and Wilson 1975).

vowel. The following three steps characterize contractions and compounds in Larike.

(150) Contraction and compounding rules:
    Step 1. If the juxtaposition of the two morphemes results in geminate vowels, the final vowel of the initial morpheme is obligatorily dropped.
    Step 2. Resyllabification occurs according to the syllabification rules in §3.2 with one slight modification: uV is an allowed VV cluster across morpheme boundaries where the second vowel in the cluster is stressed.

Thus, if morpheme boundary is represented by the symbol +, the syllable level VV constraint is revised to allow $u +$ 'V, in addition to the aV, Vi, Vu allowed by the standard syllabification rules. The allowed VV sequences are specified by the following feature matrices:

$$\begin{bmatrix} +\text{syl} \\ +\text{low} \end{bmatrix} [+\text{syl}] \; and \; [+\text{syl}] \begin{bmatrix} +\text{syl} \\ +\text{high} \end{bmatrix} \; and \; \begin{bmatrix} +\text{syl} \\ +\text{high} \\ +\text{back} \end{bmatrix} + \begin{bmatrix} +\text{syl} \\ +\text{stress} \end{bmatrix}$$

    Step 3. Stress placement occurs according to the stress assignment rules in §3.3, with primary stress falling on the surface syllable containing the underlying penultimate syllable of the right-most root in the contraction or compound.

Examples illustrating these steps for various types of contractions and compounds are shown in the following sections.

4.2. Contractions with oblique pronouns

As outlined in §4.1, oblique pronouns contracting with prepositions or modifiers illustrate the general rules of contraction and compounding. In all of the examples, the bolded letters indicate the underlying penultimate syllable of the right-most root since it is the location of this underlying stressed syllable that determines word stress on the surface. The examples below show either deletion of the unstressed geminate vowels or the coalescence of vowels at the point of contraction. For the purposes of this paper, coalescence does not refer to two underlying vowels combining into one surface vowel, but rather to two underlying vowels (each an underlying syllable) combining to form one surface syllable.

Segments, Syllables, and Stress in Larike

The examples in (151) illustrate deletion of the unstressed geminate vowel. The stressed vowel of the right-most root (bolded) determines which surface syllable is given primary stress in the resulting contraction. Each of the three steps is indicated in the following contraction.

(151)   'riʔa + 'aʔu → ri'ʔaʔu
      for   1s   'for me'

Step 1. c v c v v c v   c v c v c v
           r i ʔ a a ʔ u → r i ʔ a ʔ u

Step 2. σ   σ   σ
        /\ /\ /\
        c v c v c v
        r i ʔ a ʔ u

Step 3. u   p   u
        σ   σ   σ
        /\ /\ /\
        c v c v c v
        r i ʔ a ʔ u

Other examples involving vowel reduction are derived in a similar manner. The individual steps are omitted for simplicity.

(152)   'kisa + 'aʔu → ki'saʔu
      alone   1s   'by myself'

(153)   'aka + 'ami → a'kami
      for   1pe   'for us'

In (154), juxtaposition produces nongeminate vowel sequence. These cases illustrate vowel coalescence, using the term as previously defined.

(154) pa'pe?a + 'ite → pape'?aite
       all   1pi   'all of us'

Step 1. does not apply

Step 2.
```
      σ    σ    σ     σ
     /|\  /|\  /|\   /|\
     C V  C V  C V V C V
     p a  p e  ? a i  t e
```

Step 3.
```
      s    u    p     u
      σ    σ    σ     σ
     /|\  /|\  /|\   /|\
     C V  C V  C V V C V
     p a  p e  ? a i  t e
```

Note that in the stressed syllable /?ai/, stress originated from the underlying penultimate syllable of the root *ite*. This is characteristic of resyllabification in Larike contractions and compounds. Primary stress is always assigned to the surface syllable containing the underlying penultimate syllable of the right-most root. Secondary stress is assigned to the second syllable left of the primary stressed syllable, following the usual pattern of alternating stressed with unstressed syllables. Additional examples are given in (155)–(156).

(155) 'laku + 'ami   → la'kuami
       with   1pe   'with us'

(156) 'aka + 'imi   → a'kaimi
       for   2p   'for you'

When vv sequences are realized on the surface as a single syllable, the nuclear vowel is generally determined so as to maximize the ease of labialization. The nuclear vowel in each of the previous two examples is /a/; the stressed syllable /kua/ is pronounced [kwa], while the stressed syllable /kai/ is pronounced [kay].

4.3. Compound nouns

This section demonstrates that the contraction and compounding rules apply in the same manner to compound nouns. The stress assigned to the

Segments, Syllables, and Stress in Larike

resulting compound follows precisely the general rules outlined in §4.1. In (157)–(160), the VV sequence results in coalescence of the vowels. In (160), deletion of the juxtaposed geminate vowel occurs before resyllabification and stress assignment. These steps are illustrated in the following compound nouns.

(157) 'meita + 'udo → mei'taudo
     ocean   head   'beach'

Step 1. does not apply

Step 2.   σ   σ   σ

         C V V C V V C V
         m e i t a u d o

Step 3.   u   p   u
         σ   σ   σ

         C V V C V V C V
         m e i t a u d o

Several additional examples are given below, omitting the details of each step.

(158) 'dima + 'uru → di'mauru
     hand   length   'forearm'

(159) 'hato + 'uru → ha'touru
     rock   length   'boat dock' (lit. broken rocks; the Larike's dock is made of broken rocks)

(160) 'weidu + 'udo → wei'dudo
     river   head   'river source'

The three words in (161)–(163) clearly illustrate the compounding process, showing that both resyllabification and stress placement follow the proposed rules. The word in (161) is simply the root, showing that stress falls on the penultimate syllable as expected. The word in (162) illustrates this same root, but compounded with another root located to the right, resulting in deletion of the unstressed geminate vowel. In (163), the compound is formed from three roots, showing the deletion of unstressed geminate vowels in two locations. In each compound, primary stress has been assigned to the surface syllable containing the underlying penultimate syllable of the right-most root. Secondary stress is assigned following the usual high-low pattern of alternation, in this case falling on the second syllable to the left of the primary stressed syllable.

(161) '*hudu*
       'open area, clearing'

(162) '*hudu*   + '*uru*   → *hu'duru*
       open area   length   'mouth'

(163) '*hudu*   + '*uru*   + '*udo* → ''*hudu'rudo*
       open area   length   head   'lips'

The following examples demonstrate two compounded nouns where the final noun begins with a consonant. In this case, there is no deletion or coalescence of vowels. Primary stress is placed as expected, according to the rules for assigning stress to compounds.

(164) '*sou*   + '*tei* → *sou'tei*
       language   waste   'gossip'

(165) '*hou* + '*paka(du)* → *hou'paka*
       smell   sore   'foul smell'

A compound may be comprised of two or more nouns, modifiers, verbs, and affixes. In *souduhaha* 'wedding hat', the first two roots are contracted and the unstressed geminate vowel is dropped. The right-most root *haha*, since it begins with a consonant, is directly compounded without any alterations. The resulting compound has primary stress assigned to the underlying penultimate syllable in the right-most root. Secondary stress is then assigned in the alternating high-low pattern.

(166)   'sou + 'udo + 'haha → "soudu'haha
        sew   head   above   'wedding hat'

Step 1. c v v c v c v c v
        s o u d u h a h a

Step 2. σ   σ   σ   σ
        ⋀   ⋀   ⋀   ⋀
        c v v c v c v c v
        s o u d u h a h a

Step 3. s   u   p   u
        σ   σ   σ   σ
        ⋀   ⋀   ⋀   ⋀
        c v v c v c v c v
        s o u d u h a h a

4.4. Contractions with possessive pronouns

Contractions sometimes occur with possessive pronouns and certain nouns. The conditioning factors for these contractions have not been totally determined. Often it is the most common possessive forms which are contracted, possibly in an effort to economize the most frequently used expressions. The fact remains that the contracted form of a possessive pronoun and the following possessed noun follow precisely the general rules for contractions and compounds proposed in §4.1. Two examples showing the steps of vowel deletion (as applicable), resyllabification, and stress assignment to the resulting contracted possessive forms are given in (167)–(168).

(167) 'aku + 'ana → a'kuana
　　　 1s P　　 child　　 'my child'

　　　Step 1. does not apply

　　　Step 2.　σ　　σ　　　σ
　　　　　　　 |　 /|\　 /|
　　　　　　　 V C V　V C V
　　　　　　　 a k u　a n a

　　　Step 3.　u　　p　　　u
　　　　　　　 σ　　σ　　　σ
　　　　　　　 |　 /|\　 /|
　　　　　　　 V C V　V C V
　　　　　　　 a k u　a n a

(168) 'sena + 'ana → se'nana
　　　 INT P　　 child　　 'whose child?'

　　　Step 1. C V C V V C V　　C V C V C V
　　　　　　　 s e n a a n a → s e n a n a

　　　Step 2.　σ　　σ　　σ
　　　　　　　/|　 /|　 /|
　　　　　　 C V C V C V
　　　　　　 s e n a n a

　　　Step 3.　u　　p　　u
　　　　　　　σ　　σ　　σ
　　　　　　/|　 /|　 /|
　　　　　 C V C V C V
　　　　　 s e n a n a

Additional examples are listed without showing the details of each step.

(169) 'mana + 'ina → ma'neina
　　　 3s P　　 mother　　 'his mother'

(170) 'mana + 'ana → ma'nana
　　　 3s P　　 child　　 'his child'

Segments, Syllables, and Stress in Larike

4.5. Affixational contractions

There are not many examples of contractions of roots with affixes. The reason for this may be that there are not many words beginning with a stressed vowel that can be used with prefixes. In the two cases below, the ultimate unstressed vowel of the initial prefix and the initial stressed vowel of the following morpheme result in a VV sequence which coalesces. Resyllabification occurs and stress is assigned. The first example illustrates the process step by step.

(171) ta   +   'iya   →   'taiya
       NEG   good   'ugly, broken (no good)'

Step 1. does not apply

Step 2.
```
      σ       σ
     /|\     /|
    C V V   C V
    t a i   y a
```

Step 3.
```
      p        u
      σ        σ
     /|\      /|
    C V V    C V
    t a i    y a
```

The following example is derived in a similar manner:

(172) paka + 'iya   →   pa'kaiya
      CA   good   'repair (cause to become good)'

4.6. Contractions in the number system

The number system in Larike makes extensive use of contractions. Stress and syllable structure in these contractions give further evidence that the rules postulated for compounds and contractions in §4.1 are correct.

The first example below shows coalescence of vowels[21] and the assignment of primary stress to the surface syllable containing the stressed vowel

---

[21]Vowel coalescence in the contraction of [hu'seidana] 'eleven' changes the /ai/ vowel sequence to /ei/. This process has been noted in several other Larike words (see footnote 12).

of the right-most root. Since the morpheme *-na* meaning 'one' is a suffix, it is not part of the right-most root *ida*, and has no effect on stress assignment. The example below illustrates the steps of vowel coalescence (see footnote 12), resyllabification, and stress assignment for the number 'eleven'.

(173)   *hu'sa* +   *'ida* +   *na* →   *hu'seidana*
      ten   big   one   'eleven'

Step 1. does not apply

Step 2.
```
       σ   σ    σ   σ
       /\  /\   /\  /\
       C V C V V C V C V
       h u s e i d a n a
```

Step 3.
```
       u      p     u      u
       σ   σ    σ   σ
       /\  /\   /\  /\
       C V C V V C V C V
       h u s e i d a n a
```

The two examples below show primary stress assigned to the surface syllable containing the stressed vowel in the right-most component. Secondary stress is then assigned following the normal alternating high-low pattern.

(174)   *hu'sa* +   *'ida* +   *'itu* →   *''husei'deitu*
      ten   big   seven   'seventeen'

Step 1. does not apply

Step 2.
```
       σ   σ     σ    σ
       /\  /\    /\   /\
       C V C V V C V V C V
       h u s e i d e i t u
```

Step 3.
```
       s   u        p     u
       σ   σ     σ    σ
       /\  /\    /\   /\
       C V C V V C V V C V
       h u s e i d e i t u
```

Segments, Syllables, and Stress in Larike

(175) 'hutu + 'itu + 'ida + 'itu → hu"tuitui'deitu
     tens   six   big   six   'sixty-six'

Step 1. does not apply

Step 2.
```
     σ    σ     σ     σ     σ
    /\   /|\   /|\   /|\   /|
   C V  C V V C V V C V V C V
   h u  t u i t u i d e i t u
```

Step 3.   u s   u   p   u
```
     σ    σ     σ     σ     σ
    /\   /|\   /|\   /|\   /|
   C V  C V V C V V C V V C V
   h u  t u i t u i d e i t u
```

Several other examples show contraction of words where possible, or simple compounding of the words where the contraction is impossible because of an intervening consonant. In all the cases, the primary stress of the resulting word falls on the surface syllable containing the stressed vowel of the right-most root.

(176) 'hutu + 'dua → "hutu'dua
     tens   two   'twenty'

(177) 'hutu + 'ati → hu'tuati
     tens   four 'forty'

(178) hu'sa + 'ida + 'nene → hu"seida'nene
     ten   big   six   'sixteen'

(179) 'hutu + 'dua + 'ida + tidu → hu"tudu"aida'tidu
     ten   two   big three 'twenty-three'

4.7. Reduplication

The discussion of reduplication in this section is not an attempt to explain the process of reduplication, but rather to show that reduplicated forms obey the same rules set forth for compounds and contraction.

Reduplication takes several different forms in Larike. The most straightforward reduplication pattern is to repeat the entire root in order to emphasize or intensify the meaning of the root. For instance, *lo* 'oceanward direction' is emphasized in the reduplicated pattern *lolo* 'far in the oceanward direction'. Primary stress is assigned to the underlying penultimate syllable of the right-most root as usual. If the form to be reduplicated is monosyllabic, primary stress is still assigned to the surface syllable which has the underlying stressed syllable of the right-most root. Secondary stress is assigned as usual. Examples of this pattern of reduplication and stress assignment are given below.

(180) /lo-lo/   [lo-'lo]   'far oceanward'
       /lai-lai/   [lai-'lai]   'far landward'
       /keʔi-keʔi/   [ˌkɛʔi-'kɛʔi]   'very quickly'
       /tiwa-tiwa/   [ˌtiwa-'tiwa]   'suddenly'
       /teku-n-teku/   [ˌtekun-'teku]   'very quietly'

Another pattern of reduplication is to add a CV syllable to the beginning of the word where C is identical to the first consonant of the root and V is an /a/. When the base form has an initial glottal, the initial CV syllable of the reduplicated form would be [ʔa]. Primary stress of the resulting reduplicated word remains associated with the underlying penultimate syllable of the root, as shown in the following examples.

(181) /ra-rene-ta/   [ra'rɛneˌta]   'sickness'
       /ha-hera-ku/   [ha'heraˌku]   'opener'
       /la-loko-ta/   [la'lokoˌta]   'sitting place'
       /a-ʔese-ta/   [ʔa'ɛʔseˌta]   'task'
       /a-ʔihu-ta/   [ʔa'ʔuhuˌta]   'cough'

There are many more examples of compounds and contractions in Larike, but this discussion attempts to illustrate just a sampling from each of the two categories. The main point is that stress and syllabification patterns in Larike reduplicated forms can be understood in light of the general rules for compounds and contractions proposed in §4.1.

5. Stress shift at clause level

As demonstrated in the previous sections, stress is predictable in the vast majority of Larike words. The addition of affixes does not alter the

Segments, Syllables, and Stress in Larike

placement of stress on the root. Even in cases of contractions, compounds or reduplicated words, stress is highly predictable. There are only a few exceptions of words where the stress is not on the penultimate vowel of the root. This can all change, however, when words are part of a clause. The stress can shift from the penultimate vowel of the final root to one of the clause-final suffixes which may be present.

At the clause level, at least three clause-final particles can be suffixed to the final word of the clause. These are *-e*, a completive marker indicating completed action or certainty; *-o*, an immediacy marker implying a meaning of 'now' or 'first' and also functioning as a yes/no interrogative marker; and *-iŋ*, a tag-question marker with a meaning similar to 'isn't that right?' These particles can occur clause finally either as single suffixes or in combinations. If they occur in combinations, they appear in a specific order: *-e*, *-o*, then *-iŋ*.

When one of these suffixes is added clause finally, the primary stress shifts from the penultimate syllable of the final root to the suffix particle, while secondary stress falls on the underlying penultimate syllable of the root as shown in the following clauses.

(182)   *Au''ʔanu'e.*
        au-ʔanu-e
        1s^s-eat-COM
        I have eaten already.

(183)   *Ba Ali ka''tudokune'e.*
        ba Ali katudoku-ne-e
        Mr. Ali sleepy-2s^O-COM
        Ali, you are sleepy already.

(184)   *An''tudo'o.*
        a-n-tudo-o
        2s^s-ST-sleep-IMM
        You go to sleep right now.

(185)   *Imi''ʔeu'o?*
        imi-ʔeu-o
        2s^s-go-IMM
        Are you going?

(186) *Udata   ina   ''atata'iŋ?*
      udata   ina   ata-ta-iŋ
      mountain 3sn^P tall-NOM-TQM
      The mountain is tall, right?

Occasionally, the clause final particle *-e* and the final /a/ of the preceding word coalesce, resulting in a contraction of the particle and the preceding word. This only occurs when the particle *-e* is the only clause-final particle present. Since the VV sequence /ae/ is one that frequently coalesces in other contractions, this does not seem unusual. Stress is recognized on the syllable containing the stressed particle which follows the rules for contractions in §4.1. The following examples show this contraction process and stress placement.

(187) *Meima'tae.*
      mei-mata-e
      3s^s-die-COM
      He's dead already.

(188) *Aulaʔi   ni'dae.*
      au-laʔi   nida-e
      1s^s-arrive yesterday-COM
      I came yesterday.

(189) *Au''hiha'mae.*
      au-hiha-ma-e
      1s^s-call-3s^o-COM
      I called him already.

All of the clause-final particles are not equal with regard to stress. They are ordered according to which one receives primary, secondary and tertiary stress when used in combination clause finally. The particles are ranked below to determine which particle receives highest stress when more than one particle is suffixed to the same word.

(190) first   *-iŋ*
       second   *-e*
       third   *-o*

Thus, when a combination of *-iŋ*, *-e*, and *-o* is suffixed to the final word in a clause, primary stress is assigned according to the order in which the particles are ranked. In other words, if the particle ranked first is not present, then the particle ranked second receives primary stress and the particle ranked third receives secondary stress, etc. Examples of this process are as follows.

(191) *Akeu''eo'iŋ?*
 a-keu-e-o-iŋ
 2sˆs-go-COM-IMM-TQM
 You have already gone, right?

(192) *Auloko'e''o.*
 au-loko-e-o
 1sˆs-sit-COM-IMM
 I'm sitting first (for a while).

(193) *Imisahe ala''e'iŋ?*
 imi-sahe ala-e-iŋ
 2pˆs-buy rice-COM-TQM
 You have bought rice already, right?

6. Summary

In summary, a preliminary description of the previously uninvestigated phonological system of Larike, a Central Malayo-Polynesian language, has been presented. Even though there is evidence of heavy influence from Malay, Larike remains today a unique and distinct language on the island of Ambon.

Excluding the five borrowed phonemes, the Larike phoneme system consists of thirteen consonants and five vowels, similar to other related languages in the area.

There are four underlying syllable types: V, CV, VC, and CVC. Excluding loan words, the only constraint on the distribution of syllable types is that word-final consonants are not allowed. The VC and CVC types are rare, occurring only across morpheme boundaries. In fact, the final C in these two types can be only the morpheme *-n* (stative marker) or the morpheme *-r* (possessive marker).

In underlying representation, each vowel is associated with one syllable. In surface representation, some vv sequences are contained in a single surface syllable. Syllabification rules correctly derive the surface syllable structure from the underlying form.

Stress is highly predictable. Assigning stress requires a knowledge of the underlying root, since stress usually occurs on the underlying penultimate syllable of the root without regard to most affixes. Even in compounded or contracted words this stress rule is accurate. In a contraction, it is evident that a word-final vowel either is deleted, in the case of geminate vowels, or coalesces with an initial stressed vowel of a following word. Even though it can not be predicted when contraction will take place, when it does occur, resyllabification and stress placement follow in a predictable manner.

The only time the word-level stress placement rule is overridden is when particles carrying stress at the clause level are suffixed to the clause-final word. There are three clause-final morphemes, -e, -o and -iŋ, that receive primary stress when suffixed individually to the clause-final word. When one of these particles is present, the stress shifts from the penultimate vowel of the final word of the clause to the clause-final particle. The particles are ranked in order of stress assignment. When more than one particle appears, stress can be assigned predictably according to the particles' rank.

It is hoped that with the investigation and description of the phonology of Larike, some insight has been gained to further enhance the understanding of Central Moluccan languages and perhaps of Malayo-Polynesian languages as a whole.

Segments, Syllables, and Stress in Larike

7. Interlinearized text

In the following Larike text,[22] the first line in each set is written phonemically. Following orthographical convention, possessive pronouns and noun classifiers are shown as separate words, rather than attached to the noun which they modify. The second line in each set shows morpheme divisions and underlying morphemes. Epenthetic vowels are not separated from the root. The third line provides a morpheme-by-morpheme English gloss, using the abbreviations listed in footnote 5. An English free translation is provided at the end of the interlinearized section.

1. Waktu musim aninu timudu, musiai alei hina Rikedu matiʔeu lo
  waktu musim aninu timudu musia-i alei hina Rikedu mati-keu lo
  time season wind east person-PL here village Larike 3p^s-go seaward

  haha matisela iʔanu romu, baraŋ waktu musim timudu ma iʔanu romu
  haha mati-sela iʔanu romu baraŋ waktu musim timudu ma iʔanu romu
  far 3p^s-troll fish fish (sp) because time season east DET fish fish (sp)

---

[22]The reader who is familiar with Ambonese Malay or Standard Malay will recognize many borrowed terms in this text, often displaying segments and syllable patterns which are not typical Larike. Some examples of such words from the sample text are:

Larike	Indonesian	English Gloss
barani	berani	bold
baraŋ	barang	because
barenti	berhenti	stop
baru	baru	before
biar	biar	though
bisa	bisa	able
hanya	hanya	only
jadi	jadi	so
kastau	kasih tahu	inform
kuraŋ	kurang	less
majo	maju	forward
manahaŋ	menahan	withstand
memaŋ	memang	truly
musim	musim	season
sabe	sebab	since
sakaraŋ	sekarang	now
sanaŋ	senang	happy
subu	subuh	dawn
tagal	tegal	because
tamba	tambah	add
waktu	waktu	time
yaŋ	yang	that

lo   laute   he?e   rene. 2. *tapi ina   aninu laku   ina   kududanu iri?ida   rene*
lo   laute   he?e   rene   *tapi ina   aninu laku   ina   kududanu iri-ida   rene*
seaward ocean   many   very   but 3sn^P wind and   3sn^P wave   3pn^s-big very

si?u. 3. *Po   hanya hidi   musiai   mati biasa aninu laku ina   kududanu*
si?u   *po   hanya hidi   musia-i   mati biasa aninu laku ina   kududanu*
also   CONTR only   from   person-PL 3p   usual   wind and   3sn^P wave

idatu,   laku matinta?ue.   4. *Mati?una   ri?a biasae.* 5. *Jadi waktu hima*
ida-tu   laku mati-n-ta?u-e   *mati-puna ri?a biasa-e*   *jadi waktu hima*
big-NOM^PL then 3p^s-ST-afraid-CM 3p^s-make for usual-CM   so   time that

pito Juma?ate. 6. *Ina   hanto?ata ma musiai   elau.* 7. *Matisei   lo*
pito Juma?ate   *ina   hanto?ata ma musia-i   elau*   *mati-sei   lo*
day Friday   3sn^P morning   DET person-PL many   3p^s-paddle seaward

laute ri?a matisela   i?a romu. 8. *Narohi hima memaŋ ina   aninu i?ida*
laute ri?a mati-sela i?a romu   *narohi hima memaŋ ina   aninu i-ida*
ocean for 3p^s-troll fish fish (sp)   day   that true   3sn^P wind 3sn^s-big

rene, tapi pape?a musiai   mati sau   lo   laute. 9. *Jadi matisela-sela.*
rene tapi pape?a musia-i   mati sau   lo   laute   *jadi mati-sela-sela*
very but all   person-PL 3p   exist^at seaward ocean   so   3p^s-troll-troll

10. *Sidumai mati?adi,   sidumai tau   mati?adi.* 11. *Laku ina   aninu ma*
    sidumai mati-padi   sidumai tau   mati-padi   *laku ina   aninu ma*
    part   3p^s-pull^in part   not^yet 3p^s-pull^in   then 3sn^P wind DET

lebe iramba   kasare. 12. *Laku sidumai yaŋ matinta?u,   matisei   wela.*
lebe i-tamba   kasare   *laku sidumai yaŋ mati-n-ta?u   mati-sei   wela*
more 3sn^s-add rough   then part   that 3p^s-ST-afraid 3p^s-paddle go^home

13. *Sidumai yaŋ tau   mati?adi,   matimanahaŋ.* 14. *Matisela   saladu-saladu.*
    sidumai yaŋ tau   mati-padi   mati-manahaŋ   *mati-sela saladu-saladu*
    part   that not^yet 3p^s-pull^in 3p^s-withstand   3p^s-stroll always-always

15. *Lebe lou lebe aninu ma ina   kasare laku kudantori lebe   iramba*
    lebe lou lebe aninu ma ina   kasare laku kudanto-ri lebe   i-tamba
    more long more wind DET 3sn^P rough and wave-P^pl more 3sn^s-add

i?ida. 16. *Laku matinta?u   tarus   matinawela,   po   mati lou he?e*
i-ida   *laku mati-n-ta?u tarus   mati-na-wela   po   mati lou he?e*
3sn^s-big   then 3p^s-ST-afraid directly 3p^s-IR-go^home CONTR 3p   far very

hidi kalate. 17. *Jadi sakaraŋ matinasopa   lae.* 18. *Aninu laku kududanu*
hidi kalate   *jadi sakaraŋ mati-na-sopa lae*   *aninu laku kududanu*
from shallow   so   now   3p^s-IR-sail landward   wind and   wave

Segments, Syllables, and Stress in Larike

lebe	tamba	i?ida,	laku	undana	masa	meinala	Muhamate	meiropa
lebe	tamba	i-ida	laku	undana	masa	mei-nala	Muhamate	mei-ropa
more	add	3sn^s-big	then	male	person	3s^s^RL-named	Muhamate	3s^s^RL-sail

lae.	19. Mana	lalahari	mati?ari?ina,	tahi mana laedue.	20. Tapi mane
lae.	mana	lalaha-ri	mati-kari?i-na	tahi mana laedu-e	tapi mane
landward	3s^P	friend-P^pl	3p^s-see-EMPH	no 3s^P sail-CM	but 3s

se aninu haha,	jadi	mana	lalahari	tahi	bisa	matinamajo	ri?a
se aninu haha	jadi	mana	lalaha-ri	tahi	bisa	mati-na-majo	ri?a
at wind above	so	3s^P	friend-P^pl	no	able	3p^s-IR-forward	for

matinatanama.	21. Waktu	mati?ari?i	ri?a meimolo	pe?a,
mati-na-tana-ma	waktu	mati-kari?i-na	ri?a mei-molo	pe?a
3p^s-IR-take-3s^o	time	3p^s-see-EMPH	for 3s^s^RL-sink	finished

mati?ari?ima	meiloko	se haka haha.	22. Matimanahaŋ	matisopa
mati-kari?i-ma	mei-loko	se haka haha	mati-manahaŋ	mati-sopa
3p^s-see-3s^o	3s^s^RL-sit	at boat above	3p^s-withstand	3p^s-sail

saladusaladu	ri?anala	matila?i	lae	kalate.	23. Laku matikastau aka
saladu-saladu	ri?anala	mati-la?i	lae	kalate	laku mati-kastau aka
always-always	until	3p^s-arrive	landward	shallow	then 3p^s-inform to

pape?a musiai.	24. Laku	musiai	mati?eu lo	laute	niko
pape?a musia-i	laku	musia-i	mati-keu lo	laute	niko
all person-PL	then	person-PL	3p^s-go	seaward ocean	earlier

me,	matihule?ima.	25. Musiai matihule?i-hule?ima ri?anala
me	mati-hule?i-ma	musia-i mati-hule?i-hule?i-ma ri?anala
mentioned	3p^s-search-3s^o	person-PL 3p^s-search-search-3s^o until

narohi-rohi,	hanya dapate	mana haka mate?e.	26. Hidipo Muhamate
narohi-rohi	hanya dapate	mana haka mate?e	hidipo Muhamate
all^day	only find	3s^P boat just	but Muhamate

tadapatemae.	27. Ina	nadisa	peduke musiai	mati?eu	hule?ima.
ta-dapate-ma-e	ina	nadisa	peduke musia-i	mati-keu	hule?i-ma
NEG-find-3s^o-CM	3sn^P	tomorrow	again person-PL	3p^s-go	search-3s^o

28. Jadi	pape?a musiai	matihule?ima	ri?anala	putu	itu,	po
jadi	pape?a musia-i	mati-hule?i-ma	ri?anala	putu	itu	po
so	all person-PL	3p^s-search-3s^o	until	day	seven	but

tadapatemae.
ta-dapate-ma-e
NEG-find-3s^o-CM

29. | Jadi | kalu | musim | aninu | timudu | alei | hina | Rikedu | musiai | matisela
    | jadi | kalu | musim | aninu | timudu | alei | hina | Rikedu | musia-i | mati-sela
    | so | if | season | wind | east | here | village | Larike | person-PL | 3p^s-troll

i?anu romu, po matita?eu lou-lou lo laute. 30. Mati?eu masu-
i?anu romu po mati-ta-keu lou-lou lo laute mati-keu masu-
fish fish (sp) but 3p^s-NEG-go far far seaward ocean 3p^s-go near

masu mate?e, baraŋ matinta?u. 31. Sabe tiap aninu timudu waktu sela
masu mate?e baraŋ mati-n-ta?u sabe tiap aninu timudu waktu sela
near just because 3p^s-ST-afraid since each wind east time troll

i?a romu ma, musiai Rikedu mati masi idasa pe?a. 32. Matimata
i?a romu ma musia-i Rikedu mati masi idasa pe?a mati-mata
fish fish (sp) DET person-PL Larike 3p CLASS few finished 3p^s-die

lo haha tagal matisela i?a romu. 33. Jadi sakaraŋ hi kalu
lo haha tagal mati-sela i?a romu jadi sakaraŋ hi kalu
seaward far because 3p^s-troll fish romu so now this if

mati?ari?i aninu i?ida rene, matita?eu sela. 34. Matipapei pitosa,
mati-kari?i aninu i-ida rene mati-ta-keu sela mati-papei pito-sa
3p^s-see wind 3sn^s-big very 3p^s-NEG-go troll 3p^s-wait day-one

pitosidua. 35. Aninu laku kududanu ibarenti atau kuraŋ lohosa baru bisa
pito-si-dua aninu laku kududanu i-barenti atau kuraŋ lohosa baru bisa
day-PL-two wind and waves 3sn^s-stop or less little before able

mati?eu sela. 36. Baraŋ sela i?anu romu, musiai Rikedu matirasa
mati-keu sela baraŋ sela i?anu romu musia-i Rikedu mati-rasa
3p^s-go troll because troll fish fish (sp) person-PL Larike 3p^s-feel

matiselaya intele rene. 37. Kalu mati?eu ri?a subu-subu, masa
mati-sela-a i-n-tele rene kalu mati-keu ri?a subu-subu masa
3p^s-troll-3sn^o 3sn^s-ST-good very if-3p^s go for dawn-dawn person

meipadi anar husa ada yaŋ masaipadi anar hutudua,
mei-padi ana-r husa ada yaŋ masa-i-padi ana-r hutudua
3s^s^RL-pull^in CLASS-P ten exist that person-RL-pull^in CLASS-P twenty

baru matiwela ma kira-kira oras siwa, katahi oras husa hanto?ata.
baru mati-wela ma kira-kira oras siwa katahi oras husa hanto?ata
before 3p^s-go^home DET approximately hour nine if^not hour ten morning

38. Jadi matirasa sela i?a romu ma ina sanaŋ ri?anala musiai
    jadi mati-rasa sela i?a romu ma ina sanaŋ ri?anala musia-i
    so 3p^s-feel troll fish fish (sp) 3s^o 3sn^P like until person-PL

sidumai.	39. Biar	aninu, po	matibarani	mati?eu lo	laute.
sidumai	biar	aninu po	mati-barani	mati-keu lo	laute
part	though	wind but	3pˆs-bold	3pˆs-go	seaward ocean

40. Tapi sakaraŋ	hi,	he?e	yaŋ	musiainta?ue,	sabe	musiai
tapi sakaraŋ	hi	he?e	yaŋ	musia-i-n-ta?u-e	sabe	musia-i
but now	this	many	that	person-PL-ST-afraid-CM	since	person-PL

matimata	pe?a	tagal	sela	i?a romu.	41. Jadi	musiai	sakaraŋ
mati-mata	pe?a	tagal	sela	i?a romu	jadi	musia-i	sakaraŋ
3pˆs-die	finished	because	troll	fish fish (sp)	so	person-PL	now

hi,	matitabaranie.
hi	mati-ta-barani-e
this	3pˆs-NEG-bold-CM

Free translation

1. During the east monsoon, people from the village of Larike went out on the ocean to troll for *romu* because during that time of year there are a lot of *romu* in the ocean. 2. But the wind and waves are also very big. 3. Even though the people were used to the wind and the big waves, they were afraid. 4. They went on as usual. 5. It was a Friday. 6. That morning there were a lot of people. 7. They paddled out to sea to troll for *romu*. 8. That day the wind was truly very strong, but all the people went out to sea. 9. They trolled and trolled. 10. Some of them pulled in fish and some of them did not. 11. Then the wind got stronger. 12. Then some who were afraid paddled home. 13. Those who hadn't yet pulled in fish kept going. 14. They trolled continuously. 15. As time went on, the wind and waves became stronger. 16. Then they were afraid and wanted to go home, but they were very far from shore. 17. So now they were going to sail back. 18. The wind and waves became even stronger, and a man named Muhamate was sailing in front. 19. When his friends looked up, his sail was gone. 20. But he was upwind, so it was impossible for his friends to go and get him. 21. But when they looked up after he had sunk, they saw him sitting on top of the boat. 22. Fighting the waves, they continued to sail until they reached the shore. 23. Then they told everyone what happened. 24. Then the people went to the ocean to look for him. 25. The people searched and searched all day, finding only his boat. 26. But they didn't find Muhamate. 27. The next day they searched for him again. 28. They searched for him for seven days, but they didn't find him.

29. So if the east monsoon is here in Larike, people troll for *romu* but they don't go way far out in the ocean. 30. They stay in close because they are afraid. 31. Because each time there is an east monsoon, several people die when trolling for *romu*. 32. They die far out at sea when trolling for *romu*. 33. So now if they see a big wind, they don't go trolling. 34. They wait one or two days. 35. The wind and waves stop or decrease a little before they go trolling. 36. Because trolling for *romu* is something people from Larike really enjoy doing. 37. If they go at dawn, some people will pull in ten fish, others will get twenty fish before they return home. 38. Some people really enjoy trolling for *romu*. 39. Although it may be windy, they bravely go out on the ocean

anyway. 40. But nowadays many people are afraid, since people have died while trolling for *romu*. 41. People these days just aren't very brave.

References

Blust, Robert A. 1978. Eastern Malayo-Polynesian: A subgrouping argument. Pacific Linguistics C-61:181–221.
Bolton, Rosemary. 1989. Nuaulu phonology. In W. D. Laidig (ed.), Workpapers in Indonesian Languages and Cultures. Vol. 7, 89–119. Ambon: Summer Institute of Linguistics and Pattimura University.
Chlenov, M. A. 1976. Nasalenie Molukkskikh Ostrovov. Moscow: Nauka.
——— and U. Sirk. 1973. Merger of labial phonemes in Ambonese languages. Acta et commentationes Universitatis Tartuensis, Oriental Studies II(1).
Clements, George N. and Samuel J. Keyser. 1983. CV phonology. Cambridge: MIT Press.
Collins, James T. 1980. Laha: A language of the Central Moluccas. Indonesia Circle 23:3–19.
———. 1982. Linguistic research in Maluku: A report of recent field work. Oceanic Linguistics 21:73–146.
———. 1983. The historical relationships of the languages of Central Maluku, Indonesia. Pacific Linguistics D-47.
Crab, P. van der. 1862. De Moluksche Eilanden: Reis van Z. E. den Gouverneur-General C. F. Pahud. Batavia: Lange.
Grimes, Barbara Dix. 1988. Exploring the sociolinguistics of Ambonese Malay. Paper presented at the Fifth International Conference on Austronesian Linguistics, Auckland, January 1988.
Laidig, Wyn D. and Carol J. Laidig. 1990. Larike pronouns: Duals and trials in a Central Moluccan language. Oceanic Linguistics, in press.
Ludeking, E. W. A. 1868. Schets van de residentie Amboina. The Hague: M. Nijhoff.
Stresemann, Erwin. 1927. Die Lauterscheinungen in den Ambonischen sprachen. Zeitschrift fur Eingeborenen-Sprachen, Beiheft X.
Travis, Edgar W. 1989. A lexicostatistic survey of the languages indigenous to Ambon Island. In W. D. Laidig (ed.), Workpapers in Indonesian Languages and Cultures. Vol. 6, 65–101. Ambon: Summer Institute of Linguistics and Pattimura University.
Wallace, Alfred R. 1869. The Malay archipelago: The land of the *orang-utan* and the bird of paradise. London: Macmillan.
Wurm, Stephen A. and B. Wilson. 1975. English finderlist of reconstructions in Austronesian languages. Pacific Linguistics C-33.

A Lexical Phonology of West Tarangan

Richard Nivens
Pattimura University and The Summer Institute of Linguistics

West Tarangan is a Central Malayo-Polynesian (Austronesian) language spoken by about 7,000 people living on the west part of Tarangan island, southern Aru, southeast Maluku, Indonesia. It is closely related to the other languages in Aru. Although each village has its own linguistic idiosyncracies, there are four dialects: central west coast (Coast), River, northern west coast (North), and Plains. More detailed information on dialect and language boundaries has been given in Nivens (1989). The major portion of this paper deals with the Coast dialect as spoken in the village of Kalar-Kalar. The analysis is based on a lexicon of over 1,900 entries, collected both individually and in discourse context. Recent (unassimilated) loans from Aru Malay have been excluded from the analysis.

As with the other languages of Aru, West Tarangan has been little studied. The only studies to date are unpublished manuscripts by Takaria et al. (1982) and Pieter et al. (1984), as well as some discussion by Collins (1982) of Tarangan as a dialect of what he called Wokam-Tarangan. Hughes (1987) identified West Tarangan as a separate language on the basis of lexicostatistics. The data presented here were gathered on

Tarangan island, mostly in the Coast village of Kalar-Kalar, from 1987 to 1990, as well as in the provincial capital Ambon.[1]

The data[2] is presented in terms of the theory of lexical phonology (Mohanan 1986). This is a model in which phonology has close interaction with both morphology and syntax. Mohanan offers a diagram of lexical phonology similar to the following (147).

(1)
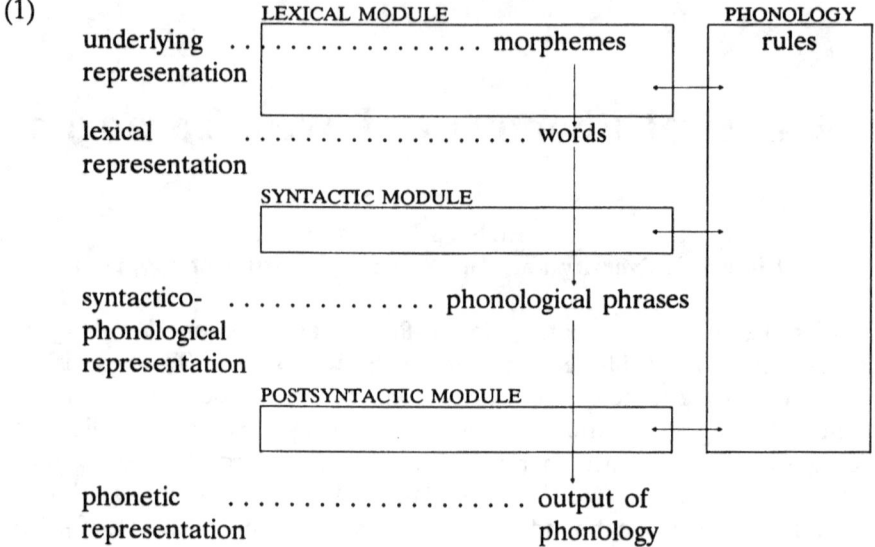

---

[1]This research was carried out under the cooperative agreement between the Summer Institute of Linguistics and Pattimura University in Ambon. Appreciation is expressed to university and government officials who expedited the work by their cooperation, and particularly to Drs. M. S. Darakay, our university counterpart who is also a native speaker of the North dialect of West Tarangan. Many thanks to Don Burquest, Jock Hughes, Ed Kotynski, and Steve Marlett, who commented on earlier versions of this paper. I take responsibility for any errors or omissions.

[2]For expository convenience, [dʒ] is written as [j], [r] represents a flap, and [t] here means voiceless dental stop. ϕ will be written as p, except when given within phonemic or phonetic brackets. Final stress, except when caused by a mid vowel in the final syllable, is indicated with a macron (ā ī ū).

The vowel /e/ is phonetically between [ɪ] and [e]; /o/ is between [ʊ] and [o]. I use diacritics [é ó] in phonetic representations to indicate the higher tongue position.

Abbreviations used in this paper include: 1s first-person singular, 2s second-person singular, 3s third-person singular, 1i first-person plural inclusive, 1e first-person plural exclusive, 2p second-person plural, 3p third-person plural, AGR subject agreement, AN animate, AP antipassive, AUX auxiliary, CONJ conjunction, DEF definite, DEG degree adverb, DUP reduplicative prefix, FUT future, IN inanimate, NF nonfinite, pl plural, PROG progressive aspect, PST past, R verb prefix r-, sp species, YNQ yes/no question tag.

A Lexical Phonology of West Tarangan

In Mohanan's diagram, the syntactic and postsyntactic modules are subsumed under a postlexical module. In addition, a module may consist of more than one stratum; each morphological operation is specified as to which stratum it takes place in, and any boundary brackets internal to the resulting string are erased at the end of each stratum. Rules of phonology are ordered and also marked as to which modules and strata they may apply in.

In West Tarangan there is evidence for the lexical/syntactic distinction, as well as for three separate strata in the lexical module.[3]

(2)   Lexical module

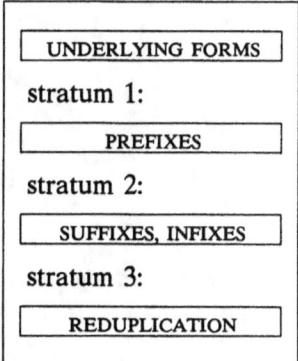

1. Stress

In most polysyllabic roots stress falls on the penultimate syllable. Affixes and clitics are never stressed, nor does affixation ever cause a stress shift.

The roots that don't have penultimate stress all have final stress; without exception the presence in the final syllable of a mid vowel causes root-final stress. It should be noted here that in this dialect there is a morpheme structure constraint prohibiting a polysyllabic morpheme from ending with a mid vowel.[4] Thus all of these morphemes with a mid vowel in the final syllable have it in a closed final syllable.

---

[3]There is some evidence that an older form of the language had a stratum of derivational prefixes prior to the stratum 1 shown here. Since these derivational prefixes are infrequent and unproductive, I ignore them in this paper.

[4]Many (if not all) cases of mid vowels in final syllables arose historically from assimilation with, and subsequent deletion of, a morpheme-final high vowel:

*aCu#   >   ɔC#   (*patu >   pɔt   'stone')
*aCi#   >   ɛC#   (*kali >   kɛl   'dig')
*oCu#   >   oC#   (*toru >   tor   'chicken')
*eCi#   >   eC#   (*peli >   pel   'price')

(3) Final mid vowel constraint[5]

$$* \quad V \quad C_0 \quad V \quad \# \\ [\text{mid}]$$

Vowel-final roots virtually always (96%) have penultimate stress. Consonant-final roots which do not have a mid vowel in the final syllable usually (89%) have penultimate stress. This holds true for every canonical shape except (C)VC.CVC: twenty of twenty-five instances in the corpus have final stress, necessitating another stress subrule for this canonical shape.[6]

(4)   *barkāt*   'lemon'
        jɛrtāy   'clothing'
        jɛlŋūt   'mollusk (sp)'
        kildūm   'sea turtle (sp)'
        karkīr   'plant (sp)'
        almūn   'shadow'

There is no synchronic rule to account for the remaining instances of final stress.[7] We do find at least one minimal pair with regard to stress.

(5)   *maŋar*   'fish (sp)'
        maŋār   'sky'

To account for these facts, a standard generative rule could be written as in (6), with disjunctively ordered subrules. Part (a) specifies that roots with a mid vowel in the final syllable have root-final stress, part (b)

---

[5]Vowel features will be discussed in §2.2.

[6]In fact, there seems to be a strange dichotomy among the (C)VCCVC roots: nearly all those with penultimate stress have /ɔ/ in the penultimate syllable.

    gɔrpan   'white hair'
    kɔrŋam   'parrot'
    tɔlŋum   'plant (sp)'

However, since the numbers are so few, I resist the temptation to include this quirk in the stress rules; for now I hold that the penultimate stress in these roots is an exception to the stress rule.

[7]Some instances of final stress are the result of the historical loss of a final high vowel, without an accompanying shift in stress.

    *paniki   >   anīk   'a large bat'

Other instances of final stress are due to the historical deletion of a glide between two low vowels.

    *puwaya   >   puwā [ɸu'ga]   'crocodile'

accounts for final stress with CVCCVC roots, while part (d) grants penultimate stress to other polysyllabic roots, and part (c) gives stress to monosyllabic roots.

(6) Stress (Lexical)

(a) $V \rightarrow [+\text{stress}] / \begin{bmatrix} \underline{\quad} \\ +\text{mid} \end{bmatrix} C \#$

(b) $V \rightarrow [+\text{stress}] / \# (C) V C C \underline{\quad} C \#$

(c) $V \rightarrow [+\text{stress}] / \# C_0 \underline{\quad} C_0 \#$

(d) $V \rightarrow [+\text{stress}] / \underline{\quad} C_0 V C_0 \#$

Under this analysis, finally stressed polysyllabic roots that do not meet the structural description of (a) or (b) would be marked [+final stress] in the lexicon.

It is generally accepted that metrical phonology explains primary and secondary stress more adequately than a generative rule-based approach does. A metrical account of stress makes use of prosodic levels above the syllable. Syllables (σ) group together into feet (F), and feet group together into prosodic words (M).

West Tarangan has bounded, quantity-sensitive feet. They are bounded in that each foot consists of at most two syllables, and they are quantity-sensitive in that syllable weight (open vs. closed) determines whether the foot consists of one or two syllables. Disyllabic feet are "left-headed"—that is, the left syllable is marked "s" (for "strong" or dominant) and the right syllable is marked "w" (for "weak" or subordinate).

Each M is binary branching, which results in the longest roots being limited to four syllables: the maximal M consists of two disyllabic feet. As will be demonstrated, this also explains why four-syllable roots may not have more than one consonant cluster.

It is important to note that the metrical tree is initially constructed on an unaffixed root. Each root has a σ, F, and M level. Affixes, however, have no M level, and only have a F level if required by the foot-construction stipulations given below. When affixes are added to a root, the M of the root is joined in a sister relationship with the metrical tree of the affix, creating a higher-level M-node.

(7) (a) (b) (c)

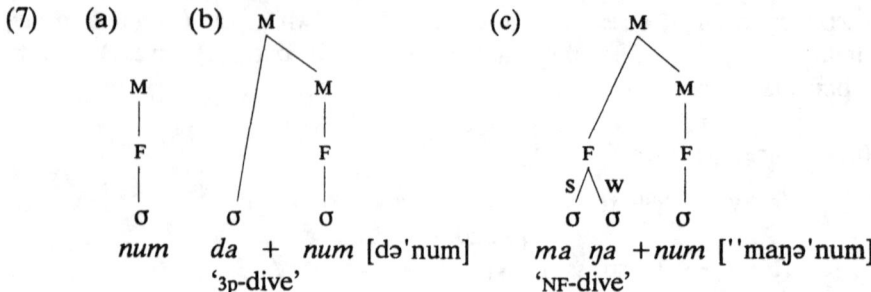

num   da + num [də'num]   ma ŋa +num [''maŋə'num]
          '3p-dive'   'NF-dive'

Thus the M-level is recursive on each cycle of morphological derivation, while the foot level is not recursive; in other words, an M-node may have another M-node below it, but a foot node may not have another foot node below it. This recursive nature of the M-level, coupled with the fact that affixes have no M-node of their own, explains why primary stress is always determined by the root, regardless of any affixation. Primary stress falls on that syllable which is linked to the topmost M-node by dominant branches alone.

Before going any further, I will demonstrate the above points with more examples.

(8) (a) (b)

(9)

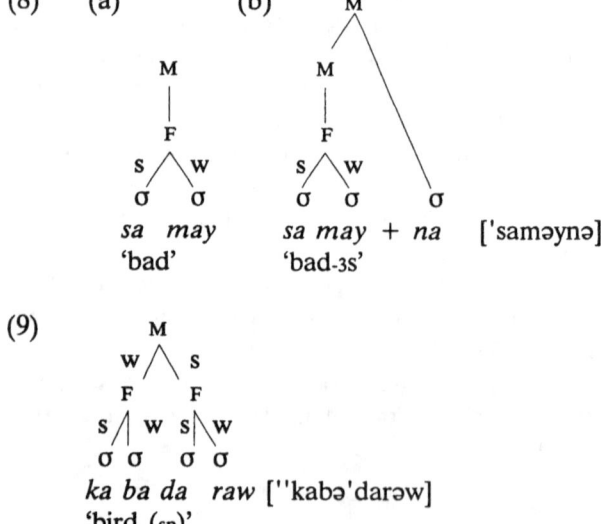

In each of the above examples, the foot consists of two syllables in a s-w configuration; note that this is true even when a light (open) syllable is

A Lexical Phonology of West Tarangan   133

followed by a heavy (closed) syllable. The M, as seen above, may consist of a single F, or two feet, or F and σ, or M and σ. (As seen below, M may also consist of M and F.) If the M consists of two constituents on the same level (i.e., two feet), they are marked w-s. Otherwise stress is assigned to the constituent whose node is at the higher level.

If the first syllable of the root is completely unstressed (i.e., has no F-node above it) then it is available to join with the prefix in forming a foot. The result of this is that the prefix syllable has secondary stress.[8]

(10) (a)   (b)

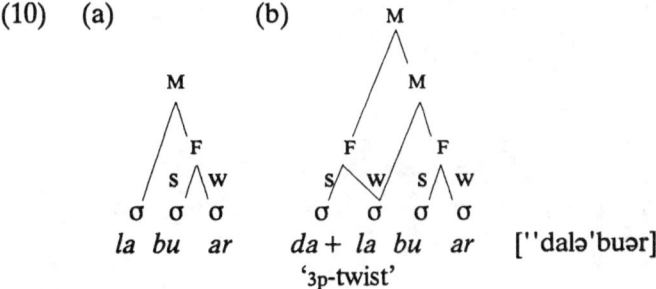

la bu ar   da + la bu ar   [ˌdalə'buər]
                '3p-twist'

All the data given up to this point seem to indicate that West Tarangan has quantity-insensitive feet, despite my earlier claim to the contrary. Since CVCVC roots have penultimate stress, it would seem that final heavy syllables do not require final stress. However, to account for regular final stress (i.e., final syllables with mid vowels, and CVCCVC roots), we must invoke the notion of syllable weight. I propose that any closed syllable preceded by either a closed syllable or a morpheme boundary may not be the weak member of a disyllabic foot. (In other words, unless a closed syllable is preceded by an open syllable, it may not be the weak member of a disyllabic foot.) As a result, no foot may contain two closed syllables. Thus I posit the following configurations.

(11)

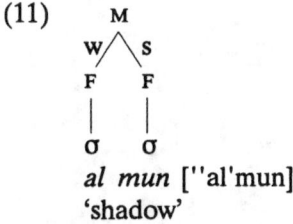

al mun [ˈalˈmun]
'shadow'

---

[8]Although I have drawn the syllable with lines both to the right and to the left, it is equally possible that the original M-node is deleted and the entire tree is redrawn, with only one M-node.

(12)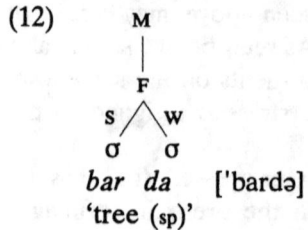
bar da ['bardə]
'tree (sp)'

(13)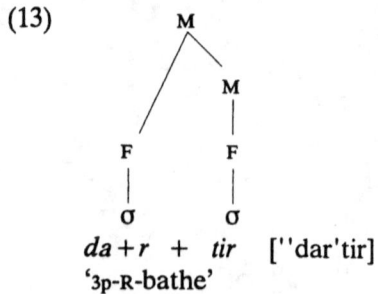
da+r + tir [''dar'tir]
'3p-R-bathe'

(14)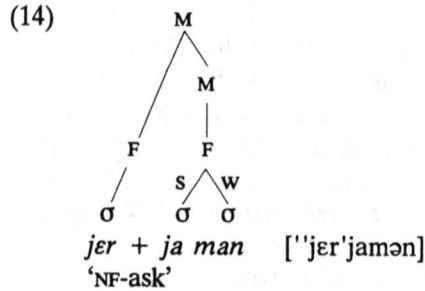
jɛr + ja man [''jɛr'jamən]
'NF-ask'

In addition, I posit that any closed syllable with a mid vowel may not be the weak member of a disyllabic foot; for some reason (to be discussed below) mid vowels are considered heavier than high and low vowels.

(15)   M
      /\
     / F
    σ   σ
    ta kɔm [tə'kɔm]
    'don't'

A Lexical Phonology of West Tarangan

(16)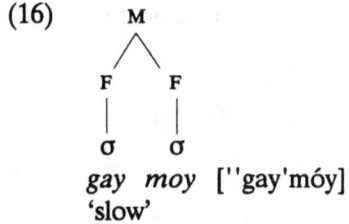
    gay moy [''gay'móy]
    'slow'

(17)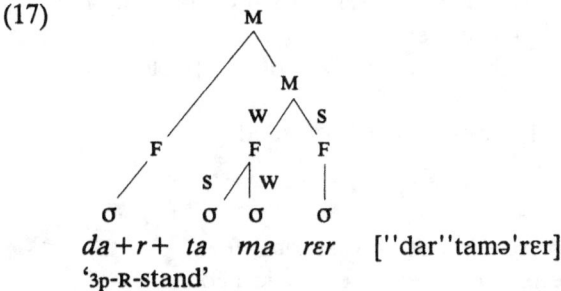
    da+r+ta ma rɛr [''dar''tamə'rɛr]
    '3p-R-stand'

To account for secondary stress, which prevents the reduction of /a/ to [ə], I posit that any syllable dominant in a foot receives (at least) secondary stress. This includes syllables marked "s" as well as those which constitute an entire monosyllabic foot. Any syllable which is paired with a constituent that dominates it (i.e., σ(s), F, or M) is completely unstressed; if the nucleus of that syllable is /a/, it reduces to [ə].

(18) *kabadaraw*   [''kabə'darəw]   *[kəbə'darəw]   'bird (sp)'
      saramina   [''sarə'minə]   *[sərə'minə]   'large gong'
      ɛr-tamarɛr [''ɛr''tamə'rɛr] *[ɛrtəmə'rɛr]   '3s-stand'
      rataŭn   [''ratə'un]   *[rətə'un]   'sago paste'

To summarize, West Tarangan has right-dominant words and left-dominant feet, and the regular instances of final stress are the result of syllable weight considerations in foot construction.

(19) Foot construction:

   (a) Feet are bounded (maximum two syllables).
   (b) Feet are quantity-sensitive (syllable weight determines whether the foot consists of one or two syllables).
   (d) Any closed syllable preceded by either a closed syllable or a morpheme boundary may not be the weak member of a disyllabic foot.

(e) Any closed syllable with a mid vowel may not be the weak member of a disyllabic foot.
(c) Disyllabic feet are left-headed (s-w).
(f) Any syllable dominant in a foot receives (at least) secondary stress.

(20) M-node construction:

(a) Each M is binary branching. (Therefore the maximal M consists of two disyllabic feet.)
(b) The M-level is recursive on each cycle of morphological derivation.
(c) An M consisting of two feet is right-headed (w-s).

(21) Maximal morphemes:

(a) The maximal root consists of two metrical feet.
(b) The maximal prefix consists of one metrical foot.
(c) The maximal suffix consists of one syllable.

Although it seems clear that a closed syllable with a mid vowel as its nucleus is classified as a "heavy" syllable, thus drawing stress to itself, this hypothesis seems rather ad hoc without some synchronic motivation. A possible explanation for this phenomenon is suggested by the theory of dependency phonology (Lass 1984:271–293):

> Dependency theorists claim that we can posit, to begin with, three 'elements' or primitives, i, u, a (primitives are given in verticals): these are respectively 'palatality', 'gravity/flatness/roundness', and 'openness/sonority' (275).

Thus /e/ is derived from "i governing a", /ɛ/ from "a governing i", and analogous statements for the back mid vowels. This notion of "two primitives in one vowel" may provide the notion of "mid-vowel weight" required for a concise treatment of stress.[9]

The heavy syllable hypothesis fails, however, to motivate the (C)VCCVC final-stress tendency. It would seem more likely for a light-heavy sequence (CV.CVC) to motivate final stress than for a heavy-heavy sequence to do so. Yet CVCVC roots have an overwhelming tendency toward penultimate stress.

Finally, what about the exceptions, those finally stressed roots that the rules predict should have penultimate stress? I propose that all roots which

---

[9]Thanks to René van den Berg for pointing this out to me.

A Lexical Phonology of West Tarangan

seem to be lexically marked exceptions in fact have two adjacent vowels in the underlying form.

(22) *pugā* /puwaa/ 'crocodile'
      maŋār /maŋaar/ 'sky'
      takūr /takuur/ 'coconut shell'
      tamīl /tamiil/ 'woodworm'

(23)

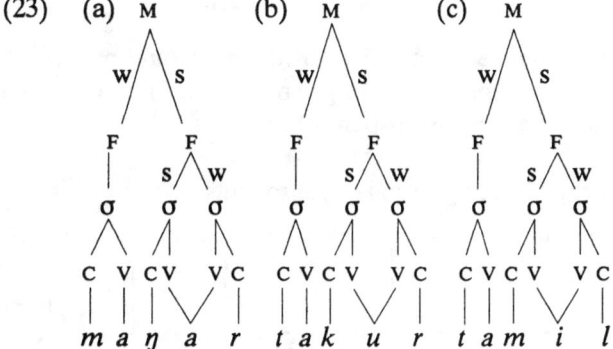

After stress has been assigned, these clusters are reduced by a degemination rule, which is well-attested elsewhere in the grammar.

A further class of exceptions, the CVCCVC roots with penultimate stress, remain unaccounted for in the analysis given above.

2. Phonemes

In lexical phonology, the underlying alphabet is distinguished from the LEXICAL ALPHABET, which consists of segments output from the lexical module. In West Tarangan, the lexical alphabet contains three more consonants than does the underlying alphabet.

2.1. Consonants

The underlying alphabet in West Tarangan contains thirteen consonants.

(24)   West Tarangan underlying consonant inventory

	bilabial	central	velar
stop vl.		t	k
vd.	b	d	
fricative	ɸ	s	
nasal	m	n	ŋ
flap		r	
lateral		l	
semivowel		y	w

The central column includes dental /t/, alveolar /d s n r l/, and palatal /y/. Distinctive features for these consonants are given in (25), followed by an explanation of the redundant features in parentheses.[10]

(25)   Distinctive features of West Tarangan consonants

	t	k	b	d	ɸ	s	m	n	ŋ	r	l	w	y
consonantal	(+)	(+)	(+)	(+)	(+)	(+)	(+)	(+)	(+)	+	+	−	−
sonorant	−	−	−	−	−	−	+	+	+	+	+	(+)	(+)
continuant	−	−	−	−	+	+	−	−	−	+	+	(+)	(+)
coronal	+	−	−	+	−	+	−	+	−	(+)	(+)	(−)	(−)
high	(−)	+	−	(−)	(−)	(−)	−	(−)	+	(−)	(−)	(+)	(+)
back	(−)	(+)	(−)	(−)	(−)	(−)	(−)	(−)	(+)	(−)	(−)	+	−
voice	−	−	+	+	(−)	(−)	(+)	(+)	(+)	(+)	(+)	(+)	(+)
lateral	(−)	(−)	(−)	(−)	(−)	(−)	(−)	(−)	(−)	−	+	(−)	(−)

(26)   Redundancy rules for consonants

    a. [−cons] → [+son, +cont, −cor, +high]
    b. [−son, +cont] → [−high]
    c. [+cons, +son, +cont] → [+cor]
    d. [+cor] → [−high]
    e. [−son] → [+cons]
    f. [−cont] → [+cons]

---

[10]The features [nasal] and [anterior] are entirely redundant:
    [+son,−cont] → [+nasal]
    (all others → [−nasal])
    [α high] → [−α anterior]

(27) Features redundant for all but one class

   g. [back] : same as [high] for all but [-cons] (glides)
   h. [voice] : same as [son] for all but [-son,-cont] (stops)
   i. [lateral]: [−lat] for all but [+cons,+son,+cont] (liquids)

The glide-to-obstruent rule. Both word initially and in the onset of a stressed noninitial syllable, the glides /w/ and /y/ are realized as [g] and [dʒ] respectively.[11]

(28) /wur/   ['gur]   'grass'
      /wɔwa/   ['gɔwə]   'blossom'
      /waymoy+na/   [gay'móynə]   'slow-3s'
      /suwakan/   [su'gakən]   'elephant tusk'

(29) /kawar/   ['kawər]   'fish (sp)'
      /lɛway/   ['lɛwəy]   'tree (sp)'
      /i+yɔw/   [i'jɔw]   '3s-see'
      /rɔraw/   ['rɔrəw]   'heat'

(30) /yɔm/   ['jɔm]   'grandparent/grandchild'
      /yabin/   ['jabin]   'many'
      /yirua/   [ji'ruə]   'tree (sp)'
      /biyarum/   [bi'jarum]   'whale'

(31) /rayan/   ['rayən]   'boat shelter'
      /woyan/   ['góyən]   'rain'
      /i+loy/   [i'lóy]   '3s-hang'
      /samay+na/   ['saməynə]   'bad-3s'

---

[11]The rule could not be stated conversely (i.e., /g/ and /ǰ/ are realized as [w] and [y] in certain positions), because the final voiced stop constraint (discussed below) would not allow /g/ and /ǰ/ to occur in syllable-final position.

To account for this process we may attempt to formulate the rule as follows, specifying two distinct environments for the change.[12]

(32)　Glide-to-obstruent rule (lexical)

$$[-\text{cons}] \rightarrow \overset{\text{C}}{\underset{}{\begin{bmatrix} +\text{cons} \\ -\text{son} \\ -\text{cont} \\ -\text{round} \end{bmatrix}}} / \left\{ \begin{array}{c} [\underline{} \\ \underline{} \; \underset{[+\text{stress}]}{V} \end{array} \right\}$$

This rule changes /w/ to [g], and /y/ to a palatal stop. We need a further redundancy rule to change the palatal stop into an alveopalatal affricate.

(33)

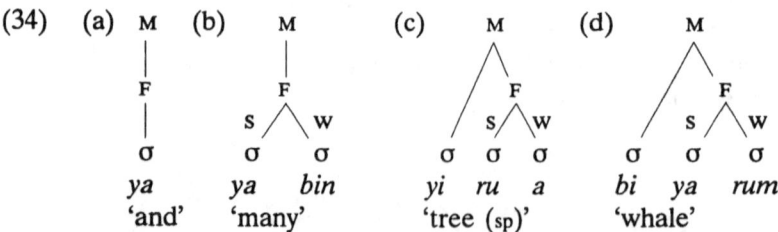

The metrical account of stress proposed in §2 enables us to simplify the structural description of the above rule. When a metrical tree is constructed on an unaffixed root, both the initial syllable and the stressed syllable are the leftmost member of a branch.

(34)　(a)　M　　(b)　　M　　　(c)　　　M　　　　(d)　　　M
　　　　　|　　　　　　|　　　　　　　／\　　　　　　　　／\
　　　　　F　　　　　　F　　　　　　　F　　　　　　　　　F
　　　　　|　　　　　／\　　　　　／／\　　　　　　／／\
　　　　　σ　　　　s　　w　　　　s　　w　　　　　s　　w
　　　　　　　　　σ　　σ　　σ　σ　σ　　　σ　σ　σ
　　　　　ya　　ya　bin　　yi　ru　a　　bi　ya　rum
　　　　'and'　'many'　　　'tree (sp)'　　　'whale'

---

[12]In lexical phonology, brackets [...] replace boundary symbols +, #, etc. I use /.../ for underlying representations, and [...] both for boundaries and to enclose phonetic transcriptions ('syntactico-phonological representations'). Within /.../ I represent morpheme boundaries with + and clitic boundaries with =. Transcriptions given without any brackets correspond to the lexical representation—i.e., lexical rules such as glide-to-obstruent have already applied.

A Lexical Phonology of West Tarangan

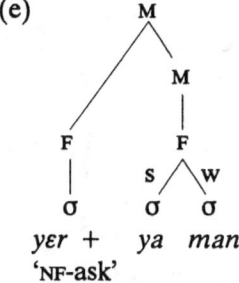

(e)

yɛr + ya man
'NF-ask'

So the rule can be stated as follows.

(35) Glide-to-obstruent rule (lexical)

$$[-\text{cons}] \rightarrow \begin{bmatrix} +\text{cons} \\ -\text{son} \\ -\text{cont} \\ -\text{round} \end{bmatrix} \bigg/ \underset{\{M,F\}}{[\underline{\quad\quad}}$$

(with an associated C above [−cons])

As will be demonstrated in §5.2, the glide-to-obstruent rule applies prior to reduplication; therefore it is necessary to posit that it applies in the lexical module.

According to the theory of CV phonology (Clements and Keyser 1983), /w/ and /y/ actually represent /u/ and /i/ linked to C-elements instead of V-elements. This linking to C and V elements obviates the need for the feature [syllabic]. Lexical entries consist of strings of melody elements unassociated to C and V elements, and there are universal principles of associating the skeletal (CV) tier with the melody tier.

> Permissible core syllable associations between elements of the CV-tier and elements of the segmental tier are determined in part by universal principles. Unless otherwise stipulated in the grammar or lexicon of a given language, V-elements of syllable structure are freely allowed to dominate [−consonantal] segments, and C-elements are freely allowed to dominate both [+consonantal] segments and [+high, −consonantal] segments. Other associations are possible only when admitted by language specific rules. (Clements and Keyser 1983:32)

So, when C and V elements are linked to the melody tier, any high vowel is linked to a C-element if language-specific constraints permit. Thus we would posit the following derivation for *gar* 'water'.

(36)   Underlying   Association   Glide-to-obstruent
           form

skeletal tier: CVC   CVC
                        ||| |||
melody tier: *uar* → *uar* (= war)   →   *gar*

However, West Tarangan apparently has a contrast between /u/ and /w/.

(37) (a) *gar*   /war/   ['gar]   'water'
         uar   /uar/   ['uər]   'wound'
     (b) *nawa*   /nawa/   ['nawə]   'sugar palm'
         ŋauan /ŋauan/ [ŋə'uən]   'honey'

Words like *uar* and *ŋauan* seem to be violations of the universal principle mentioned above.

There are two ways of solving this dilemma. First, we could propose that the underlying form of *uar* is /uuar/; that of *ŋauan*, /ŋauuan/. The second /u/ would be linked to a C-element, leaving the first /u/ to be linked to a V-element. Subsequently, the glide /w/ would be deleted from the geminate vowel-glide cluster, which is trivial, since geminate reduction is attested throughout the phonology of West Tarangan.

(38)   VCVC   VVC
           |||| |||
    uuar → *uuar* (= *uwar*) → *uar*

However, since vowel clusters are permissible, we would also have to provide some mechanism for preventing /uuar/ from being associated to a CVVC skeleton, giving */wuar/ *[guar].

An alternative proposal is to say that the underlying form of *uar* is simply /uar/, and that the /u/ is pre-linked to a V-element. Mohanan (1986:30) suggests that in certain lexical items, high vowels may be pre-linked to C or V elements in order to bypass the default linking of high vowels to C-elements as outlined above. Thus, we could posit the following derivation for *uar*:

A Lexical Phonology of West Tarangan

(39) V VVC

  | |||
  uar → uar

With the /u/ in this word (but not in *gar*) pre-linked to a V-element, the linking algorithm fails to link it to a C-element as universal principles would dictate. I see this analysis as more desirable than the first.

It should be noted here that the Clements and Keyser linking algorithm and the obligatory contour principle (OCP) cannot both work for West Tarangan. There are dozens of roots containing the sequences /wu/ and /yi/; the Clements and Keyser derivation for *gun* 'blood' and *jir* 'cockatoo' would be as follows.

(40) Underlying Association Glide-to-obstruent
     form

a.
            C V C   C V C
       → | | | → | | |
    u u n   u u n   g u n

b.
            C V C   C V C
       → | | | → | | |
     i i r   i i r   j i r

But the OCP holds that there are no geminate sequences like /uu/ or /ii/ on the melody tier in the underlying forms of morphemes; rather, underlying geminates must be of the form:

(41) x x skeletal tier
    \\/
    [ ]   melody tier

In order to maintain both the OCP and Clements and Keyser's hypothesis about linking conventions, we must assume that the underlying forms of morphemes include not only phonemic material but a skeletal tier comprised of X-elements and association lines already drawn between the skeletal tier and the phonemic material. The Clements and Keyser algorithm, then, is that which assigns the feature [syllabic] to the X-elements of the skeletal tier, deriving C and V elements. We would therefore posit that underlying forms of the morphemes mentioned above are as follows.[13]

---

[13]For expository convenience, I will continue to write /w/ and /y/ to represent high vowels linked to C-elements.

(42) (a) x x x   (b) v x x   (c) x x x   (d) x x x
          | | | | | | \ / | \ / |
          u a r   u a r   u n   i r
          gar   uar   gun   jir

The fricative-to-obstruent rule. The phoneme /ɸ/ is pronounced as [p] syllable-finally, and usually [ɸ] syllable-initially. It may occasionally be pronounced as a lightly articulated stop [p] in syllable-initial position.

(43) pit   ['ɸit] ~ ['pit]   'night'
      papa   ['ɸaɸə] ~ ['papə]   'ground'
      ε-tapaka   [εta'ɸakə] ~ [εta'pakə]   '3s-capsize'
      ɔlpɔt   [ɔl'ɸɔt] ~ [ɔl'pɔt]   'egret'
      na=k-pɔ   [nak'ɸɔ] ~ [nak'pɔ]   'FUTURE=1s-carry'
      pɔp   ['ɸɔp] ~ ['pɔp]   'pig'
      gurep   [gurép]   'nail'

Since [s] never occurs syllable-finally, contrast between /t/ and /s/ is apparently neutralized in that position. But some words show evidence of having syllable-final /s/ in the underlying form.[14]

(44) /las/   ['lat]   'three'
      /las+kim/   ['latkim]   'three-2p (the three of you)'
      /las+ay/   ['lasəy]   'three-3p (the three of them)'
      /jεr+later/   [jεr'la'tér]   'the third day after today'

(45) /us/   ['ut]   'her female genitals'
      /us+am/   ['usəm]   'your female genitals'

(46) /pes/   ['ɸét]   'breath'
      /pes+am/   ['ɸésəm]   'your breath'

Note that a rule changing /t/ to [s] intervocalically would not be appropriate, either morpheme-internally or at a morpheme boundary.

(47) lεtan   ['lεtən]   *['lεsən]   'far out to sea'
      let-let-ay ['lét'létəy] *['lét'lésəy]   'DUP-male-3p'

---

[14]Note also that in the closely related language Manumbai, there is no fricative-to-obstruent rule; /ɸ/ is always [ɸ], and words cognate with the forms under discussion here have [s].

A Lexical Phonology of West Tarangan

I propose the following strengthening rule to represent the fact that underlying fricatives are pronounced as stops in syllable-final position.[15]

(48) Fricative-to-obstruent rule (lexical)

$$[-son] \rightarrow [-cont] \; / \; \underline{\qquad}]_\sigma$$

From *jɛrlat er* 'three days from now' we see that the rule does not apply across word boundaries. Noting that resyllabification occurs when words are concatenated into phrases, it is clear that the rule must apply on the word level, i.e., lexically.

(49)   /yɛr+las#er/   [jɛr'la'tér]   *[jɛr'la'sér]

I also propose the following rule to account for those occasions when /ɸ/ is pronounced [p] syllable-initially.

(50) Voiceless bilabial stop formation (post-syntactic) (optional)

ɸ → [−cont]

This strengthening rule seems to spread across the entire word or phrase, since *[paɸə] and *[ɸapə] are apparently not possible pronunciations of /ɸaɸa/ 'ground'.

As a result of the glide-to-obstruent rule and the fricative-to-obstruent rule, the lexical alphabet of West Tarangan has three more consonants than the underlying alphabet.

(51)   West Tarangan lexical consonant inventory

	bilabial	apical	(alveo)palatal	velar
obstruent vl.	p	t		k
vd.	b	d	j	g
fricative	ɸ	s		
nasal	m	n		ŋ
flap		r		
lateral		l		
semivowel			y	w

---

[15]Alternatively, we could propose that the environment of the rule is morpheme-final rather than syllable-final; since fricatives cannot be the first member of a consonant cluster, all syllables ending with an underlying fricative are necessarily morpheme-final syllables. However, a rule that only refers to phonological constituents like foot or syllable is preferable to one that refers to morpheme boundaries.

/k/-**weakening.** In fast or casual speech /k/ may become glottal stop between two nonhigh vowels. This cannot happen at a word boundary, although it may occur at a clitic boundary.

(52)   *gaka*   ['gakə] ~ ['gaʔa]   'swamp'
      ka=kama   [kakə'ma] ~ [kaʔa'ma] 'our(s) (exclusive)'
      ɔk=kanāŋ   [ɔkə'naŋ] ~ [ɔʔə'naŋ] 'my, mine'

In some words (possibly high-frequency functors) it may even drop out altogether in fast speech.

(53)   *sakali*   [sə'kali] ~ [sa'ʔali] ~ [sa'ali]   'not'
      aka   ['akə] ~ ['aʔa] ~ ['aa] ~ ['a] 'for, because'

This weakening may be symbolized by the following two rules.

(54)   /k/-weakening (syntactic) (optional)

      k → ʔ /   V   —   V
                  [−high]   [−high]

(55)   Glottal deletion (syntactic) (optional)

      ʔ → ∅

The /k/-weakening rule can be expressed autosegmentally as deletion of the supralaryngeal tier.

(56)

$$\begin{bmatrix} -\text{son} \\ -\text{cont} \\ -\text{cor} \\ +\text{high} \end{bmatrix} \quad \emptyset \qquad [-\text{high}] \qquad [-\text{high}] \quad \Big\} \text{ supralaryngeal tier}$$

           | | | |
           C → C / V — V   CV tier
           | |
     [−voice] [+constr]   laryngeal tier

I posit that these rules apply in the syntactic module for two reasons: first, they apply at a clitic boundary, and cliticization of personal pronouns takes place early in the syntactic module; secondly, since they do not apply word initially (between two full words), they must apply prior to the concatenation of words into phrases (which takes place later in the syntactic module). Thus I propose the following derivations.

(57)

[gaka]	[ɔk] [kanāŋ]	[aka] [kama]	lexical representation
—	[[ɔk] [kanāŋ]]	—	cliticization
—	[[ɔ] [kanāŋ]]	—	geminate reduction
[gaʔa]	[[ɔ] [ʔanāŋ]]	[aʔa] [kama]	/k/-weakening
—	—	[[aʔa] [kama]]	phrase construction
[gaʔa]	[ɔʔanāŋ]	[aʔakama]	bracket erasure
'swamp'	'my, mine'	'for us (excl.)'	

Morpheme structure constraints. There are no voiced obstruents in syllable-final position, at any level of analysis (underlying, lexical, or phonetic). So I propose the following negative constraint, the asterisk indicating that the specified structure is prohibited.

(58) Final voiced stop constraint

$$*\begin{bmatrix} -son \\ +voice \end{bmatrix}_\sigma$$

This constraint on syllable-final stops could alternatively be stated as a constraint on morpheme-final stops, since a separate morpheme-structure constraint restricts the first member of a consonant cluster within a morpheme to /r l y/. So, the only syllable-final stops are those which occur at a morpheme boundary.

I propose the following constraint on underlying consonant clusters.[16] This is a positive constraint; that is, it specifies a structure which is allowed rather than one which is prohibited.

---

[16]Actually, I do have four or five examples of words with *m* or *n* as the first member of a consonant cluster, but these are probably either loan words or compounds. The related language Dobel (Hughes and Hughes 1989) does allow nasals as the first member of a consonant cluster.

(59) Consonant cluster constraint

$$C\ C \Rightarrow C\quad C$$
$$\quad\quad\quad\ \ |$$
$$\quad\quad\quad \begin{bmatrix} +\text{son} \\ +\text{cont} \\ -\text{back} \end{bmatrix}$$

This is a constraint on underlying structure alone; consonant clusters resulting from affixation and reduplication do not conform to this constraint.

There are no syllable-internal consonant clusters. Possible morpheme-internal consonant clusters, then, are shown in (60).

There are also phonotactic (co-occurrence) restrictions apparent in the corpus. There is no morpheme containing both /b/ and /ɸ/, and no morpheme has /d...t/ or /t...s/. Other co-occurrences are rare, although not prohibited, such as /t...d/, /s...t/, /s/ and /d/, /s/ and /s/, /w/ and /w/, and /y/ and /y/. In addition, it is nearly unattested for a velar consonant to be immediately followed by /i/.

(60) Consonant clusters

		C1 = /r/		C1 = /l/	
C2	/t/	kartɔw	'rat'	siɲalŋalta	'fungus (sp)'
	/k/	garkɔw	'orphaned'	ɛlkɛy	'black cockatoo'
	/b/	korkorba	'bat (sp)'	kaybɛlbɛlbal	'bird (sp)'
	/d/	barda	'shrimp (sp)'	kildūm	'turtle (sp)'
	/ɸ/	gɔrpan	'white hair'	ɔlpɔt	'heron'
	/s/	garsi	'crab (sp)'	galsɛrasɛran	'tuber (sp)'
	/m/	ɔrmol	'seasnake'	almŭn	'shadow'
	/n/	marnām	'turtle (sp)'	sɛlnɔr	'mollusk (sp)'
	/ŋ/	kɔrŋam	'parrot'	tɔlŋum	'plant (sp)'
	/r/	[geminate]		??	
	/l/	irlow	'cassava'	[geminate]	
	/w/	??		??	
	/y/	ɔrjɛla	'tree (sp)'	maljamajaman	'bed'

A Lexical Phonology of West Tarangan

              c₁ = /y/
    c₂ /t/   kaytɛa   'corn'
        /k/   gaykapa   'crab (sp)'
        /b/   gaybūn   'large'
        /d/   ??
        /ɸ/   ŋaypep   'womb'
        /s/   ??
        /m/ gaymoy   'slow'
        /n/   gaynaka   'sago leaf'
        /ŋ/   ayŋɔtay   'difficult'
        /r/   payrɔra   'bird (sp)'
        /l/   maylɛwa   'tree (sp)'
        /w/ ??
        /y/   [geminate]

Phonemic contrasts. Listed below are minimal pairs showing contrasts between similar consonants.[17] Initial and final here refer to morphemes, not necessarily phonological words, since what we are mainly interested in is contrasts between the underlying forms.

Labial consonants:

(61)   ɸ/b   initial
                    i-pɔ   '3s-carry'   i-bɔ   '3s-nurse'
                    i-para   '3s-bake'   bara   'lung'
                    pɛl   'with'   bɛl   'coast'

                medial
                    i-tɔpa   '3s-wash'   i-toba   '3s-chop'
                    da-apal   '3s-cross'   abal-di   'inside-3p'

(62)   b/m   initial
                    bɛl   'coast'   i-mɛl   '3s-laugh'

                medial
                    aba-y   'leg-3s'   ama-y   'father-3s'
                    taba   'carrying stick' tama   'flesh'

---

[17]The morphemes prefixed with *i-* or *da-* can also occur without these prefixes; they are given here to illustrate typical affixation.

(63) b/w initial[18]
            bara   'sago patch'   i-gara   '3s-born'
            ba   'what'   ga   'until'
            boy   'father'   i-goy   '3s-die'

            medial
            kabar   'pufferfish'   kawar   'fish (sp)'
            goba   'basket'   gɔwa   'blossom'

(64) m/w initial
            maŋar   'a fish'   gaŋar   'rattan'
            mar   'river'   gar   'water'
            i-ma   '3s-come'   ga   'until'

            medial
            kamar   'bird (sp)'   kawar   'fish (sp)'

            final
            jɔm   'grandparent'   i-jɔw   '3s-see'

Alveolar consonants:

(65) t/d initial
            ta-   '1i'   da-   '3p'

            medial
            bɔtam   'sacred'   dɛdɛdam   'afternoon'

(66) t/s initial
            taba   'carrying stick'   saba   'a kind of song'
            ɛr-tir   '3s-bathe'   ɛr-sir   '3s-speak'

            medial
            gatan   'just'   i-gasan   '3s-carry'

(67) d/n initial
            -da   '1i'   -na   '3s'
            dum   'six'   i-num   '3s-dive'
            din   'these (IN)'   i-nin   '3s-sleep'

            medial
            dɛdɛdam   'afternoon'   anam   'door'

(68) d/r initial
            i-dua   '3s-howl'   i-rua   '3s-plant'

            medial
            kada   'pants'   i-kara   '3s-bite'

---

[18]The reader is reminded that the underlying form of [g] is /w/.

A Lexical Phonology of West Tarangan

(69) d/l initial
i-doy	'3s-watch'	i-loy	'3s-hang'
i-dɛm	'3s-make'	i-lɛman	'3s-love'

medial
bɛda	'machete'	bɛla	'song (sp)'

(70) n/r initial
nor	'coconut'	ror	'stove'

medial
bana	'from'	bara	'sago patch'

final
gun	'blood'	gur	'grass'
din	'these (IN)'	dir	'those (IN)'
i-jaman	'3s-ask'	jamar	'mackerel'

(71) n/l initial
i-nar	'3s-hit'	i-lar	'3s-sail'
i-nɛr	'3s-spit'	lɛr	'foliage'

medial
kɔnar	'woman'	kɔlar	'breadfruit'
kanar	'remora'	kalar	'pandanus (sp)'

final
gun	'blood'	gul	'hair'
kɛn	'2s'	i-kɛl	'3s-dig'

(72) r/l initial
rat	'hundred'	lat	'three'
ra	'forest'	ɛ-la	'3s-run'

medial
kara-y	'urine-3s'	kala-y	'skin-3s'
rɔraw	'heat'	ɔlaw	'sago bowl'

final
gur	'grass'	gul	'hair'
gaŋar	'rattan'	gaŋal	'marsupial (sp)'
i-nar	'3s-hit'	i-nal	'3s-take/give'

Velar consonants:

(73) k/ŋ   initial
                kɔnar   'woman'   ŋɔnar   'a berry'
                -ka   '2s'   -ŋa   '1s'
                i-kɛl   '3s-dig'   ŋɛl   'light'

            medial
                gakar   'medicine'   gaŋar   'rattan'
                i-laka   '3s-carry'   i-laŋa   '3s-draw (water)'

            final
                gɔk   'bird (sp)'   gɔŋ   'game'

(74) k/w   initial
                i-kara   '3s-bite'   i-gara   '3s-born'
                ka   'so that'   ga   'until'
                i-kul   '3s-bend'   i-gul   '3s-gather'

            medial
                i-naka   '3s-tell'   nawa   'sugar palm'

            final
                ɔk   '1s'   ɔw   'fire'

(75) ŋ/w   initial
                ŋar   'woven box'   gar   'water'

            medial
                naŋa   'deck'   nawa   'sugar palm'

            final
                tɔŋ   'mollusk (sp)' tɔw   'fish (sp)'

2.2. Vowels

West Tarangan has seven vowels in both the underlying and lexical alphabets. Although this is historically derived from a five-vowel system, there is no nonabstract way to synchronically reduce it to such (see Nivens 1990).

(76)   i   u
        e   o
        ɛ   ɔ
            a

There are a number of things that make /a/ stand out as distinct from the other vowels. First, /a/ accounts for over half the vowels in the corpus;

A Lexical Phonology of West Tarangan

in fact, there are five times as many instances of /a/ than of the next-most-frequent vowel. Next, there are epenthesis rules that insert a vowel, and in each case the vowel is /a/. Further, /a/ is deleted in various environments. Finally, there is a vowel cluster constraint specifying that one of the vowels in a cluster must be /a/. (These rules and constraints will be discussed in subsequent sections.)

Pulleyblank (1988) pointed out that in Yoruba, the vowel /i/ behaves differently from other vowels: it is the vowel inserted by epenthesis rules, it fails to trigger rules that other vowels trigger, and it fails to undergo rules that other vowels undergo. Yet there are other ways in which /i/ does pattern as a vowel. To account for this asymmetry, Pulleyblank posits that /i/ is a V-element with no specified features in its underlying representation, and all of its surface features are assigned by redundancy rules.

I posit a similar analysis for West Tarangan /a/. Conventional distinctive features for vowels, then, would be as follows, with redundant features in parentheses.

(77) West Tarangan vowel features

	i	e	ɛ	a	ɔ	o	u
high	+	(−)	(−)	(−)	(−)	(−)	+
low	(−)	−	−	(+)	−	−	(−)
back	−	−	−	(+)	(+)	(+)	(+)
ATR	(+)	(+)	−	(+)	−	(+)	(+)

(78) Redundancy rules for vowels:

    a. [   ] → [−high]
    b. [   ] → [+low]
    c. [   ] → [+back]
    d. [   ] → [−ATR]
    e. [+high] → [−low]
    f. [+high] → [+ATR]

Notice that /a/ has no underlying features, and all of its surface features are provided by redundancy rules (a)-(d). Note too that mid vowels are the only ones underlyingly specified for [low]; this may be what the stress rule is sensitive to.

We may, however, reduce the number of features needed by following Wang's (1968) proposal, using the feature [mid] instead of [low]; the feature [ATR] would then be completely redundant, and only three redundancy rules would be needed.

(79) West Tarangan vowel features

	i	e	ɛ	a	ɔ	o	u
high	+	+	(−)	(−)	(−)	+	+
mid	(−)	+	+	(−)	+	+	(−)
back	−	−	−	(+)	(+)	(+)	(+)

(80) Redundancy rules for vowels:
    a. [ ] → [−high]
    b. [ ] → [−mid]
    c. [ ] → [+back]

Since the notion MID VOWEL is crucial to West Tarangan stress, I will follow Wang's proposal.

High vowel laxing. High vowels /i/ and /u/ tend to be slightly lowered (laxed) in closed syllables, especially unstressed syllables closed by /r/; in other unstressed closed syllables, and in stressed syllables closed by /r/, the lowering is very slight.

(81)   *sirlawun* [sɪrˈlaun] 'basket (sp)'
      takir [ˈtakɪr] 'ear 3s'
      ɛpur-ka [ˈɛɸʊrkə] 'good 2s-2s'
      ŋur [ˈŋur] ~ [ˈŋʊr] 'rotten'
      abil [ˈabil] ~ [ˈabɪl] 'under 3s'

(82) High vowel laxing (post-syntactic) (optional)

$$\begin{bmatrix} +\text{high} \\ -\text{mid} \end{bmatrix} V \rightarrow [-\text{ATR}] \; / \; [\underline{} \; C]_\sigma$$

/a/-weakening. The low vowel /a/ is almost always mid [ə] in an unstressed syllable, except in very careful speech. As noted in the discussion on stress, unstressed here means either there is no foot node over the syllable, or else the syllable is the weak member of a foot.

All syllables following the stressed syllable are completely unstressed, and require weakening of /a/.

A Lexical Phonology of West Tarangan

(83) waka   ['gakə]   'swamp'
    abal-di   ['abəldi]   'inside-3p'
    mata-y   ['matəy]   'eye-3s'
    tɔp-ay   ['tɔɸəy]   'short-3p'
    rɔraw   ['rɔrəw]   'heat'
    samay-na ['saməynə]   'bad-3s'

An open syllable immediately preceding the stressed syllable cannot have secondary stress either, and in this position /a/ is usually weakened, although it seems that the weakening may be optional if the next syllable contains a stressed /a/.

(84) sariba   [sə'ribə]   'knife'
    tamata   [tə'matə] ~ [ta'matə]   'person'
    balār   [bə'lar] ~ [ba'lar]   'garden'

As noted in the discussion of stress, /a/ is not weakened if it carries secondary stress.

(85) kabadaraw [ˌkabə'darəw] *[kəbə'darəw] 'bird (sp)'
    saramina   [ˌsarə'minə]   *[sərə'minə]   'large gong'

(86) da-r-tir   [dar'tir]   *[dər'tir]   '3p-R-bathe'
    gaymoy-na [gay'móynə]   *[gəy'móynə]   'slow-3p'
    almūn   [al'mun]   *[əl'mun]   'shadow'

I propose the following rule.

(87) /a/-weakening (post-syntactic)

   a → ə / ──
          [−stress]

(where [−stress] includes both primary and secondary stress)

This rule is blocked, however, in the case of an unstressed /a/ next to a stressed /a/ (even if [ʔ] intervenes).

(88) da-akay [da'akəy]   '3p-climb'
    aka   ['akə] ~ ['aʔa] ~ ['aa] ~ ['a]   'for'

This will be discussed further in §2.3.

If the sequence [dʒədʒ] occurs, for example, as the result of reduplication, the [ə] is fronted to [ɪ].

(89)   /DUP+yawa+na/   [jɪ'jawənə]   'DUP-Java-3s'

(90)   [ə]-fronting (post-syntactic)

   ə → ɪ / j —— j

/si/-devoicing. Unstressed /i/ often devoices after /s/.

(91)   kɔsi   ['kɔsi] ~ ['kɔsi̥]   'cat'
       si   [si] ~ [si̥]   'already'
       sikali   [si'kali] ~ [si̥'kali]   'not'
       lɛsilɛsir   ['lɛsɪ'lɛsɪr] ~ ['lɛsi̥'lɛsɪr] 'intestine'

I propose the following rule to devoice unstressed [i] or [ɪ] after [s].

(92)   /si/-devoicing (post-syntactic) (optional)

$$\begin{bmatrix} +\text{high} \\ -\text{mid} \\ -\text{back} \\ -\text{stress} \end{bmatrix} \rightarrow [-\text{voice}] / s \underline{}$$

Phonemic contrasts. Some vowel contrasts are given below. Most of these are in stressed syllables due to the infrequency of mid vowels in unstressed syllables.

(93)   ir   'those (AN)'   er   'that (IN)'
       jir   'cockatoo'   jer   'mollusk (sp)'
       ɛr-tir   '3s-bathe'   ɛr-ter   '3s-walk'
       idā   'their'   esā   'I don't know'

(94)   i-kel   '3s-buy'   i-kɛl   '3s-dig'
       pel   'price'   pɛl   'with'
       ner   'that (AN)'   i-nɛr   '3s-spit'
       esā   'I don't know'   lɛbā   'what'

A Lexical Phonology of West Tarangan

(95)   *i-gul*   '3s-collect'   *i-gol*   '3s-hunt'
       bum   'sago beetle'   *bom*   'bamboo (sp)'
       i-but   '3s-pluck'   *bot*   'house'

(96)   *ow*   'sago leaf'   *ɔw*   'fire'
       kola   'sand'   *kɔla*   'mud'
       kotan   'maybe'   *kɔtan*   'window'
       jow   'far'   *i-jɔw*   '3s-see'
       da-or   '3p-chop'   *ɔr*   'kangaroo'

2.3. Degemination

A sequence of two identical consonants or vowels within a phonological word is pronounced as one. Such geminate clusters arise from affixation and cliticization.

(97)   /tin+na/   ['tinə]   'itch-3s'
       /guyak+ka/   ['guyəkə]   'deaf-2s'
       /rua+ay/   ['ruəy]   'two-AN'
       /ku+tɔra=ay/   [ku'tɔrəy]   '1s-accompany=3p (AN)'

When the second member of the geminate cluster is a stressed vowel, geminate reduction does not occur. But if the first member of the cluster is a stressed vowel, geminate reduction does occur.

(98)   *da-akay*   [da'akəy]   *['dakəy]   '3p-climb'
       sakali   [sa'kali] ~ [sa'ali]   *['sali]   'no, not'
       /ka+ay/   ['kay]   'four-3p'

As noted in the discussion of /a/-̆ ̇kening, an unstressed /a/ next to a stressed /a/ does not become [ə] (even if [ʔ] intervenes).

(99)   *da-akay*   [da'akəy]   '3p-climb'
       aka   ['akə] ~ ['aʔa] ~ ['aa] ~ ['a]   'for'

This would be predicted by the autosegmental model of degemination. The reduction of geminate clusters created by affixation is the result of two processes: first, a STRONG FORM of the obligatory contour principle (OCP), which may be stated as follows.

(100) Strong form of OCP:
Geminates that arise from the output of a rule automatically undergo reduction of the two identical melody elements to one, bringing about double association of one melody element to two skeletal elements.

Secondly, two skeletal elements linked to a single melody element are reduced by the following rule.[19]

(101) Geminate reduction (lexical, syntactic)

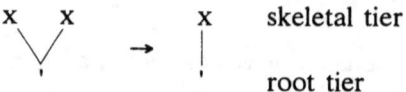

So it is natural that an unstressed /a/ in a geminate cluster would not be weakened to [ə]. Since both the stressed and the unstressed v-element are linked to the same /a/, the unstressed /a/ could not change to [ə] without altering the stressed /a/ as well.

(102)   [+stress]   [+stress]
                 | |
          c v + v c v c   c v + v c v c
          | | | | | | | | \/ | | |
          d a   a k a y   d a   a k a y

In addition, it is evident that the strong OCP examines the supralaryngeal tier to find identical melody elements while disregarding the laryngeal tier, with the result that any intervening glottal stop (which has no supralaryngeal features) is ignored.

(103) supralaryngeal tier: ' ' '   (k-to-ʔ)   ' '   (OCP)   '
                            | | | | | /\
       cv tier: v c v   →   v c v   →   v c v
                            | | | | | | | | |
       laryngeal tier: ' ' '   ' ' '   ' ' '

                            a k a   a ʔ a   a ʔ a

---

[19]If the geminate cluster reduced is a vowel cluster, an extra syllable node is left over; it is subsequently removed by resyllabification. If the geminate cluster is a glide-vowel sequence, the resulting skeletal element must be a V-element in order to obey morpheme structure constraints.

This is merely a way of formalizing the fact that since the tongue is not involved in making a glottal stop, it doesn't move.

Geminate reduction has also been observed to occur across a full word boundary, but data is insufficient at present to determine whether the rule is optional in this context. It may be that geminate reduction is not associated with a particular module or stratum, but applies wherever and whenever the conditions are met.

3. Syllable and root structure

Having discussed the phonemes of the language, we now discuss the structures (that is, the underlying forms) in which these phonemes may be grouped. The following syllable types are found in West Tarangan.

(104)
    V   ε   (yes/no question enclitic)
    VC   εm   'mother-of-pearl'
    CV   bɔ   'breast'
    CVC   bam   'chest'

These constitute exactly the "primary set of core syllable types" proposed by Clements and Keyser (1983:28). In their terms, then, West Tarangan is a "type IV" language. These core syllables are not expanded by the addition of further C-elements; that is, there are no syllable-internal consonant clusters.

All possible two-syllable combinations occur, although CVCV and CVCVC far outnumber the rest.

(105) Structure of two-syllable roots

V.V	ua-m	'nail-2s'	CV.V	rua	'two'
V.VC	aεy	'spouse'	CV.VC	dɔam	'pound'
V.CV	aka	'for'	CV.CV	gaka	'swamp'
V.CVC	anam	'door'	CV.CVC	bεbar	'afraid'
VC.CV	ɔrsa	'bunch'	CVC.CV	garsi	'crab (sp)'
VC.CVC	irlow	'cassava'	CVC.CVC	gɔrpan	'white hair'

Word-medial vowel clusters do occur across syllable boundaries, both within a morpheme and across a morpheme boundary.

(106) da-εt   [da'εt]   '3p-spear'
         maεra   [ma'εrə] 'sun, day'

Almost all morpheme-medial intersyllabic vowel clusters encountered in the corpus consist of unstressed /a/ and a stressed vowel.

(107) (a) ai: airan 'gall bladder' (b) ia: garia 'island'
ae: kaelay 'difficult' ea: ??
aɛ: maɛra 'sun, day' ɛa: kaytɛa 'corn'
aɔ: naɔy 'hawk' ɔa: dɔam 'pound'
ao: ?? oa: koay 'sketch'
au: ŋauan 'honey' ua: pua 'heart'

Thus a positive constraint may be proposed as follows (apparent exceptions are discussed below).

(108) Vowel cluster constraint (mirror-image)

v v ⇒ v a
　　　　[+stress]

One problem with this constraint is that it rules out geminate /ii/ and /uu/ proposed to account for exceptional final stress in forms like *tamīl* 'woodworm' and *takūr* 'coconut shell'. Recalling the hypothesis presented in the discussion on vowels that /a/ has no underlying features, we may state the constraint as a negative constraint.

(109) Vowel cluster constraint (mirror-image)

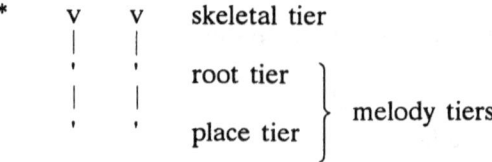

Stated this way, the constraint forbids a sequence of v-elements which each have a distinct place feature specification in their underlying representations. This constraint does not, however, rule out geminate /ii/ and /uu/ proposed to account for exceptional final stress, since these geminates, following the obligatory contour principle, consist of one root node doubly linked to two skeletal nodes.

A Lexical Phonology of West Tarangan

(110)   v   v   skeletal tier
         \/
          u   melody tiers

There exist words like ['bail] 'flexible' and ['mair] 'weak' which seem to violate the above constraint. However, the [i] in these cases is actually the third-person singular infix, and the underlying form has a medial /y/.

(111) *bayil*   /bayal+i/   'flexible-3s'   *bayal-di*   'flexible-3p'
       mayir   /mayar+i/   'weak-3s'   *mayar-di*   'weak-3p'

Since native speakers identify the two syllables of *bail* as [ba] and [il], with no medial [y], I propose that the degemination rule described earlier reduces /yi/ to [i] and /wu/ to [u].

(112)   c   v   →   v   skeletal tier
         \/ |
                            root tier

This degemination of a glide-vowel sequence must not occur before the glide-to-obstruent rule applies, since words like the following are not reduced.

(113) *gur*   /wur/   'grass'
       jir   /yir/   'cockatoo'
       gurep   /wurep/   'nail'
       jikodam   /yikodam/   'snake (sp)'

This is automatic if degemination applies only in the post-syntactic module, since the glide-to-obstruent rule applies in the lexical module.

There are also a handful of monomorphemic words which apparently have vowel clusters violating the above constraint; for these I also posit intervening glides which are deleted by degemination.

(114) *juyir*   ['juir]   'native'
       bitawur   [bi'taur]   'tree (sp)'

The most common vowel cluster is [uə]; second is [iə]. For these one could actually posit an intervening glide, such as /wariya/ or /puwa/ for *garia* and *pua* respectively.[20] However, there is clear evidence for vowel clusters in forms like *ŋauan* and *rataūn*, for which it is impossible to posit an underlying glide because of the glide-to-obstruent rule.

(115)   *ŋauan*   */ŋawuan/*   *[ŋə'guən]   'honey'
        rataūn   */ratawūn/*   *[rata'gun]   'sago paste'

As stated above, the glide-to-obstruent rule clearly applies prior to degemination, so we cannot say the glide is deleted before the glide-to-obstruent rule can apply. I will continue to assume underlying forms like /waria/ and /pua/.

In syllables closed with a glide, if the vowel is [−back], the glide must be [−back]. (This rules out rimes /ew/, /εw/, and /iw/.) This may be stated formally as follows:

(116) Vowel-glide constraint

$$* \left[\begin{array}{cc} V & C \\ | & | \\ [-\text{back}] & \begin{bmatrix} -\text{cons} \\ +\text{back} \end{bmatrix} \end{array} \right]_\sigma$$

There is also a morpheme structure constraint requiring that any non-final syllable closed with a glide have /a/ (the vowel with no underlying place features) linked to the V-slot. (By the consonant cluster constraint, the glide must be /y/.)

(117) Non-final vowel-glide constraint

$$* \begin{array}{ccc} V & C & C \\ | & | & \\ [\text{place}] & [-\text{cons}] & \end{array}$$

For each vowel-glide sequence one must ask whether it is in fact a monosyllabic vowel-glide sequence or a disyllabic vowel-vowel sequence. In terms of CV phonology, is the high vowel linked to a C-element or a V-element? In West Tarangan the evidence is clearly in favor of a

---

[20]Cognate forms in related languages (e.g., East Tarangan) do have consonants in this position.

A Lexical Phonology of West Tarangan 163

vowel-glide sequence. Some examples of roots ending in [y] and [w] are as follows.

(118) (a) *tay*   'salt water'   (b) *raw*   'language'
          galāy 'house'   *kulāw* 'pearl'
      (c) *boy*   'father'   (d) *ɔy*   'rice'
          aroy 'ironwood'   *naɔy* 'hawk'
      (e) *ɔw*   'fire'   (f) *ow*   'sago leaf'
          tarɔw 'dog'
      (g) *kɛy*   'wood'   (h) *ey*   (none in corpus)
          maɲey 'leaf'

The disyllabic VV hypothesis is really not feasible. Consider first the mid vowels. Since the reverse sequences /uɔ/, /iɔ/ and /iɛ/ never occur, it makes more sense to stick with our earlier constraint on vowel clusters, which stipulated that one of the vowels must be /a/. Furthermore, since there are no instances of /ɔu/, /ɔi/, or /ɛi/ with stress on the second vowel, it seems unlikely that these could be allowable VV sequences. In addition, such an analysis would leave an inexplicable hole in the distribution of /y/ and /w/, namely that they would not occur in the coda of a syllable.

It is tempting, however, to posit disyllabic vowel-vowel sequences for cases like *galāy* and *kolāw*, since this would explain the apparent final stress.

(119) *ga.la.i* [gə'lay] 'house' (cf. *sa.may* ['saməy] 'bad')
      ku.la.u [ku'law] 'pearl' (cf. *kɔ.law* ['kɔləw] 'squash')

But such an analysis conflicts with the vowel cluster constraint given earlier, which states that one member of the cluster must be unstressed /a/. The apparent contrast between final vowel-glide and final vowel-vowel shown above is probably best explained by examining the frequency of exceptions to the penultimate stress rule. Polysyllabic C-final roots (excluding CVCCVC roots and those with mid vowels) are stressed on the penultimate syllable in 89% of such roots, finally in 11%. The same statistics hold for roots ending in [aw] and [ay]: 87% of such roots (as *samay*, *kɔlaw* above) are stressed on the penultimate syllable, while 13% (as *galāy*, *kulāw*) are stressed on the final syllable. Since these forms fit the statistical probability of exceptions to the stress rule, they lose their strength as evidence for a vowel-vowel analysis.[21]

4. Lexical rules for affixation

In addition to the rules mentioned in the discussion above on consonants, there are various rules related to affixation and cliticization that apply in the lexical module.

The phonological phrase surrounding the West Tarangan finite verb may be represented as follows.

(120) Verbal phonological phrase =
       (CONJ) (AUX) (AGR) (R) ROOT1 (ROOT2) (DEG) (ENCLITICS)
  where ENCLITICS = (OBJECT) (PERFECT) (YNQ)

Nonfinite verbs are formed via a prefix on the verb. Adjectives participate in a phonological phrase that includes the following.

(121) Adjectival phonological phrase =
       (CONJ) (AUX) ROOT (AGR) (DEG) (ENCLITICS)
  where ENCLITICS = (PERFECT) (YNQ)

This information has been given to provide a framework for the discussions that follow.

4.1. Agreement prefix allomorphy

A predicate verb normally agrees with the subject of the clause by means of an unstressed agreement prefix. The underlying forms of verb agreement prefixes are as follows.

(122)
1s	2s	3s	1e	1i	2p	3p
ku-	*mu-*	*i-*	*ma-*	*ta-*	*mi-*	*da-*

However, there are a variety of conditions that alter the pronunciation of these prefixes, as noted below.

---

[21]The vowel cluster constraint also demands that we posit:
    tay   ['tay] 'seawater' (*tai*)
    raw   ['raw] 'language' (*rau*)

A Lexical Phonology of West Tarangan

Singular prefix vowel deletion. If the verb root is vowel-initial and AGR is affixed directly to the verb root (i.e., *r-* does not intervene), the vowel drops out of the singular prefixes (leaving ∅ for 3s).

(123) Singular prefix vowel deletion (lexical [stratum 1])

$$V \rightarrow \emptyset \;/\; \begin{bmatrix} (C) \underline{\quad} \\ \text{[+singular]} \end{bmatrix}_{\text{AGR}} \begin{bmatrix} \quad \\ \end{bmatrix}_{\text{VERB}} [V$$

Resyllabification subsequently makes *k-* and *m-* the onset of the verb-initial syllable. This rule yields paradigms such as the following.

(124)
	1s	2s	3s	1e	1i	2p	3p
'poke'	k-ɛt	m-ɛt	ɛt	ma-ɛt	ta-ɛt	mi-ɛt	da-ɛt
'pluck'	k-abak	m-abak	abak	ma-abak	ta-abak	mi-abak	da-abak

Prefix vowel lowering. If the first syllable of the root is unstressed, or if *r-* is affixed, the prefix vowels /i/ and /u/ are lowered to [ɛ] and [ɔ] respectively. This yields the following prefix set and paradigms.

(125)
1s	2s	3s	1e	1i	2p	3p
kɔ-	mɔ-	ɛ-	ma-	ta-	mɛ-	da-

(126)
	singular	plural	
1e	kɔ-tapaka	ma-tapaka	'capsize'
1i		ta-tapaka	
2	mɔ-tapaka	mɛ-tapaka	
3	ɛ-tapaka	da-tapaka	

(127)
	singular	plural	
1e	kɔ-r-tir	ma-r-tir	'bathe'
1i		ta-r-tir	
2	mɔ-r-tir	mɛ-r-tir	
3	ɛ-r-tir	da-r-tir	

(128)
	singular	plural	
1e	kɔ-r-ɛt	ma-r-ɛt	'poke'
1i		ta-r-ɛt	
2	mɔ-r-ɛt	mɛ-r-ɛt	
3	ɛ-r-ɛt	da-r-ɛt	

This vowel lowering also occurs with the verb root *y* 'go'.

(129)
1s	2s	3s	1e	1i	2p	3p
kɔy	mɔy	ɛy	may	tay	mɛy	day

We could posit the following rule, stating that high vowels become mid lax vowels before either an unstressed syllable or a morpheme that consists of a single consonant.

(130)

$$\begin{matrix} V \\ | \\ [+\text{high}] \end{matrix} \rightarrow \begin{bmatrix} -\text{high} \\ +\text{mid} \end{bmatrix} / \underline{}]\,[\left\{ \begin{matrix} \sigma\,[-\text{stress}] \\ | \\ C \\ \\ C] \end{matrix} \right\}$$

Considering the metrical analysis of stress presented above, however, we can simply state that this lowering occurs if the prefix receives primary or secondary stress; in other words, if the prefix syllable is below a foot node.

(131) Prefix vowel lowering (lexical [stratum 1])

$$V \rightarrow \begin{bmatrix} -\text{high} \\ +\text{mid} \end{bmatrix} / \begin{bmatrix} \underline{} & [+\text{stress}] \end{bmatrix}_{\text{AGR}}$$

(where [stress] includes both primary and secondary stress)

In order for this account to work for vowel-initial roots with *r-* affixed (e.g., *kɔ-r-ɛt*), we must propose that *r-* is syllabified as the coda of the prefix syllable, in order for that syllable to receive secondary stress[22] (cf. *ku-ret* '1s-aground'). However, the behavior of reduplication clearly shows *r-* to be syllabified as the onset of the root-initial syllable in these cases (e.g., *kɔ-rɛt-r-ɛt*). So it may be that *r-* is ambisyllabic when affixed to a vowel-initial root.

(132)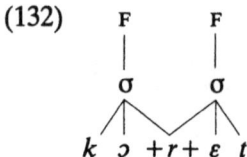

---

[22]This may be necessary in any case; if *r-* were prefixed to a consonant-initial root, and then resyllabification took place before AGR were prefixed, the *r-* would be lost. So it may be best to consider AGR+*r-* as a compound prefix or prefix stem.

A Lexical Phonology of West Tarangan 167

The verb *la* 'run' idiosyncratically takes lowered prefixes *kɔ-*, *mɔ-*, *ɛ-*, *mɛ-*. I conclude that it is marked in the lexicon as undergoing the rule, even though it doesn't meet the structural description.

Agreement prefix reduction in the syntactic module. There are four rules that delete portions of certain agreement prefixes if the morpheme to the left of the prefix meets the structural description of the rule. The morphemes that trigger deletion are not part of the verb word; in fact, some are not even part of the verb phrase. This presents an interesting problem for the theory of lexical phonology, since the boundary between the prefix and the verb root would have been erased before phrase construction brings the separate words together.[23]

/u/-deletion. If a vowel immediately precedes the agreement prefix *ku-* (1s), the /u/ of the prefix is deleted. (This occurs only if the /u/ has not been lowered to [ɔ].) The consonant of the prefix is then resyllabified as the coda of the preceding syllable. One set of morphemes that triggers this is the set of vowel-final auxiliaries *sɔ* 'yesterday', *ma* 'awhile ago', *nɔ* (progressive aspect), *mɔ* 'now' or 'want to', *na* (future),[24] and *bisa* 'can'.

(133) ɔk   sɔ =   k-si
       1s   yesterday = 1s-go
       I went yesterday

(134) ɔk   sikali ma =   k-say-say   = ∅
       1s   not   PST = 1s-DUP-take^apart   = it
       I didn't take it apart

---

[23]In the data which follows, I use the clitic boundary symbol '=' to link the deletion-triggering morpheme with the agreement prefix. However, it is not entirely clear that cliticization is involved. What is clear is that the two morphemes are combined into one syllable.

[24]The monosyllabic auxiliaries are stressed weakly if at all. However, I believe them to be separate words, not prefixes, because they can precede adjectives, time nouns, and other words, not just verbs:

      ma lɔlɔar   'awhile ago this morning'   (lɔlɔar = 'morning')
      sɔ dedɛdam   'yesterday evening'   (dedɛdam = 'evening')
      na jow   'far in the future'   (jow = 'long (time)')
      na jɛy ba?   'when will... ?'   (jɛy ba = 'when?')

The apparent lack of stress is probably due to the fact that these morphemes can never be in a position to receive phrase stress; in fact they commonly occur adjacent to the phrase-stressed syllable.

(135) ɔk   nɔ=   k-tok-tok
     1s   PROG=   1s-DUP-dance
     I'm dancing

(136) ɔk   mɔ=   k-jɔw   =ay
     1s   now=   1s-see   =3p
     I want to see them now

(137) sikali bisa na=   k-tɔra   =y
     not   can   FUT=   1s-accompany   =AP
     I won't be able to go along

The vowel-final conjunctions *ja* 'then', *ka* 'so', and *tɛ* 'or' also trigger /u/-deletion.

(138) ja=   k-tɔra   =na
     then= 1s-accompany   =3s
     then I accompany her

(139) k-ɛla ka=   k-ma
     1s-go so=   1s-come
     I come and go

(140) ɔk   na=   k-tɛn, tɛ=   k-dɛm lɛr   gɔŋar
     1s   FUT=   1s-cry or=   1s-do voice cord
     (if) I cry, or make a big fuss

Vowel-final verbs can also trigger this deletion.

(141) ma=   k-dɛm   =na
     come=   1s-do   =3s
     Here, I'll do it[25]

In a standard generative framework, a fairly straightforward rule could be written as follows.

---

[25]Devoid of any pragmatic context, the *ma* in this sentence could be interpreted as the auxiliary *ma* 'awhile ago'. In order for *ma* to be understood as the verb *ma* 'come', as in this example, the utterance would be accompanied by some indication that an offer was being made (e.g., a gesture).

A Lexical Phonology of West Tarangan

(142) /u/-deletion

u → ∅ / v ## k —— +

The use of the full word boundary /##/ and the morpheme boundary /+/ ensure that this rule will affect only prefixes. In lexical phonology, however, there is only one type of boundary, [...]. Rules that would make use of /##/ are those which apply in the syntactic module, while those which would have /+/ are those which apply in the lexical module. Since the above rule makes use of both types of boundaries, lexical phonology is left with a paradox; the rule must apply in the syntactic module in order for the vowel-final trigger morpheme to be present, but before the verb word enters the syntactic module, its internal boundaries (corresponding to the traditional /+/) will have been erased.

(143) Lexical module:

[na]	[ku]	[dεm]	underlying forms
[na]	[[ku]	[dεm]]	affixation
[na]	[kudεm]		bracket erasure

Syntactic module:

[[na] [kudεm]]		phrase construction
[[na] [kdεm]]		/u/-deletion
[nakdεm]		bracket erasure and resyllabification

'I will make'

Thus the following rule, referring to brackets as the rule above does, will not work in lexical phonology.

(144)

$$u \rightarrow \emptyset \ / \ v] \ [k \underline{\quad}]_{AGR}$$

There are two alternatives: first, we could propose that the agreement prefixes are in fact phrase constituents which cliticize to the verb word, attaching in the syntactic module. Then the derivation would be as follows.

(145) Lexical module:

    [na] [ku] [dɛm]   underlying forms

Syntactic module:

    [[na] [ku] [dɛm]]   phrase construction
    [[na] [k] [dɛm]]   /u/-deletion
    [nakdɛm]   bracket erasure and resyllabification

'I will make'

One problem with this hypothesis is that, as shown in the discussion on prefix vowel lowering, there is a close connection between the agreement prefixes and the verb prefix r-; if the agreement morphemes are actually clitics, then r- would probably have to be a clitic as well. The hypothesis fails completely when we consider that reduplication, a process which clearly takes place in the lexical module, quite obviously follows the prefixation of the agreement morphemes.

(146) Lexical module:

    STRATUM 1
    [DUP] [ku] [ɛla]   underlying forms
    [DUP] [ku] [ɛla]   affixation
    [DUP] [k] [ɛla]   singular prefix vowel deletion
    [DUP] [kɛla]   resyllabification and bracket erasure
    STRATUM 3
    [[kɛla] [kɛla]]   reduplication
    [kɛlakɛla]   bracket erasure

'I am going'

The alternative hypothesis is to frame the rule so that it refers to stress, rather than to a word-internal boundary. I propose the following rule.

(147) /u/-deletion (syntactic)

$$u \rightarrow \emptyset \; / \; v]_{VERB} \; [k \; \underline{\quad} \; [-stress]$$

(where [−stress] refers to either primary or secondary stress)

This rule is not intuitively pleasing in that it does not make explicit the fact that only a prefix vowel is being deleted, not part of the verb root. This is because the rule applies in the syntactic module, at which point there is no longer a boundary between the prefix and the verb root. Recall, however, that

A Lexical Phonology of West Tarangan 171

in the discussion on stress I proposed that affixation involves the addition of an M-node above the M-node of the root; this means that the internal morphological structure of the word is preserved, at least temporarily, in the metrical tree. Since /u/-deletion results in resyllabification of the remaining /k/ with the preceding syllable, the metrical tree would be redrawn as follows.

(148)

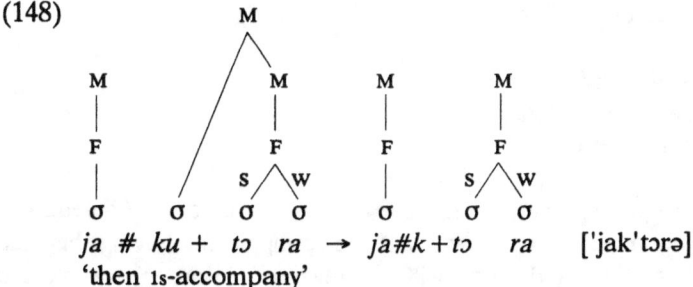

ja # ku + tɔ ra → ja#k+tɔ ra ['jak'tɔrə]
'then 1s-accompany'

So the notation [−stress] in the rule proposed above could be replaced by reference to the metrical structure of the verb word, thus making explicit the fact that the morpheme being altered is merely a prefix. And since verbs are the only syntactic category that can be prefixed, the boundary no longer needs to be marked VERB.

(149) /u/-deletion (syntactic)

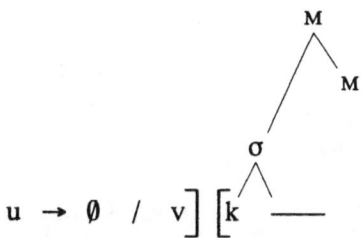

u → ∅ / v] [k ⎯⎯

/k/-deletion. The /u/-deletion triggers given above fail to delete the /u/ from *ku-* in one case: that is, if the verb root begins with /k/. In this case the /k/ is deleted from *ku-* instead of the /u/.

(150) ɔk sɔ-u-kel   roko
       1s yesterday-1s-buy cigarette
       yesterday I bought cigarettes

(151) ɔk ma-u-kel roko
    1s PST-1s-buy cigarette
    I bought cigarettes awhile ago

(152) ɔk mɔ-u-kel roko
    1s now-1s-buy cigarette
    I'm going to buy cigarettes now

(153) ɔk na-u-kel roko
    1s FUT-1s-buy cigarette
    I will buy cigarettes

I propose the following rule, which must be ordered before /u/-deletion in order for /u/-deletion not to apply. In fact, the rationale for having this rule at all is obviously so that /u/-deletion will be prevented, in order to avoid the formation of a geminate /k+k/. The same problems regarding bracket erasure mentioned above complicate the formulation of this rule as well.

(154) /k/-deletion (syntactic)

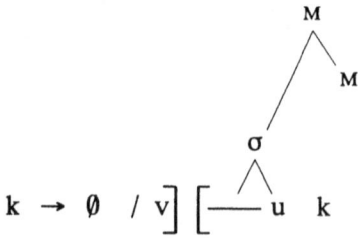

Contrast the following two derivations.[26]

(155) Lexical module: Lexical module:

    [na] [ku] [kel]   underlying forms   [na] [ku] [dɛm]
    [na] [[ku][kel]]   affixation   [na] [[ku][dɛm]]
    [na] [kukel]   bracket erasure   [na] [kudɛm]

---

[26]The derivation given here assumes that resyllabification does not occur, which would change [nau'kél] to [naw'kél]. Although it is difficult to tell, I think that [u] is the correct pronunciation.

A Lexical Phonology of West Tarangan 173

Syntactic module: Syntactic module:

[[na][kukel]]   phrase construction   [[na][kudɛm]]
[[na][ukel]]   /k/-deletion
———   /u/-deletion   [[na][kdɛm]]
[naukel]   bracket erasure   [nakdɛm]

'I will buy'   'I will do'

/m/-deletion. In some cases, [m] is deleted from *mi-* (2p), but data is insufficient to determine exactly what triggers this. It may be the presence of labial consonants in both syllables before and after the prefix syllable.

(156) *ma i= ma =si   =ɛ?*
      PST 2p=come=already=YNQ
      You (pl) have come already, have you?

(157) *ma i=pɔ   lɛbā nɔ?*
      PST 2p=carry what that
      What was that you (pl) were carrying?

This is obviously similar to /k/-deletion, and it may be that one rule could be written to cover both phenomena.

Omission of agreement prefixes. In the Coast dialect an agreement prefix is typically omitted if a subject NP or pronoun immediately precedes the verb (i.e., no auxiliaries, time phrases, etc.) and the prefix syllable is completely unstressed. In other words, contiguous tokens for the same subject referent are superfluous. Singular prefixes, rather than plural prefixes, are more commonly deleted in this context. This rule is statable as follows.

(158) Agreement prefix omission (syntactic) (optional)

$$\sigma \rightarrow \emptyset \ / \ ]_{NP} \ [_{VERB} \ [-\text{stress}]$$

(where [−stress] includes both primary and secondary stress)

The optionality of this deletion may be related to discourse-level selection of pronominal reference. Again, this rule could be framed in terms of metrical structure.

(159) Agreement prefix omission (syntactic) (optional)

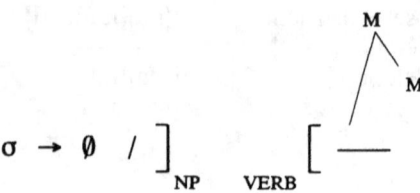

mu- reduction. The prefix *mu-* (2s) is never realized as [mu] in this dialect. If the /u/ is not lowered to [ɔ] by prefix vowel lowering—that is, if it is completely unstressed—it must be deleted. The resulting /m/ is then deleted as well unless preceded by a vowel-final syllable with which it may syllabify.

(160) ∅-kor   ka mɔ-r-sir   pεy   =∅   ka era
      2s-beat so 2s-R-speak about it to 3p
      Beat (the gong) and talk to them about it.

(161) mol   kεkanām badi ɔt-ɔtay   nɔ, ka= m-si=   m-sεtak =∅
      2sˆtake your   sword DUP-long   that so= 2s-go= 2s-sever =it
      Take that long sword of yours, and go cut it off.

In (160), the first instance of *mu-* is completely deleted because it is phrase-initial, while the second instance of *mu-* surfaces as [mɔ]. In (161), there are two instances of *mu-* reduced to [m] and resyllabified as the coda of the preceding syllable: [ˈkamˈsimˈsεtək]. It should be noted that the deletion in (160) is not due to imperative mood, as the following example demonstrates.

(162) mol   gur   nɔ   tarεy-di, ka= m-garay =∅
      2sˆtake grass that some-pl   so= 2s-dry   =it
      Take some of that grass, and dry it in the sun.

If a vowel-final conjunction is followed by a pause, as often happens, a new phonological phrase begins and the [m] cannot resyllabify with the preceding syllable.

(163) m-εla ka mol   gur   er   tarεy, ka, garay =∅
      2s-go so 2sˆtake grass DEF some   so   dry   =it
      Go get some grass, and dry it.

(cf. *ka=m-garay* above)

A Lexical Phonology of West Tarangan   175

As the examples below demonstrate, the same morphemes that trigger the deletion of /u/ from *ku-* (1s) (and subsequent resyllabification of [k] as coda) also allow resyllabification of [m] from *mu-* as coda. Despite this superficial similarity, there are indeed two rules in operation here, since *ku-* does not completely delete in the same environments that *mu-* does.[27]

(164) *kɛn   sɔ =   m-si   = ɛ?*
      2s   yesterday= 2s-go = YNQ
      Did you go yesterday?

(165) *ma = m-dɛm lɛbā?*
      PST= 2s-do   what
      What did you do a while ago?

(166) *kɛn nɔ =   m-jama-jaman ɔk*
      2s   PROG = 2s-DUP-ask   1s
      You're asking me.

(167) *boy,   mɔ =   m-jaman nɛy*
      father now=   2s-ask   3s
      Dad, ask her now.

(168) *kɛn na =   m-jɔw-jɔw nɔ*
      2s   FUT=   2s-DUP-see that
      You'll see that.

(169) *dɛdɛdam er, ja =   m-kor   aka nata   ɔn   abil*
      evening DEF then= 2s-beat for village this inside^3s
      This evening, beat the gong to call the village inhabitants.

(170) *ja   m-ɛla ka =   m-tɔra   era*
      then   2s-go   so=   2s-accompany 3p
      Then go and accompany them.

If the verb is /m/-initial, *m-* is deleted by degemination, even if preceded by an open syllable. (This is another contrast with *ku-*, which reduces to *u-* if the verb is /k/-initial.)

---

[27]The *mu-* reduction rule is an older rule, occurring in all dialects of West Tarangan, while /u/-deletion (affecting *ku-*) is an innovation of this dialect.

(171) kɛn ma ∅-ma =si =ɛ?
2s PST 2s-come already YNQ
You've already come, have you?

The following rule accounts for the reduction of *mu-* to *m-*.

(172) *mu-* reduction (lexical [stratum 1])

$$u \rightarrow \emptyset \ / \ \begin{bmatrix} m \underline{\qquad} \\ [-\text{stress}] \end{bmatrix}_{\text{AGR}}$$

(where [stress] refers to either primary or secondary stress)[28]

Once again, we could follow the pattern of the other prefix allomorphy rules.

(173) *mu-* reduction (lexical)

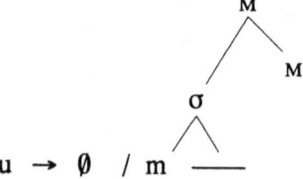

u → ∅ / m ____

4.2. Other prefixes

With some roots, an epenthetic [ə] is inserted after *r-* and *jɛr-* (a prefix for making a verb nonfinite); included are all roots beginning with /r/, and some other roots which begin with /ɸ/.

(174) *i-rua*   'he/she plants (transitive)'
      ɛ-r[ə]-rua   'he/she plants (antipassive)'

(175) *da-ru*   'they bark'
      da-r[ə]-ru=ay 'they bark at each other'

(176) *i-pun*   'he/she kills'
      da-r[ə]-pun=ay 'they kill each other'
      jɛr[ə]-pun   'killing'

---

[28]If we stipulate that this rule is ordered after prefix vowel lowering, the designation [−stress] is unnecessary.

A Lexical Phonology of West Tarangan

I assume that [a] is inserted between two /r/'s, and that the [a] subsequently becomes [ə] by /a/-raising.

(177) /a/-epenthesis after r- (lexical [stratum 1])

∅ → a / r —— r

I will assume for now that non-r-initial verbs that exhibit this epenthesis are idiosyncratically marked by the lexicon as undergoing the rule.

Because this rule applies in the lexical module, it applies only at word-internal morpheme boundaries. (There are no underlying geminate consonants.) It does not apply in the syntactic module, i.e., across word boundaries; here, degemination is likely to occur.

(178) *gar ra-raray*   ['gara'raray] 'water DUP-hot'

This rule therefore offers evidence of lexical compounding in at least one instance.

(179) (a) *ɛ-r-sir pɛy*   (b) *ɛ-r-sirapɛy*
         3s-R-talk about   3s-R-talk^about
         'he/she talks about (it)' 'he/she talks about (it)'

I interpret *ɛrsirapɛy* as a compound formed in the lexical module, marked as such by the epenthesis of [a].

The /r/ of *r-* and *jɛr-* may be deleted if the first syllable of the verb root is unstressed.

(180) /i+r+lalū=na/   [ɛlə'lunə]   '3s-R-descend=3s'
      /i+r+kalɛka=na/   [ɛkə'lɛkənə] ~ [ɛrkə'lɛkənə]   '3s-R-hide=3s'
      /ku+r+taɸaka=ŋa/   [kɔtə'ɸakəŋə]   '1s-R-overturn=1s'
      /jɛr+palɔw/   [jɛɸə'lɔw] ~ [jɛrɸə'lɔw]   'NF-naked'

Note that the prefix *r-* is obligatory if the verb is in a reflexive or reciprocal clause, as the first three verbs above are. Therefore it seems clear that the lack of [r] is based on phonological rather than morphosyntactic considerations. I posit a rule as follows.

(181) /r/-deletion (lexical [stratum 1]) (optional)

r → ∅ / ——] [C   V
                    [−stress]

The nominalizing prefix *sin-* occurs on only a few roots, all of which begin with an alveolar consonant. The root-initial alveolar consonant is deleted.

(182)   ɛ-r-tamarɛr   '3s-R-stand'   sinamarɛr   'standing'
        i-talar   '3s-sit'   sinalar   'sitting'
        ɛ-r-sir   '3s-R-speak'   sinir   'speech'
        i-tor   '3s-call'   sinornor   'constantly calling'
        i-tɛn   '3s-cry'   sinɛn   'constantly crying'

The following rule is posited:

(183) Alveolar deletion (lexical [stratum 1])

    C → ∅ / [sin] [──

Note that this phenomenon provides a classic example of paradoxical rule ordering with regard to reduplication. We have *sinornor*, not **sinortor*, which implies that alveolar deletion occurs prior to the prefixation of the reduplicative morpheme.

(184)   [DUP] [sin] [tor]   underlying forms
        [DUP] [[sin][tor]]   affixation
        [DUP] [[sin][or]]   alveolar deletion
        [DUP] [sinor]   bracket erasure
        [sinornor]   reduplication

(185)   [sin] [DUP] [tor]   underlying forms
        [sin] [tortor]   reduplication
        [[sin] [tortor]]   affixation
        [[sin] [ortor]]   alveolar deletion
        *[sinortor]   bracket erasure

This is a classic problem for linguistic theory because it appears that a phonological rule applies prior to affixation of a morpheme. In lexical phonology this is no problem at all, however, since the lexical module may be subdivided into consecutive strata, each with its own set of morphemes and phonological rules. I have already posited that agreement prefixes are affixed in a stratum prior to the stratum in which reduplication takes place; therefore I posit that *sin-* also is affixed in stratum 1, where alveolar deletion occurs, while the reduplicative template is affixed in a later stratum.

4.3. Suffix allomorphy

Two kinds of roots typically take suffixes: adjectives and inalienably possessed (IP) nouns. IP nouns are those which are normally inflected for the person of the possessor. The paradigm used for all vowel-final (and some consonant-final) IP nouns is as follows.

(186)
1s	2s	3s	pl
-ŋ	-m	-y	-in

A typical paradigm is that of *mata* 'eye'.[29]

(187)
1s	2s	3s	1e	1i	2p	3p
mata-ŋ	mata-m	mata-y	mat-in	mat-in	mat-in	mat-in

To account for the loss of /a/ in plural forms I propose a rule, which will be necessary in the context of infixation as well, to delete unstressed /a/ before a high vowel if a morpheme boundary intervenes.

(188) /a/-deletion before high vowel (lexical [stratum 2])

$$a \rightarrow \emptyset \;/\; \underset{[-\text{stress}]}{\underline{\quad\quad}} \; \begin{bmatrix} V \\ +\text{high} \\ -\text{mid} \end{bmatrix}$$

This rule applies in the lexical module stratum where suffixation and infixation take place. However, the rule does not apply in the lexical stratum of prefixation.[30]

(189)
/da+inal/	[də'inəl]	*['dinəl]	'3p-hate'
/ta+urar/	[tə'urər]	*['turər]	'1i-enter'

---

[29]The reader may wonder if the underlying form of 'eye' is in fact *mat*, with no deletion of final /a/ in the plural forms. However, *mata* can also occur in an uninflected form.

    mata bar-bar   'eye discharge'
    mata jara-jara 'eye infection'

(Cf. *pua*-y 'fruit-3s,' *pu-in* 'fruit-3p,' *ɛr-pua* '3s-bearfruit'.) Apparently all vowel-final IP nouns end in /a/.

[30]Designating the high vowel as [−stress] would obviate the need for the boundary symbol in the rule, and would also prevent these prefixes from reducing. In any event, however, the rule applies in the lexical module only, since this deletion does not occur across full word boundaries.

Adjectives agree with their subject or head noun by means of agreement suffixes, the underlying forms of which are as follows.

(190)
	SG	PL
1e	-ŋa	-kam
1i		-da/-ay[31]
2	-ka	-kim
3 (AN)	-na	-ay
3 (IN)	-∅	-di[32]

(191)
	SG	PL	
1e	kamarɛy-ŋa	kamarɛy-kam	'embarrassed'
1i		kamarɛy-da	
2	kamarɛy-ka	kamarɛy-kim	
3	kamarɛy-na	kamarɛy-ay	

Roots that end in unstressed /a/ or /ay/ take the suffix *-in* (3p), which occurs to the left of *-ay* (3p AN) and instead of *-di* (3p IN). When *-in* is affixed, the root-final /a/ or /ay/ is deleted. The paradigms for *jɛsa* 'not want' and *tɔbay* 'weak' are as follows.

(192)
	SG	PL	
1e	jɛsa-ŋa	jɛsa-kam	'not want'
1i		jɛsa-da	
2	jɛsa-ka	jɛsa-kim	
3	jɛsa-na	jɛs-in-ay	

(193)
	SG	PL	
1e	tɔbay-ŋa	tɔbay-kam	'weak'
1i		tɔbay-da	
2	tɔbay-ka	tɔbay-kim	
3	tɔbay-na	tɔb-in-ay	

To account for the deletion of final /a/ and /ay/, we need only invoke two rules which have independent motivation elsewhere in the grammar. First,

---

[31]The traditional 1i suffix is *-da*, but in this dialect speakers use both *-da* and *-ay* interchangeably. The use of *-ay* for 1i is obviously the result of broadening the semantic range of *-ay* (3p AN).

[32]*-di* is omitted as redundant if the following morpheme conveys the same information:

uɲatin lɔar-∅ da-uk-uk
not^yet clear-3p 3p-DUP-very
not completely clear yet

A Lexical Phonology of West Tarangan

the geminate glide-vowel reduction rule, mentioned earlier in the discussion of vowel clusters, reduces /yi/ to /i/. Then /a/-deletion before high vowel reduces the resulting vowel cluster.

(194) [[samay] [in] [ay]]   affixation
      [[sama] [in] [ay]]   geminate glide-vowel reduction
      [[sam] [in] [ay]]   /a/-deletion before high vowel
      [saminay]   bracket erasure

'they are bad'

4.4. Infixes

Most adjectives and IP nouns whose root-final segment is [+cons] take an agreement infix, in singular forms, just before the final consonant of the root. IP nouns that take infixes take no suffixes for singular forms, and take the suffix -di for all plural forms.[33] Adjectives that take these infixes, however, have them in addition to the adjective agreement suffixes given above. The infixes are as follows.[34]

(195) 1s   2s   3s
       -u-   -u-   -i-

Typical paradigms are those of *jɛmal* 'wet' and *tubar* 'belly'.[35]

(196)   SG   PL
      1e *jɛmul-ŋa* *jɛmal-kam*   'wet'
      1i   *jɛmal-da*
      2   *jɛmul-ka* *jɛmal-kim*
      3   *jɛmil-na* *jɛmal-ay*

---

[33]Again, *-di* is usually omitted if the following morpheme conveys the same information.

  pɔp bɔbar(di)   di-nɔ
  pig offspring(-pl) 3p^IN-that (near)
  those piglets

I posit that *di-* (3p IN) which is used to form demonstrative articles is the same morpheme which occurs as a suffix on IP nouns and adjectives.

[34]These infixes arose historically from suffixes which metathesized with the final consonant. In the neighboring language Manumbai, the corresponding morphemes are suffixes.

[35]The third-person singular form of roots that take infixation is the citation form. Sometimes the IP-noun form with *-i-* is used as a regular (non-IP) noun.

(197)   SG   PL
     1e *tubur*   *tubar-di*   'belly'
     1i   *tubar-di*
     2 *tubur*   *tubar-di*
     3 *tubir*   *tubar-di*

Monosyllabic IP noun roots never take -*u*-, but they do take suffixes -*aŋ* (1s) and -*am* (2s); I interpret these as -*ŋ* and -*m* (from the other IP noun paradigm) with an epenthetic [a]. Several of these paradigms are irregular; some monosyllabic IP nouns are completely uninflected for third-person singular, while in others the root vowel is deleted by the infix -*i*-.

(198) 1s   2s   3s   pl
      pes-aŋ   *pes-am*   *pet*   *pet-di*   'breath'
      jɛl-aŋ   *jɛl-am*   *jɛl*   *jɛl-in*   'younger sibling'
      lɛr-aŋ   *lɛr-am*   *lir*   *lɛr-di*   'voice'
      nɛn-aŋ   *nɛn-am*   *nin*   *nɛn-di*   'tooth'
      gul-aŋ[36] *gul-am*   *jil*   *gul-di*   'hair'
      tul-aŋ   *tul-am*   *tul*   *tul-di*   'bone'
      ɛr-aŋ   *ɛr-am*   *ɛr*   *ɛr-di*   'life'

The insertion of [a] may be described by the following rule, which serves to make forms acceptable to the syllable structure constraints of the language.

(199) Vowel epenthesis before -C suffix (lexical [stratum 2])

     ∅ → a / [c] —— [c]

The examples presented thus far could be interpreted as involving some kind of vowel mutation rather than true infixation. However, there are at least two roots with /ɔ/ in the final syllable, which provide evidence that this is in fact true infixation.

---

[36]There is also the inexplicable form *gul-ŋa* 'hair-1s', using the adjective agreement suffix. Conversely, at least one adjective takes IP-noun suffixes.

    aūr-aŋ   'worried-1s'
    aūr-am   'worried-2s'
    aūr-na   'worried-3s'

(200)
	SG	PL	
1e	*kanɔur-ŋa*	*kanɔr-kam*	'hungry'
1i		*kanɔr-da*	
2	*kanɔur-ka*	*kanɔr-kim*	
3	*kanɔir-na*	*kanɔr-ay*	

(201)
	SG	PL	
1e	*karɔun-ŋa*	*karɔn-kam*	'old'
1i		*karɔn-da*	
2	*karɔun-ka*	*karɔn-kim*	
3	*karɔin-na*	*karɔn-ay*	

For these roots it is impossible to say that a vowel simply mutates because the inflectional /u/ and /i/ are clearly inserted between two segments.

The deletion of /a/ from *tubar* 'belly' and *jɛmal* 'wet' above is accounted for by /a/-deletion before high vowel, as described above in the discussion on suffix allomorphy. The rule is repeated here for the reader's convenience.

(202) /a/-deletion before high vowel (lexical [stratum 2])

$$a \rightarrow \emptyset\ /\ \underline{\quad}_{[-stress]}\ \begin{bmatrix} V \\ +high \\ -mid \end{bmatrix}$$

Designating the /a/ as [-stress] is motivated by the fact that when *gar* 'water' is inflected as an IP noun with the *-i-* infix, the stressed /a/ is not deleted.

(203) (a) *gar* 'water' (b) *nor gair* 'coconut milk'
                              mata-m gar-di 'your tears'

I therefore propose the following derivations.

(204)
[jɛmal] [i]	[na]	underlying forms
[[jɛma [i] l]]	[na]	infixation
[jɛm [i] l]	[na]	/a/-deletion before high vowel
[jɛmil]	[na]	bracket erasure
[jɛmilna]		affixation and bracket erasure

'he/she is wet'

(205) [kanɔr] [u] [ka]   underlying forms
      [kanɔur] [ka]   infixation and bracket erasure
      [kanɔurka]   affixation and bracket erasure

   'he/she is hungry'

The infixation itself may be diagrammed as follows, with each morpheme on a separate tier.

(206) j ε m '   l   melody tier of root
       | | | |
       [c v c v [v] c]   skeletal tier
                |
                i   melody tier of infix

As posited in the discussion on vowels, the /a/ in /jɛmal/ has no features in the underlying representation. The rule of /a/-deletion before high vowel, then, is a process of a high vowel capturing the featureless v-element to its left; this is followed by degemination, bracket erasure, and resyllabification.

(207) j ε m ' l   j ε m   l   j ε m   l
       | | | | | | | | | | | |
       [c v c v [v] c] → [c v c v [v] c] → [c v c v c]
                | \/ |
                i   i   i

Finally with regard to infixes, there are several roots whose infixing paradigms seem to suggest a glide insertion rule.

(208) 1s   2s   3s   3p
       lɔur-ŋa   lɔur-ka   lɔir-na   lɔar-ay/lɔyar-ay   'clean'
       sour-ŋa   sour-ka   soir-na   soyar-ay   'dead'
       joun-ŋa   joun-ka   join-na   joyan-ay   'quick'
       ɛul-ŋa   ɛul-ka   ɛil-na   ɛal-ay/ɛyal-ay   'evil'

(209) 3s   3p
       oyoir   oror-di[37]   'finger'

For each of the 3s forms above, native speakers tend to believe there is a /y/ prior to the infix -i-, even though the first-person singular and

---

[37]This pair will be discussed further in the section on reduplication.

second-person singular forms indicate there is none. Since I have not investigated this phenomenon, I will not attempt to write a rule for it.

5. Reduplication

5.1. Phonological forms

The phonological form of reduplication depends entirely on the phonological shape of the base. Although there are many morphosyntactic functions of reduplication, they all use the same forms. A more complete description of the forms and functions of reduplication in all four major dialects of West Tarangan will be found in Nivens (to appear); here I will present the basic phonological facts of reduplication in this dialect and demonstrate how reduplication relates to the rest of the phonology.

Many recent works have taken the view that "reduplication is a special case of ordinary affixational morphology, where the affixes are phonologically underspecified, receiving their full phonetic expression by copying adjacent segments" (Broselow and McCarthy 1983:25). That is, a reduplicative affix consists of a structural "template" with no phonetic content. Here, as in Nivens (to appear), I adopt the "prosodic model" of McCarthy and Prince (1986). As in many languages of Maluku, the reduplicative prefix is attached not to the left edge of a morpheme but to the left edge of the stressed metrical foot. The stressed metrical foot is then the base of reduplication, i.e., the source of copied phonemic material. West Tarangan makes use of three distinct templates, which are selected based on the canonical shape of the base. If the base is other than CVCV(C), the template is simply σ. Since the maximal syllable in West Tarangan is CVC, the reduplicative process will attempt to fill up a CVC syllable with whatever phonemic material is available from the base.

If the base is of the form CVCV(C), the template is defined in terms of the core syllable CV, symbolized σ_c. The template will be $\sigma_c\sigma_c$ unless certain conditions described below are met, in which case the template will be σ_c.

Once the appropriate template is selected, it is inserted to the left of the stressed metrical foot. Then the entire base melody is copied to the left of the stressed foot melody. Next, the copied melody elements are associated to the empty template from left to right until a melody element is unable to associate with the template. At this point association stops and any leftover melody segments are discarded.

In this dialect of West Tarangan, a stressed vowel in the base usually yields a stressed vowel in the reduplicative affix, resulting in two stress groups. However, when the surface form of the reduplicative prefix is CV, it is unstressed.

(210) *tuntun*   ['tun'tun]   'mosquito'
      da-ɔn-ɔn   [da'ɔn'ɔn]   '3p-DUP-shoot'

(211) *juju*   [dʒu'dʒu]   'cockroach (sp)'
      da-la-lar [dala'lar]   '3p-DUP-sail'

The stress on the reduplicative prefix is primary, not secondary stress. Apparently the reduplicative prefix in this dialect must constitute a separate phonological word if it contains two morae (i.e., either two syllables or a closed syllable).

One-syllable bases, vowel-initial bases, and bases with intersyllabic vowel and consonant clusters take σ as a reduplicative prefix. Since CVC is the maximal syllable in West Tarangan, the prefix consists of as much of a CVC structure as can be constructed beginning with the first segment of the stressed syllable. Thus, one-syllable bases (CV, VC, and CVC) reduplicate entirely.

(212) CV:
      dɛdɛ   'song (sp)'
      juju   'cockroach (sp)'

(213) VC:
      ilil   'Manta ray'
      ɛ-tailīl   '3s-DUP bounce'
      da-ɔn-ɔn   '3p-DUP-shoot'

(214) CVC:
      kɛy-kɛy   'DUP-wood'
      maŋɛyŋɛy-di   'DUP leaf-3p'
      tibɔybɔy-na   'DUP new-3s'
      tɔp-tɔp   'DUP-short'
      ɛ-lajirjīr   '3s-DUP white'

The following diagrams illustrate how the McCarthy and Prince model handles the West Tarangan data.[38]

---

[38] Actually, McCarthy and Prince stipulate that each morpheme is on a separate tier. For convenience I diagram them on the same tier.

A Lexical Phonology of West Tarangan

(215) σ + σ → σ σ
       d ε   d ε   d ε

(216) σ + σ → σ + σ   σ — resyllabification → σ σ
       ɔ n   ɔ n   ɔ n   ɔ n ɔ n

(217) σ + σ → σ σ
       t ɔ p   t ɔ p t ɔ p

vcv and vcvc bases satisfy the σ template by reduplicating only the first vc.

(218) vcv:
     da-εl-εla   '3p-DUP-go'
     ak-aka   'DUP-for'
     da-ɔp-ɔpa   '3p-DUP-wrap'

(219) vcvc:
     da-εt-εtar   '3p-DUP-ride'
     da-εk-εkar   '3p-DUP-receive'
     εp-εpir   'DUP-good 3s'

This is predicted by positing σ as the prefix template (and assuming left-to-right association).

(220) σ + σ σ → σ + σ σ — resyll. → σ σ σ
          ɔ p a   ɔ p a   ɔ p a   ɔ p ɔ p a

(221) σ + σ σ → σ + σ σ — resyll. → σ σ σ
          ε k a r   ε k a r   ε k a r   ε k ε k a r

Two-syllable bases of the form CVV or CVVC reduplicate only the first syllable. As McCarthy and Prince (1986:94) predict, the σ template does not "reach across" the second V in a CVVC base in order to complete the maximal CVC structure by using the second C.

(222) CVV:
  ru-rua 'DUP-two'
  i-du-dua 'DUP-3s-howl'

(223) CVVC:
  bɛ-bɛir 'DUP-red 3s' (*bɛr-bɛir)
  su-suar 'DUP-pole' (*sur-suar)
  dɔ-dɔam 'DUP-pound' (*dɔm-dɔam)

(224) σ + σ σ   σ σ σ
   /\ | /\ /\ |
   r u a → r u a r u a = *rurua*

(225) σ + σ σ   σ σ σ
   /\ /\   /\ /\ /\
   d ɔ a m → d ɔ a m d ɔ a m = *dɔdɔam*

The infixation of *-i-* (3s) and *-u-* (1s/2s) sometimes creates vowel clusters.

(226) /kanɔr/ 'hungry'   /karɔn/ 'old'
  kanɔur-ŋa 'I'm hungry' *karɔun-ŋa* 'I'm old'
  kanɔur-ka 'you're hungry' *karɔun-ka* 'you're old'
  kanɔir-na 'he/she is hungry' *karɔin-na* 'he/she is old'
  kanɔr-ay 'they are hungry' *karɔn-ay* 'they are old'

The reduplicated forms of these words also follow the pattern given above.

(227) *kanɔnɔur-ŋa* 'DUP hungry-1s'
  kanɔnɔir-na 'DUP hungry-3s'
  kanɔrnɔr-ay 'DUP hungry-3p'

Bases with a stressed CVC syllable reduplicate only that syllable.

(228) cvccv:
    gɔrgɔrsa   'coconut stem'
    korkorba   'bat (sp)'
    siɲalɲalta   'flying fish'

(229) cvccvc:
    kaybɛlbɛlbal   'bird (sp)'

With CVCV and CVCVC bases, reduplication consists of a $\sigma_c\sigma_c$ prefix, or in segmental terms a CVCV prefix. Thus, most CVCV bases also reduplicate entirely, and CVCVC bases usually reduplicate the first CVCV.

(230) cvcv:
    i-para-para   '3s-DUP-bake'
    kɛla-k-ɛla   'DUP-1s-go'[39]
    mɔna-mɔna-na   'DUP-first-3s'
    milamila   'coconut oil'
    jɛr-kɛru-kɛru   'NF-DUP-scrape'
    alemalema   'DUP right'

(231) cvcvc:[40]
    kɔla-kɔlat   'DUP-spoon'
    i-tubu-tubuk   '3s-DUP-punch'
    ɛ-r-dɔsa-dɔsam '3s-R-DUP-trip'
    jaba-jaban   'DUP-dried'
    i-gɔla-gɔlal   '3s-DUP-howl'
    bora-borar-na   'DUP-small-3s'
    jora-joraw   'DUP-scoop'
    i-gara-garay   '3s-DUP-hang'
    kɔni-kɔnir-na   'DUP-female 3s-3s'

In the case of CVCV and CVCVC bases, however, there are two conditions under which the final form of reduplication must be (unstressed) CV only. The first condition is if the second C is [+high], i.e., a velar or glide.

(232) cvcv:
    ɛy-lɛ-lɛka   '3s-DUP-play'
    paylalawa-na   'DUP-talkative-3s'
    jilalaŋa   'worm'

---

[39] The relationship between reduplication and other affixation will be discussed below.
[40] Note that no matter what the final C of a CVCVC base is, it is not included in the reduplicative prefix.

(233) CVCVC:
    *baba*kir   'DUP-small 3s'
    ma-m-akay   'DUP-2s-climb up'
    ja-jaŋil   'DUP-rotten 3s'
    ɛ-r-ga-gayat=na   '3s-R-DUP-lying down=3s'

Note that this restriction applies only to σ$_c$σ$_c$-type reduplication, not to σ-type (CVC) reduplication.

(234) *kɔwkɔw*   (**kɔkɔw*)   'butterfly'
    bɔŋbɔŋ   (**bɔbɔŋ*)   'gong (sp)'
    bɔybɔy   (**bɔbɔy*)   'hermit crab'
    nuynuy   (**nunuy*)   'great-grandparent'
    kaykuykuy-na (**kaykukuy-na*) 'DUP complete-3s'
    ak-akay   (**aakay*)   'DUP-climb up'

The second condition requiring a CV prefix with CVCV and CVCVC bases is if the first two Cs in the base are the same phoneme, or at least make use of the same articulator and share a certain number of distinctive features. It is apparently impossible, however, to specify which features or even how many features must be the same; *j ... s* in the base requires the reduced prefix while *t ... d* does not, even though [t] and [d] share more features than [j] and [s] do. Thus the sets of sounds which interfere with one another and require the shorter prefix must simply be listed.

(235) *ma-mama*   'DUP-chew'
    ra-raray   'DUP-hot'
    i-bɛ-bɛbar   '3s-DUP-afraid'
    dɛdɛdam   'afternoon'
    ɛ-r-nɔ-nɔnaw   '3s-R-DUP-crawl'
    ŋu-ŋuŋim   'DUP-damp 3s'
    ɛ-salalala   '3s-DUP watch'

(236) *lɛ-lɛray*   'DUP-sift'   (l/r)
    da-rɔ-r-ɔlay   '3p-DUP-R-argue' (r/l)
    i-sɛ-sɛtak   'DUP-3s-sever'   (s/t)
    sɛ-sɛtin-di   'DUP-severed pl-3p' (s/t)
    ji-jisin   'DUP-flesh 3s'   (j/s)
    pɔpjejetur-na 'DUP-Popjetur-3s' (j/t)
    ma-m-abak   'DUP-2s-pluck'   (m/b)
    ma-m-apan   'DUP-2s-measure' (m/p)

(237)   *i-tuda-tuda*   '3s-DUP-prop up'   (t/d)
       ɛ-r-dɔsa-dɔsam   '3s-R-DUP-trip'   (d/s)
       sɛrasɛrat   'insect (sp)'   (s/r)
       mata jarajara   'pink eye'   (j/r)
       i-tala-talar   '3s-DUP-sit'   (t/l)
       lɛsalɛsar-di   'intestine-pl'   (l/s)
       jɛna-jɛna   'DUP-tide rising'   (j/n)
       i-jila-jilal   '3s-DUP-trill'   (j/l)
       sɔlasɔlan   'harpoon (sp)'   (s/l)
       i-tɔra-tɔra   '3s-DUP-accompany'   (t/r)
       i-jora-joraw   '3s-DUP-draw (water)' (j/r)

I take these two cases of CV prefixes as an indication of phonetic difficulty restricting reduplication to the first syllable only. In Nivens (to appear) I consider positing reduction rules to delete the final CV from the reduplicative prefix; however I reject these ad hoc rules in favor of positing two distinct prefixes σ_cσ_c and σ_c.

There are a few CVCV(C) bases for which the reduplicative prefix is CVC rather than the expected CVCV. In these bases, both consonants are voiced alveolars.

(238)   *nɛlnɛla*   'lower back'   (cf. *nɛla-y* 'waist-3s')
       sinalnalar   'sitting'   (from /sin + talar/)
       manɛlnɛlay   'DUP sour'
       jin-jinay   'DUP-large'
       jin-jinin-ay   'DUP-large pl-3p'
       ɛ-tanirnira   '3s-DUP have diarrhea'
       da-ran-r-anat   '3p-DUP-R-child'

(Contrast *sinalnalar* 'sitting' with *i-tala-talar* '3s-DUP-sit'.)

However, there are also bases that fit the above criteria but take a full CVCV prefix.

(239)   *jɛna-jɛna*   'DUP-tide rising'
       i-jila-jilal   '3s-DUP-trill'
       jɛlajɛla low   'eel (sp)'

Since /a/-deletion takes place in a variety of other contexts as well, it seems reasonable in this case to posit a reduction rule applying to forms with two alveolar sonorants /n r l/. Apparently it is also idiosyncratically extended to the forms *jinjinay* and *jinjininay*.

(240) /a/-deletion between alveolar sonorants (lexical [stratum 3])

$$V \rightarrow \emptyset \;/\; C \underline{} + C \quad\quad V$$
$$\begin{bmatrix} +\text{cor} \\ +\text{son} \end{bmatrix} \quad\quad \begin{bmatrix} +\text{cor} \\ +\text{son} \end{bmatrix} \quad\quad [+\text{stress}]$$

To summarize the range of forms that attach to CVCV(C) bases, I present the following chart ('?' indicates that no base of this form exists in my corpus).

(241) Affixes that attach to CVCV(C) bases

Base = $C_1VC_2V(C)$:

	C_2		
C_1	b	p	m
b	CV	?	?
p	?	CV	?
m	CV	CV	CV

	C_2					
C_1	t	d	s	n	l	r
t	CV	CVCV	?	?	CVCV	CVCV
d	?	CV	CVCV	?	?	?
j	CV	?	CV	CVC/CVCV	CVCV	CVCV
s	CV	?	?	CVCV	CVCV	CVCV
n	CVCV	?	?	CV	CVC	CVC
l	?	?	CVCV	?	CV	CV
r	CVCV	?	CVCV	CVC	CV	CV

Although certain combinations seem to require a CV prefix (e.g., both consonants are bilabial, or both consonants are liquids), I will not attempt to write a rule until some of the above holes are filled in by further research.

If reduplication results in a geminate consonant cluster, the cluster undergoes geminate reduction, which is a rule attested in many other (nonreduplicative) environments as well.

(242) i-*tu-tut*   '3s-DUP-hammer'
     i-*ni-nin*   '3s-DUP-sleep'
     lɔ-lɔl-na   'DUP-deep-3s'
     ε-*marerer*   '3s-DUP stand'

A Lexical Phonology of West Tarangan

In addition, certain other homorganic clusters are reduced, losing the first member of the cluster.

(243)   *da-la-lar*   '3p-DUP-sail'   (r+l)
       dɛ-dɛn   'DUP-near'   (n+d)
       babaw   'egg yolk'   (w+b)
       kabɔbɔm-na   'DUP swollen-3s'   (m+b)

But the vast majority of homorganic clusters are not reduced.

(244)   *i-tɛn-tɛn*   '3s-DUP-cry'   (n+t)
       tɛl-tɛl   'DUP-savannah grass'   (l+t)
       tur-tur   'DUP-leak'   (r+t)
       tuytuy   'whistle'   (y+t)

(245)   *del-del-na*   'DUP-sound-3s'   (l+d)
       dɛrdɛr matin   'heat rash'   (r+d)
       i-doy-doy   '3s-DUP-watch'   (y+d)

(246)   *ɛ-rajitjit*   '3s-DUP urinate'   (t+j)
       i-jan-jan   '3s-DUP-shake off'   (n+j)
       i-jɛl-jɛl   '3s-DUP-walk around'   (l+j)
       jɛrjɛr   'biting gnat'   (r+j)
       i-jɛy-jɛy   '3s-DUP-sew'   (y+j)

(247)   *i-guk-guk*   '3s-DUP-suck'   (k+g)
       i-gɔŋ-gɔŋ   '3s-DUP-sell'   (ŋ+g)

(248)   *i-sun-sun*   '3s-DUP-poke'   (n+s)
       sɛl-sɛldi   'DUP-prawn'   (l+s)
       ɛ-r-sir-sir   '3s-R-DUP-speak'   (r+s)
       kapal sɛysɛy   'cumulus cloud'   (y+s)

(249)   *i-nal-nal*   '3s-DUP-take'   (l+n)
       i-nar-nar   '3s-DUP-hit'   (r+n)
       i-nay-nay   '3s-DUP-cook'   (y+n)

(250) *let-let-na*   'DUP-male-3s'   (t+l)
      i-lan-lan   '3s-DUP-light'   (n+l)
      i-loy-loy   '3s-DUP-hang'   (y+l)

(251) *i-ret-ret*   '3s-DUP-aground'   (t+r)
      ranran   'branch'   (n+r)
      ɛ-ril-r-il   '3s-DUP-R-pick up'   (l+r)
      i-ray-ray   '3s-DUP-think'   (y+r)

(252) *pɔw-pɔw-na*   'DUP-stink-3s'   (w+p)
      mɔwmɔw   'louse larva'   (w+m)

While true geminate reduction is a rule found throughout the language, reduction of these clusters has only been observed in this context. To summarize, I present the following table.

(253) Affixes that attach to CVC bases

Base = c_1vc_2:

c_1	c_2 p	m	w
b	?	CV	CV
p	?	?	CVC
m	?	?	CVC

c_1	c_2 k	ŋ
k	?	?
g	?	CVC
ŋ	?	?

c_1	c_2 t	n	l	r	y
t	CV	CVC	CVC	CVC	CVC
d	?	CV	CVC	CVC	CVC
j	CVC	CVC	CVC	CVC	CVC
s	?	CVC	CVC	CVC	CVC
n	?	CV	CVC	CVC	CVC
l	CVC	CVC	CV	CV	CVC
r	CVC	CVC	CVC	CV	CVC

In summary, I have proposed three distinct prosodic templates: σ, $σ_cσ_c$, and $σ_c$. The question remains as to how this variety of templates developed

A Lexical Phonology of West Tarangan

historically. Since nearly all languages in southern Maluku have σ (CVC) as the reduplicative template, prefixed to the stressed syllable, it appears certain that the disyllabic reduplication in this dialect is an innovation. The apparent motivation is that a syllable structure constraint not be violated, namely that voiced stops may not occur in syllable codas. CVCV(C) bases are exactly those which would potentially violate the constraint, since the onset of the second syllable would end up as the coda of a σ (CVC) prefix. North dialect allows voiced stops to occur in the coda of the reduplicative σ prefix, while River has a rule devoicing syllable-final stops; Coast, however, expands the prefix to σ$_c$σ$_c$ (CVCV) in order not to violate the constraint.

5.2. Reduplication and other morphophonemic processes

The picture of West Tarangan phonology and morphology that emerges from consideration of these facts is that of a lexical module with at least three distinct strata.

(254) Lexical module

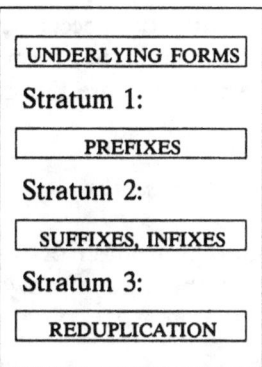

I have already noted at least two differences between prefixes and suffixes: first, while some prefixes may be below a foot-node in metrical structure and thus receive secondary stress, suffixes may not lie under a foot-node. Secondly, /a/-deletion before high vowel occurs between root and suffix or infix, but not between prefix and root. These facts argue for prefixation occurring in a stratum distinct from suffixation or infixation; however it is unclear at this point whether these two strata are ordered with respect to each other.

Now I will demonstrate that reduplication must occur in a stratum subsequent to any of the above affixation. From forms like *kɛla-k-ɛla*

'DUP-1s-go' it is clear that prefixation and prefix allomorphy rules must occur prior to reduplication. Without the reduction of *ku-* (1s) and subsequent resyllabification of /k/ as the onset of the root-initial syllable, the reduplicative template would be σ, not σ_cσ_c, and neither would /k/ be available for copying into the reduplicative prefix, since it would not be part of the stressed metrical foot. (Cf. *da-ɛl-ɛla* '3p-DUP-go'.) Thus I propose the following derivation:

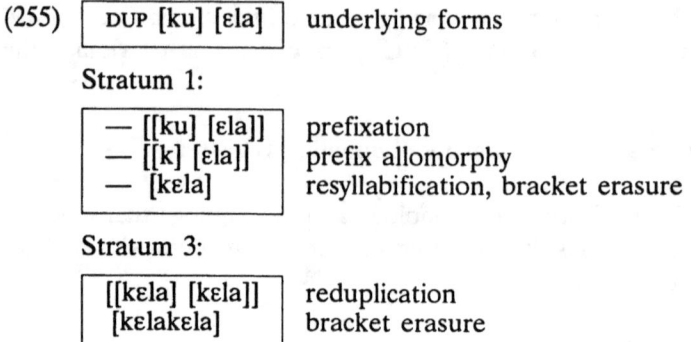

(255) DUP [ku] [ɛla]   underlying forms

Stratum 1:

— [[ku] [ɛla]]   prefixation
— [[k] [ɛla]]   prefix allomorphy
— [kɛla]   resyllabification, bracket erasure

Stratum 3:

[[kɛla] [kɛla]] reduplication
[kɛlakɛla]   bracket erasure

We can also see that the prefix vowel lowering rule occurs prior to reduplication; when the reduplicative prefix takes the form of an unstressed syllable, the prefix vowel remains [+high] because the rule does not apply in stratum 3.

(256) *i-sɛ-sɛtak*   '3s-DUP-sever'   (not *ɛ-sɛ-sɛtak*)

It is also clear that reduplication occurs after prefixation of *r-* and its resyllabification as part of the metrical foot, in the case of vowel-initial roots. This prefixation would also take place in stratum 1.

(257) *kɔ-rɔk-r-ɔk*   '1s-DUP-R-look for'
      da-ran-r-anat '3p-DUP-R-child'
      ko-raba-r-abak '1s-DUP-R-pluck'

Reduplication also occurs after suffixation of *-in* (3p) and the resulting deletion of root-final /ay/.

(258) *jɛla-jɛlay-na* 'DUP-full-3s'
      jɛli-jɛlin-ay 'DUP-full pl-3p'

A Lexical Phonology of West Tarangan 197

However, *-ay* (3p AN) exhibits anomalous behavior. If affixed to a number root, it is included as part of the base; but if affixed to regular adjectives it cannot be a part of the base.[41]

(259) *lasa-las-ay*   'DUP-three-3p'
      kay-ka-y   'DUP-four-3p'

(260) *tibɔybɔy-ay*   'DUP new-3p'   (*tibɔbɔyay)
      tapɛrpɛr-ay   'DUP old-3p'   (*tapɛrapɛray)

The failure of suffixes to be considered part of the base falls out naturally from the metrical account of stress proposed above. Recall that suffix syllables may not lie under a foot node, even if the final foot of the root is monosyllabic.

(261)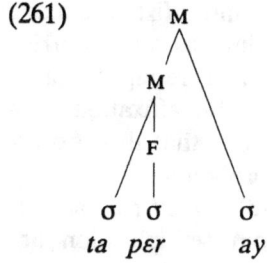

However, because affixation of *-in* results in the replacement of the root-final syllable's nucleus with the /i/ of the suffix, resyllabification is required, resulting in this /i/ being part of the stressed metrical foot (which is the base for reduplication).

(262) affixation: degemination: /a/-deletion:

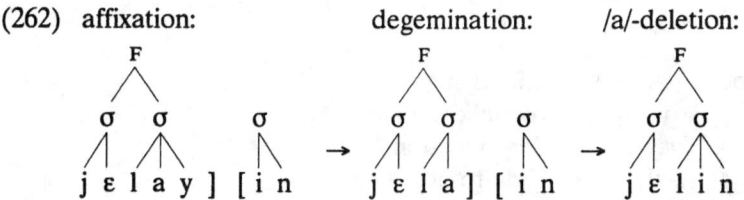

---

[41]As one would expect, when *-ay* (3P) functions as an object enclitic, attached in the syntactic module (after reduplication), it cannot be taken as part of the base:
   da-rɔk-r-ɔk=ay   (*darɔrɔkay)
   3P-DUP-R-seek=3P
   they sought each other

A similar situation holds for *ka-y* 'four-3p'. The underlying form is /ka+ay/; degemination forces the resyllabification of /y/ with the root, thus making it part of the base.⁴² But *las-ay* 'three-3p' is a special case. Being formed from one of the few /s/-final roots, resyllabification of -*ay* with the root is the only way to prevent the /s/ from undergoing the fricative-to-obstruent rule and changing to [t]. Apparently the language condones breaking a principle of metrical structure in order to avoid the undesirable **lat-lat-ay*.

As the following example shows, DUP is prefixed after infixation of [u] (1s, 2s) and [i] (3s).

(263) *arumarumak-ay*   'DUP sweaty-3p'
       arumirumik-na   'DUP sweaty 3s-3s'
       arumurumuk-ka   'DUP sweaty 2s-2s'

Since the data above shows prefixation, suffixation, and infixation, along with related phonological rules, to occur prior to reduplication, we arrive at the multistratal lexical module proposed above. Since reduplication is fundamentally a different kind of affixation, namely the affixation of a phonetically empty prosodic template, it is not surprising that this process occurs in a separate stratum from the rest of the morphology.

It is evident from *jey-jey* 'DUP-sew' that the glide-to-obstruent rule applies before reduplication, since geminates resulting from reduplication are reduced.

(264) a. [DUP]   [yɛy]   underlying forms
         [DUP]   [jɛy]   glide-to-obstruent
         [[jɛy] [jɛy]]   reduplication
         ———————   degemination
         ['jɛy'jɛy]

       b. [DUP]   [yɛy]   underlying forms
         [[yɛy] [yɛy]]   reduplication
         [[yɛ] [yɛy]]   degemination
         [[jɛ] [jɛy]]   glide-to-obstruent
         *[jɛ'jɛy]

More evidence for the glide-to-obstruent rule applying before reduplication comes from *oy-oir* 'DUP-finger 3s'.

---

⁴²The root *ka* 'four' is the only number or adjective root of the form CV.

A Lexical Phonology of West Tarangan   199

(265) *or-or-di*   'DUP-finger/toe-3p'
       oy-oir   'DUP-finger/toe 3s'

This is the only inalienably possessed noun in our corpus which requires reduplication. The infix *-i-* (3s) is affixed to the root or 'finger/toe' to form *oir*, after which reduplication occurs. Let us assume for now that there is a glide insertion rule (mentioned at the end of §4), changing *oir* to *oyir* before σ is prefixed. Then the derivation is as follows.[43]

(266) σ + σ σ   σ   + σ σ   σ   + σ σ
      | /|\   → | /|\   →   /| | /|\
      V C V C   V C V C   V C   V C V C
      | | | | | | | | | | | | | |
      o y i r   o y i r   o y i o y i r

Without the glide insertion rule we must assume that, since high vowels can be associated to C-elements, the high vowel /i/ of *oir* is taken as the coda of the reduplicative syllable, producing the prefix *oy-*.

(267) σ + σ σ   σ   + σ σ   σ   + σ σ
      | /| → | /| →   /| | /|
      V V C   V V C   V C   V V C = *oyoir*
      | | | | | | | | | | |
      o i r   o i r   o i   o i r

However, this capture of a high vowel in the base to form a glide in the reduplicative prefix is not possible with other bases (cf. *kanɔnɔir* 'DUP hungry 3s', not **kanɔynɔir*). This raises a serious problem for the CV-theory of Clements and Keyser (1983). Since only the melody is copied to associate with the reduplicative template, theoretically any high vowel should be available for associating with the coda of the σ template.

---

[43]The adjective *ɛal* 'evil' would also shed some light on the existence of a glide insertion rule and the behavior of glides and high vowels with regard to reduplication. However, my present data is tentative, being taken from a single elicitation session

unreduplicated:		reduplicated:
ɛul-ka	'evil 2s-2s'	['ɛ'ɛulkə] ~ ['ɛ'wɛulkə]
ɛil-na	'evil 3s-3s'	['ɛ'yɛilnə]
ɛal-da/ɛyal-da	'evil-1i'	['ɛ'ɛəldə] ~ ['ɛ'yɛyəldə]

(268)

$$\begin{array}{c} \sigma + \quad \sigma \\ \wedge \\ C\ V\ C \\ |\ \ |\ \ | \\ b\ \mathfrak{o}\ i \end{array} \rightarrow \begin{array}{c} \sigma + \quad \sigma \\ \wedge \quad \wedge \\ C\ V\ C\quad C\ V\ C \\ |\ \ |\ \ |\quad |\ \ |\ \ | \\ b\ \mathfrak{o}\ i\quad b\ \mathfrak{o}\ i \end{array} \rightarrow \begin{array}{c} \sigma \quad \sigma \\ \wedge \quad \wedge \\ C\ V\ C\quad C\ V\ C \\ |\ \ |\ \ |\quad |\ \ |\ \ | \\ b\ \mathfrak{o}\ i\quad b\ \mathfrak{o}\ i \end{array} = \boldsymbol{b\mathfrak{o}yb\mathfrak{o}y}$$

(269)

$$\begin{array}{c} \sigma + \sigma + \quad \sigma\ \sigma \\ \wedge \quad \wedge\ \wedge \\ C\ V\quad C\ V\ V\ C \\ |\ \ |\quad |\ \ |\ \ |\ \ | \\ k\ a\quad n\ \mathfrak{o}\ i\ r \end{array} \rightarrow \begin{array}{c} \sigma\quad +\sigma+\quad \sigma\ \sigma \\ \wedge \quad\quad \wedge\ \wedge \\ C\ V\quad\quad C\ V\ V\ C \\ |\ \ |\quad\quad\ |\ \ |\ \ |\ \ | \\ k\ a\ \ n\ \mathfrak{o}\ i\ r\ \ n\ \mathfrak{o}\ i\ r \end{array}$$

$$\rightarrow \begin{array}{c} \sigma\quad +\sigma+\quad \sigma\ \sigma \\ \wedge\quad \wedge\quad \wedge\ \wedge \\ C\ V\quad C\ V\ C\quad C\ V\ V\ C \\ |\ \ |\quad |\ \ |\ \ |\quad |\ \ |\ \ |\ \ | \\ k\ a\quad n\ \mathfrak{o}\ i\ r\quad n\ \mathfrak{o}\ i\ r \end{array} = *\boldsymbol{kan\mathfrak{o}yn\mathfrak{o}ir}$$

Thus it is evident that reduplication sees the difference between glides and vowels in the melody; therefore the feature [syll] must be part of the melody, which is what Clements and Keyser argued against. It may be that Clements and Keyser's algorithm for linking segments to C and V elements actually assigns [syll] both to x-elements and to the segments under them.

No matter how the reduplicative prefix gets its /y/, however, *oyoir* provides evidence that the glide-to-obstruent rule applies in a stratum previous to that of reduplication. Assuming that *oy.o.ir* (or *o.yo.yir*) is resyllabified as *o.yo.ir*, the failure of the glide-to-obstruent rule to change this to *ojoir* is an indication that the rule does not apply either in the stratum where reduplication occurs or in any subsequent stratum.

6. Cliticization and other syntactic processes

In lexical phonology, the output of the lexical module is a word. These words are then concatenated into phrases in the syntactic module, where phonological rules may apply to each word as a unit. Cliticization is a process which occurs in the syntactic module.

6.1. Object enclitics

When the object of a transitive verb or preposition is given or non-focused, a pronominal object enclitic is used, attaching to the end of the verb or preposition. The object enclitics are homophonous with the set of adjective agreement suffixes.

(270) 1s   2s   3s AN   3s IN   1e   1i   2p   3p AN   3p IN
       ŋa   ka   na   ∅   kam   da   kim   ay   di

I propose that these are in fact the same morphemes as the adjective agreement suffixes (not merely homophonous). A lexical affixation process attaches them to adjectives, while a postsyntactic cliticization process attaches them to transitive verbs and prepositions.

If a root ends in a stressed [−high] vowel, a [y] is inserted between the root and 3p AN enclitic *ay*.

(271) /da+ka=ay/   [də'kayəy]   'they eat them'
      /ku+pɔ=ay/   [ku'ɸɔyəy]   'I carry them'
      /da+mɛ=ay/   [də'mɛyəy]   'they were in them'

(272) /i+ru=ay/   [i'ruəy]   'it barks at them'

(273) /ku+tɔra=ay/   [ku'tɔrəy]   'I accompany them'

(274) /y/-epenthesis (syntactic [cliticization])

∅ → y / v $\begin{bmatrix} -\text{high} \\ +\text{stress} \end{bmatrix}$] —— [ay]

This rule does not apply in the lexical module. Numbers also take the adjective agreement suffixes when they modify an animate noun, and if *-ay* (3p^AN) is affixed to a number ending in a stressed [−high] vowel, [y] is not inserted, and degemination occurs.

(275) /ka+ay/   ['kay]   'four-3p AN (the four of them)'
      /ka+kim/   ['kakim]   'four-2p (the four of you)'

6.2. Cliticized personal pronouns

There are two contexts in which certain personal pronouns are reduced to an abbreviated form. I interpret this as a cliticization process.[44]

The first context is immediately preceding the verb agreement prefixes.

(276) seta tadɛm   ['sétə tə'dɛm] ~ [sétə'dɛm]   'we (incl.) make'
       kama madɛm   ['kamə mə'dɛm] ~ [kamə'dɛm]   'we (excl.) make'

In cases like this, it may just as well be mere omission of the agreement prefix. But if r- is prefixed to the verb root, the situation is more complex, since the /r/ is syllabified as the coda of the syllable preceding the verb root.

(277) seta tarsir   ['sétə tar'sir] ~ [sétar'sir]   'we (incl.) speak'
       kama marsir   ['kamə mar'sir] ~ [kamar'sir]   'we (excl.) speak'

Again, it may appear from the above two examples that the personal pronoun is cliticizing directly to r+verb, with no intervening agreement morpheme. However, the third-person plural form argues against this.

(278) era dadɛm   ['érə də'dɛm] ~ [érdə'dɛm]   'they make'
                    ~ [érə'dɛm]
       era darsir   ['érə dar'sir] ~ [érdar'sir]   'they speak'
                    *[érar'sir]

The form [érə'dɛm] is apparently a case of agreement prefix omission. But since *[érar'sir] is unacceptable, I posit that the pronoun is not simply replacing the agreement prefix, but cliticizing to the left of it, and the final /a/ of the pronoun is deleted as part of the cliticization process. In the case of séta (1i) and kama (1e), a geminate cluster is created, which is then reduced.

---

[44]These are simple clitics, i.e., "the reduced forms occur in the same positions as the full forms" (Zwicky 1977:6). Note that Zwicky (p. 10) lists personal pronouns as one of the most common types of simple clitics.

A Lexical Phonology of West Tarangan   203

(279)   LEXICAL MODULE
       [kama] [ma] [r] [sir]   underlying forms
       [kama]   [marsir]   affixation and bracket erasure

                                   SYNTACTIC MODULE
       [[kama] [marsir]]   cliticization
       [[kam] [marsir]]   pronoun /a/-deletion
       [[ka] [marsir]]   geminate reduction
       [kamarsir]   bracket erasure

(280) Pronoun /a/-deletion (syntactic [cliticization]) (optional)

       a → ∅ / ───]$_{\text{PRONOUN}}$ [

The second context where a personal pronoun cliticizes is immediately preceding a possession word.

(281) era da   ['érə 'da] ~ ['érda]   'their(s)'
      seta da   ['sétə 'da] ~ ['sétda]   'our(s) (incl.)'
      kama kamā   ['kamə kə'ma] ~ [kaka'ma]   'our(s) (excl.)'
                    ~ [kaʔa'ma]
      kɛn kanām   ['kɛn kə'nam] ~ [kɛkə'nam] 'your(s) (singular)'
                    ~ [kɛʔə'nam]
      kɛm kimā   ['kɛm ki'ma] ~ [kɛki'ma]   'your(s) (plural)'[45]
      ɔk kanāŋ   ['ɔk kə'naŋ] ~ [ɔkə'naŋ]   'my, mine'
                    ~ [ɔʔə'naŋ]

The 1s pronoun plus possession word undergo degemination, optionally followed by /k/-weakening. Again, I posit pronoun /a/-deletion for the 1i, 1e, and 3p forms, as well as a nasal deletion rule for the 1e, 2s, and 2p forms.

(282) Nasal deletion (syntactic [cliticization])

       [+nasal] → ∅ / ─── C

This rule may be related to the consonant cluster constraint, which prevents nasals from being the first member of a consonant cluster. However, when a nasal plus consonant cluster results from suffixation or

───────────────
[45]Some speakers use the pronunciation [kiki'ma], an apparent case of vowel harmony. Zwicky (1977:28) points out that although the relationships between simple clitics and their corresponding full forms are often the result of regular phonological rules observed in other contexts (e.g., /a/-deletion), "hosts as well as clitics may show exceptional phonology."

reduplication, the geminate is not reduced. As seen above, this rule feeds the /k/-weakening rule in the case of 2s and 1e forms.

6.3. Clausal enclitics

Perfect aspect is usually expressed by the unstressed enclitic *si(n)*, which either cliticizes to the end of the clause, or to the (synonymous) perfect aspect auxiliary *jaw*, or both.

(283) (a) *kɔ-r-tir =sin*   (b) *jaw   =sin   kɔ-r-tir   =sin*
           1s-R-bathe =already   already=already 1s-R-bathe=already
           I have already bathed *or* I am already bathing

The following examples demonstrate that *si(n)* cliticizes to the clause and not to the verb.

(284) *era da-manām sɛna   =sin*
        3p   3p-eat   finish =already
        They have finished eating.

(285) *ariran er   ɛ-r-or   tan   papa   =sin*
        bird   DEF 3s-R-fall   GOAL ground =already
        The bird has fallen to the ground.

Yet *si(n)* comes before the sentence-level question tag *tɛy*.

(286) *sandāl din   jow-di   =sin,   tɛy?*
        sandal these old-3p   =already   TAG
        These sandals are already old, aren't they?

Another clausal enclitic is the yes/no question enclitic *ɛ*, which follows enclitic *si(n)* if it occurs. This question enclitic expects agreement with the proposition being questioned.

(287) *kɛn sikali mɔy-mɔy   nɔ   =ɛ?*
        2s   not   DUP-2s^go   there YNQ
        So you're not going there, eh?

(288) *kɛn mɔ-r-tir   =si   =ɛ?*
        2s   2s-R-bathe   already   YNQ
        So you've already bathed, have you?

(289) kɛn jɔar nɛn =ɛ?
 2s in^law this YNQ
 So this is your in-law, is it?

(290) kɛn nɔ mɔ-manamnām =ɛ?
 2s PROG 2s-DUP^eat YNQ
 So you're eating, are you?

6.4. /a/-deletion before stressed vowel

The vowel /a/, if unstressed, will be deleted before a full word boundary if the next segment is a stressed vowel.

(291) kola-kolay-na ina ['kólə'kóləy'ninə]
 DUP-blind-3s one
 a blind person

(292) ɛpir-na uk ['ɛɸɪr'nuk]
 good-3s very
 very good

(293) maɛra ɔn [ma'ɛ'rɔn]
 day this
 today

(294) maɛra er [ma'ɛ'rér]
 day DEF
 that day

(295) galāy laguya er [gə'lay lə'gu'yér]
 house meeting DEF
 the meeting house

I posit the following rule, noting that once again it is the default vowel /a/, which has no underlying feature specifications, that is deleted.

(296) /a/-deletion before stressed vowel (syntactic)

$$a \rightarrow \emptyset\ /\ \underline{\quad}\ ]\ [\ \ V$$
$$[-\text{stress}]\quad [+\text{stress}]$$

7. Postsyntactic processes

According to the theory of lexical phonology, phrases exit the syntactic module with no internal boundaries, and may then undergo phonological rules marked as postsyntactic or phonetic implementation rules. Several of these rules have already been discussed.

7.1. Intonation

Intonation contours may be roughly described in terms of the three pitch levels high (H), mid (M), and low (L). Distinct intonation contours may be described for phrase and sentence levels.

In a phonological phrase, the last syllable that has word stress is the phrase nucleus and receives phrase stress. Therefore I posit that a right-headed metrical tree is drawn on the phrase level. All syllables preceding the phrase nucleus have mid pitch. The phrase nucleus has high pitch, as do any following syllables in the phrase (unless that phrase nucleus is also the sentence nucleus). The phrase nucleus is louder than other stressed syllables.

(297) M M M   H   M M H
       era pit   ɔn da-kor-kor, ...
       3p night this 3p-DUP-beat
       This night they beat [the drums], ...

Note that if a subject pronoun is followed by a time phrase, they constitute a single phonological phrase.

The final phrase nucleus in a phonological sentence constitutes the sentence nucleus. In declarative and imperative moods, the sentence nucleus is marked by a low pitch after the high pitch which it has by virtue of being a phrase nucleus. If the sentence nucleus is not the final syllable in the phonological sentence, the low pitch begins on the syllable after the sentence nucleus and continues until the end of the phonological sentence. Thus the sentence-level metrical tree is also right-headed.

(298)   M M H   M   M M M H   M M M   M HL
       da-lalū   kɔ   maɛra nɔ   da-antam kor-kor.
       3p-descend then day   that 3p-begin DUP-beat
       They come down, then on that day they begin beating [drums].

(299)   M M   M H H M   H   M   M   M M   M HL
da-tɔm da-sɛna, kɔ puy, ja dal kanɛy ramiaŋ.
3p-roof 3p-finish then done then 3p^take 3s^POSS party
After roofing it, and it's done, they throw a party for it.

Yes/no questions with question enclitic ɛ have this same M...HL pitch contour. Content questions sometimes have this contour or perhaps M...HM, but usually end with the high pitch only.

(300)   M   M M H   M   M   H L   L
kɛm maɛrɔn mɛy-mɛy Dobo =ɛ?
2p today DUP-2p^go Dobo YNQ
So you're going to Dobo today, are you?

(301)   M   M   M H
dɛm-dɛm lɛbā?
DUP-do what
What are you doing?

(302)   H   M   M H   M M M H
kɛn nɔ-m-tɛn-tɛn aka lɛbā?
2s PROG-2s-DUP-cry for what
Why are you crying?

(303)   M M   M H H M M M M   H
ɔna karter-na bana-bana ba?
PROG sound-3s DUP-from what
Where is the sound coming from?

(304)   M   M M   H   M M   M HM
kɛm mi-ma ɔn aka lɛbā?
2p 2p-come here for what
What have you come here for?

(305)   M M H   M   M M M HM
lɛbā ɔn ɛy natapɛn ɔn?
what this LOC village this
What's this in this village?

(306)   M   H   M   H   M   M M H H M HL
        ga   kɛm pit   ɔn   kɛm ma-mi-dɛŋar lɛbā?
        relative 2p   night this 2p   PST-2p-hear   what
        You relatives, what did you hear this (last) night?

(307)   M M   M H H
        nar-nar nɛy aka?
        DUP-hit 3s   for
        why are you hitting him?

Vocative intonation, that is, the intonation used when calling a person, follows the M...HL pattern as well.

(308)   M   H L   M MM   HL
        Kris jina-y!   Kris jina-y   ɔ!
        Kris mother-3s Kris mother-3s hey
        Kris's mom! Hey, Kris's mom!

7.2. Markers of phonological phrase boundaries

If the final segment in a phonological phrase is a stop, a homorganic syllabic nasal may be inserted after the stop. The nasal takes whatever pitch is appropriate for a syllable in that position of an intonation contour.

(309) *da-tar   kubaŋ, anakɔta, dɔit [n], jɛrtāy.*
       3p-bring gong   plate   money   clothing
       They bring gongs, plates, money, clothes.

(310) *da-r-kel tuak   [ŋ], da-r-dɛm manām...*
       3p-R-buy liquor   3p-R-make food
       They buy liquor, they make food...

(311) *da-ɛla da-sika ŋerat   [n].*
       3p-go 3p-get   tree (sp)
       They go get a certain kind of tree.

(312) *i-rua   =di   ɛy   nɛy kanɛy mama kanɛy pɔw tit [n].*
       3s-plant =3p^IN LOC 3s   3s^POSS mother 3s^POSS grave top
       She planted them on top of her mother's grave.

A Lexical Phonology of West Tarangan

(313) tor   da-uk   [ŋ], japūn ε-r-loŋar, ...
chicken 3p-crow   then 3s-R-get^up
The chickens crowed, and then she got up, ...

(314) ε-r-tip   [m], nεy ja-jaga, ...
3s-R-sprout   3s DUP-watch
It sprouted, she was watching it, ...

I posit a rule to insert a homorganic nasal after a phrase-final voiceless stop. (Since the rule is postsyntactic, the boundary it refers to is a phonological phrase boundary.)

(315) Nasal epenthesis (postsyntactic) (optional)

$$\emptyset \rightarrow \begin{bmatrix} +\text{nasal} \\ \alpha \text{ point} \end{bmatrix} / \begin{bmatrix} -\text{cont} \\ -\text{voice} \\ \alpha \text{ point} \end{bmatrix} \underline{\quad} \;]$$

Vowel clusters across syllable boundaries are not separated by a glottal stop, even if a morpheme boundary intervenes, but vowel-initial words are generally preceded by a (nonphonemic) glottal stop, when occurring phrase initially. (I have been conveniently ignoring this in phonetic transcriptions throughout this paper.) The rule is fairly straightforward, as follows:

(316) Glottal stop epenthesis (post-syntactic)

$$\emptyset \rightarrow \text{?} \;/\; [\; \underline{\quad} \; V$$

Again, the boundary in this postsyntactic rule refers to a phonological-phrase boundary.

8. Summary of rules

I present here the rules posited in this paper for West Tarangan Coast dialect. The rules are marked as to their domain of application, in accordance with the following diagram.

(317) Lexical module

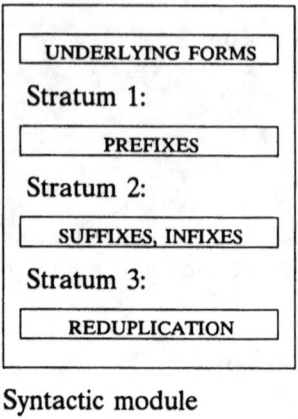

Syntactic module

Postsyntactic module

8.1. Underlying forms

First, there are a variety of constraints on underlying morpheme structure:

(318) Underlying alphabet

```
            t      k
     b      d
     ɸ      s
     m      n      ŋ
            r
            l
            y      w
            i      u
            e      o
            ɛ      ɔ
              a
```

(319) Syllable types: CV, V, CVC, VC

(320) Final mid vowel constraint

$$* \ V \ C_0 \ \underset{[\text{mid}]}{V} \ \#$$

A Lexical Phonology of West Tarangan 211

(321) Final voiced stop constraint

$$*\begin{bmatrix}\begin{bmatrix}-son\\+voice\end{bmatrix}\end{bmatrix}_\sigma$$

(322) Consonant cluster constraint

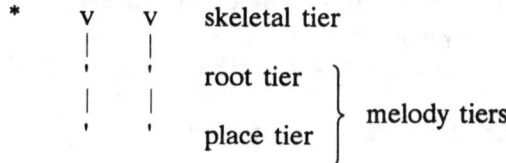

(323) Vowel cluster constraint (mirror-image)

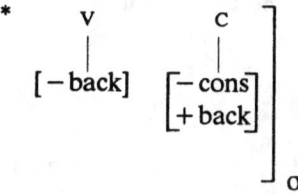

(324) Vowel-glide constraint

$$*\begin{bmatrix}V & C\\ | & |\\ [-back] & \begin{bmatrix}-cons\\+back\end{bmatrix}\end{bmatrix}_\sigma$$

(325) Nonfinal vowel-glide constraint

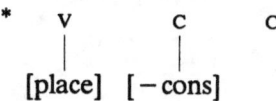

The above constraints can be seen as filters which exclude ill-formed sequences. The length of a morpheme is limited by stipulations of metrical structure.

(326) Foot construction:

    (a) Feet are bounded (maximum two syllables).
    (b) Feet are quantity-sensitive (syllable weight determines whether the foot consists of one or two syllables).
    (d) Any closed syllable preceded by either a closed syllable or a morpheme boundary may not be the weak member of a disyllabic foot.
    (e) Any closed syllable with a mid vowel may not be the weak member of a disyllabic foot.
    (c) Disyllabic feet are 'left-headed' (s-w).
    (f) Any syllable dominant in a foot receives (at least) secondary stress.

(327) M-node construction:

    (a) Each M is binary branching—therefore the maximal M consists of two disyllabic feet.
    (b) The M-level is recursive on each cycle of morphological derivation.
    (c) An M consisting of two feet is right-headed (w-s).

(328) Maximal morphemes:

    (a) The maximal root consists of two metrical feet.
    (b) The maximal prefix consists of one metrical foot.
    (c) The maximal suffix consists of one syllable.

8.2. Lexical module

Once a morpheme has run the gauntlet of underlying structure constraints, it undergoes the rules which apply in the lexical module.

(329) Glide-to-obstruent rule (Lexical)

$$[-\text{cons}] \rightarrow \begin{bmatrix} +\text{cons} \\ -\text{son} \\ -\text{cont} \\ -\text{round} \end{bmatrix} \bigg/ \underset{\{M,F\}}{[\underline{}}$$

(with a C associated above the [−cons])

A Lexical Phonology of West Tarangan

(330) Fricative-to-obstruent rule (lexical)

$$[-\text{son}] \rightarrow [-\text{cont}] \ / \ \underline{\hspace{1em}}]_\sigma$$

These two rules result in the lexical alphabet having three more consonants than the underlying alphabet does.

(331) Lexical alphabet

```
p    t         k
b    d    j    g
ɸ    s
m    n         ŋ
     r
     l
          y    w
          i    u
          e    o
          ɛ    ɔ
             a
```

Some rules apply only in one stratum of the lexical module. The following rules apply in the stratum of prefixation (stratum 1).

(332) Singular prefix vowel deletion (lexical [stratum 1])

$$V \rightarrow \emptyset \ / \ \left[(C) \ \underline{\hspace{1em}} \right]_{\text{AGR} \atop [+\text{singular}]} \left[V \right]_{\text{VERB}}$$

(333) Prefix vowel lowering (lexical [stratum 1])

$$V \rightarrow \begin{bmatrix} -\text{high} \\ +\text{mid} \end{bmatrix} \ / \ \underline{\hspace{1em}} \ [+\text{stress}] \Big]_{\text{AGR}}$$

(where [stress] includes both primary and secondary stress)

(334) *mu-* reduction (lexical [stratum 1])

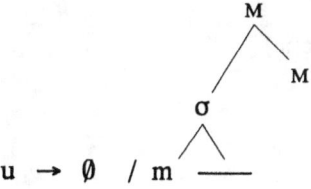

$$u \rightarrow \emptyset \ / \ m \ \underline{\hspace{1em}}$$

(335) /a/-epenthesis after *r-* (lexical [stratum 1])

∅ → a / r —— r

(336) /r/-deletion (lexical [stratum 1]) (optional)

r → ∅ / ——] [c   v
                    [−stress]

(337) Alveolar deletion (lexical [stratum 1])

c → ∅ / [sin] [——

The following rules apply only in stratum 2, the stratum of suffixation and infixation.

(338) /a/-deletion before high vowel (lexical [stratum 2])

a → ∅ / ——   [v
         [−stress]
                  $\begin{bmatrix} +\text{high} \\ -\text{mid} \end{bmatrix}$

(339) Vowel epenthesis before *-c* suffix (lexical [stratum 2])

∅ → a / c] —— [c]

Reduplication takes place in lexical stratum 3; there is one rule relating specifically to reduplication.

(340) /a/-deletion between alveolar sonorants (lexical [stratum 3])

v → ∅ /   c   ——   + c   v
                              [+stress]
       $\begin{bmatrix} +\text{cor} \\ +\text{son} \end{bmatrix}$ $\begin{bmatrix} +\text{cor} \\ +\text{son} \end{bmatrix}$

Geminate reduction applies in both the lexical and syntactic modules.

(341) Geminate reduction (lexical, syntactic)

x x   x   skeletal tier
 \/   → |
  •   •   root tier

A Lexical Phonology of West Tarangan 215

8.3. Syntactic module

The following rules take place in the syntactic module, where words are combined into phrases.

(342) /k/-weakening (syntactic) (optional)

k → ʔ / v   —   v
         [−high]   [−high]

(343) Glottal deletion (syntactic) (optional)

ʔ → ∅

(344) /a/-deletion before stressed vowel (syntactic)

a → ∅ /   —   ] [v
        [−stress]   [+stress]

In the syntactic module, the internal morphological structure of words has been erased, so any alteration of prefixes must refer to the M-nodes of the metrical tree.

(345) /u/-deletion (syntactic)

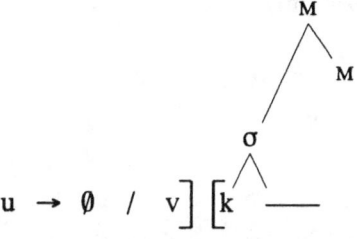

(346) /k/-deletion (syntactic)

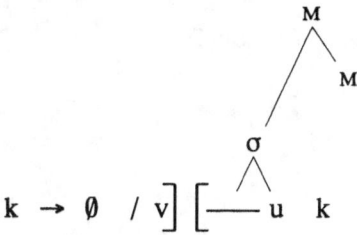

(347) /m/-deletion (syntactic)

   m → ∅ / ...

(348) Agreement prefix omission (syntactic) (optional)

$$\sigma \rightarrow \emptyset\ /\ ]_{NP}\ \overset{\displaystyle M \atop \displaystyle M}{[\ \underline{\quad}\ }_{VERB}$$

There are three rules which apply only in that part of the syntactic module where cliticization takes place:

(349) Pronoun /a/-deletion (syntactic [cliticization]) (optional)

   a → ∅ / ___]$_{PRONOUN}$ [

(350) Nasal deletion (syntactic [cliticization])

   [+nasal] → ∅ / ___ C

(351) /y/-epenthesis (syntactic [cliticization])

$$\emptyset \rightarrow y\ /\ \begin{bmatrix} V \\ -high \\ +stress \end{bmatrix}]\ \underline{\quad}\ [\ ay\ ]$$

8.4. Postsyntactic module

After phrases are formed, a variety of rules apply in the postsyntactic module, including rules that assign intonation contours.

(352) High vowel laxing (post-syntactic) (optional)

$$\begin{bmatrix} V \\ +high \\ -mid \end{bmatrix} \rightarrow [-ATR]\ /\ \underline{\quad}\ C]_{\sigma}$$

A Lexical Phonology of West Tarangan

(353) /a/-weakening (postsyntactic)

a → ə / ___
          [−stress]

(where [−stress] includes both primary and secondary stress)

(354) [ə]-fronting (postsyntactic)

ə → ɪ / j ___ j

(355) /si/-devoicing (postsyntactic) (optional)

$$\begin{bmatrix} +\text{high} \\ -\text{mid} \\ -\text{back} \\ -\text{stress} \end{bmatrix} \rightarrow [-\text{voice}] / s \underline{\quad}$$

(356) Voiceless bilabial stop formation (postsyntactic) (optional)

ɸ → [−cont]

There are two rules that refer to phrase boundaries, and therefore must apply postsyntactically.

(357) Glottal stop epenthesis (postsyntactic)

∅ → ʔ / [___ v

(358) Nasal epenthesis (postsyntactic) (optional)

$$\emptyset \rightarrow \begin{bmatrix} +\text{nasal} \\ \alpha \text{ point} \end{bmatrix} / \begin{bmatrix} -\text{cont} \\ -\text{voice} \\ \alpha \text{ point} \end{bmatrix} \underline{\quad}]$$

9. Summary of River dialect phonology[46]

9.1. Consonant inventory

In River dialect, there is no glide /w/, although there is a glide /y/; /g/ is phonemic, while /y/ undergoes the glide-to-obstruent rule. Words in Coast

---

[46]Most of the data presented in this section were gathered during a three-month residency in Doka Timur village in 1987–88.

with syllable-final [w] have no [w] in the corresponding River words; Coast words with intervocalic [w] either drop the [w] or have [g] in its place.

(359)   rɔra   'heat'   (cf. Coast rɔraw)
        taro   'dog'   (cf. Coast tarɔw)
        lɛgay   'tree (sp)' (cf. Coast lɛway)

In terms of CV phonology, underlying /u/ is never linked to a C-element. Thus in this dialect words like ŋauan 'honey' and uar 'wound' need no idiosyncratic stipulation that /u/ is linked to a V-element; rather, a dialect-specific constraint prevents /u/ from linking to a C-element.

9.2. Devoicing

In this dialect, not only is there a constraint on underlying structure prohibiting voiced stops from occupying the coda of a syllable, there is an active rule to devoice any stop which may be placed there (e.g., by reduplication).

(360)   /DUP+jaban/ [jip'jabən] 'DUP-dry'
       /DUP+kudam/ [kit'kudəm] 'cloud'

9.3. Assimilation

In River, unlike Coast and North, nasals may assimilate to a following consonant. In the case of the verb agreement prefix m- (from /mu/) (2s), the assimilation is obligatory. If the verb begins with a nasal, after assimilation the resulting geminate is reduced.

(361) | | | | | | | |
|---|---|---|---|---|---|---|
| m-bana | '2s-leave' | n-tɔra | '2s-accompany' | ŋ-ka | '2s-eat' |
| m-pan | '2s-fall' | n-dɛm | '2s-make' | ŋ-ga | '2s-arrive' |
| ∅-ma | '2s-come' | ∅-nun | '2s-drink' | ∅-ŋɛtal | '2s-know' |
| | | n-jɛmar | '2s-sweep' | | |
| | | n-si | '2s-go' | | |
| | | n-rɔka | '2s-overloaded' | | |
| | | n-la | '2s-run' | | |

If reduplication places a nasal to the left of a consonant, nasal assimilation sometimes occurs; data is insufficient at present to determine whether or not the rule is optional for all forms or combinations.

A Lexical Phonology of West Tarangan

(362) Assimilated in all instances:

mt	/DUP+bitem/	[bin'tém]	'DUP-small'
ŋp	/DUP+kalɸaŋar+i/	[kalpim'paŋir]	'DUP-obstinate 3s'

(363) Optional assimilation:

mj	/DUP+ɸaɸa+jɛm+na/	[ɸaɸam'jɛmnə] ~ [ɸaɸan'jɛmnə]	'overcast-3s'
mg	/DUP+jɛr+gum/	[jɛrgim'gum] ~ [jɛrgiŋ'gum]	'DUP-NF-rub'
ms	/DUP+simar/	[sim'simər]	'DUP-east'
	/DUP+sima/	[sin'simə]	'ant (sp)'
nk	/DUP+kinir/	[kan'kinɪr] ~ [kaŋ'kinɪr]	'DUP-female'
ŋr	/DUP+maraŋam/	[maŋ'raŋəm]	'praying mantis'
	/DUP+ruŋan+i/	[rin'ruŋin]	'section of fruit'

The following sequences have not been observed to undergo assimilation. Some of these may be due merely to the fact that the assimilation rule is optional for these sequences. However, it is apparent that a nasal never assimilates to a following nasal, since this would result in degemination.

(364) Not assimilated in any instances:

mk	/DUP+jɛr+kɔm/	[jɛrkim'kɔm]	'DUP-NF-dislike'
md	/DUP+dum+di/	[dim'dumdi]	'DUP-six-pl'
mn	/DUP+nam/	[nim'nam]	'berry (sp)'
ml	/DUP+lema+in/	[lim'lémin]	'DUP-five-pl'
mr	/DUP+ruma+y/	[rim'rumɛ]	'sheath-3s'
nb	/DUP+bɔn/	[bin'bɔn]	'DUP-shut'
nm	/DUP+mɔna+na/	[min'mɔnənə]	'DUP-first-3s'
ŋm	/DUP+muŋar+i/	[miŋ'muŋɪr]	'DUP-dirty 3s'
ŋn	/DUP+sin+tɔŋar/	[siŋ'nɔŋar]	'house beam (sp)'
ŋl	/DUP+i+lɛŋan/	[iŋ'lɛŋan]	'DUP-3s-pass by'

(365) Heterorganic sequences unattested in the corpus:

/mŋ/, /np/, /ng/, /nŋ/, /ŋt/, /ŋb/, /ŋd/, /ŋy/, /ŋs/

An adjective root ending in /n/ may assimilate to agreement suffix -ka (2s), but not to agreement suffix -ŋa (1s); this provides more evidence that nasals never assimilate to a following nasal.

(366) tin-ka   ['tinkə] ~ ['tiŋkə]   'you itch'
      tin-ŋa   ['tinŋə]   'I itch'

I posit the following rule, which states that a nasal will take on the point of articulation of a following nonnasal.

(367) Nasal assimilation (lexical, postsyntactic) (optional)

$$[+\text{nasal}] \rightarrow [\alpha \text{ point}] / \underline{\quad} \begin{bmatrix} c \\ -\text{nasal} \\ \alpha \text{ point} \end{bmatrix}$$

This rule is apparently optional in its postsyntactic application, but obligatory in its lexical application (in the stratum of prefixation, affecting the agreement prefix m- (2s)).

There is another type of assimilation for which our data is insufficient to formulate a rule precisely. When /ɸ/ or /b/ occur syllable finally as a result of reduplication, they both become [p] either by the fricative-to-obstruent rule or by devoicing. If this [p] is followed by a liquid, [p] may optionally assimilate to that liquid. If the liquid is /r/, the [p] may become [t]; but if the liquid is /l/, the [p] may become [r].[47]

(368) [gup'raɸər] ~ [gut'raɸər] 'sago thorn'

    [guraɸar]   underlying form
    [guɸraɸar]   reduplication
    [gupraɸar]   fricative-to-stop rule
    [gutraɸar]   [p]-assimilation (optional)

(369) [kép'labə] ~ [kér'labə] 'plank'

    [kelaba]   underlying form
    [keblaba]   reduplication
    [keplaba]   devoicing
    [kerlaba]   [p]-assimilation (optional)

---

[47]These are the only two examples of this phenomenon in our corpus.

A Lexical Phonology of West Tarangan

If the [p] is followed by a nasal, assimilation to that nasal is apparently obligatory, although we have only one example in our corpus.

(370) [akˈŋaɸə] 'left'

[aŋaɸa]	underlying form
[aɸŋaɸa]	reduplication
[apŋaɸa]	fricative-to-stop rule
[akŋaɸa]	[p]-assimilation

For now I posit the following rule, which specifies that [p] assimilates to a following nasal or liquid.

(371) [p]-assimilation (lexical)

$$p \rightarrow \begin{bmatrix} \alpha \text{ point} \\ <+\text{son}> \\ <+\text{cont}> \end{bmatrix} / \underline{} \begin{bmatrix} +\text{son} \\ \alpha \text{ point} \\ <+\text{lat}> \end{bmatrix}$$

This rule applies in the lexical stratum of reduplication; it does not affect [p]-final adjectives when a nasal-initial suffix is added (e.g., *tɔp-ŋa* [ˈtɔpŋə] *[ˈtɔkŋə] 'short-1s').

9.4. /y/-lowering

In this dialect, the syllable rime /ay/ is never realized as [ay] or even [əy]. Instead, it occurs as [aɛ] if it carries any stress (primary or secondary), or [ɛ] if completely unstressed (which could only be in morpheme-final position due to the stress rules of West Tarangan). In addition, /ɔy/ is pronounced [ɔɛ] (although /oy/ remains [óy]).

(372) *bɔray-na*   [ˈbɔrɛnə]   'big-3s'
   mata-y   [ˈmatɛ]   'eye-3s'
   tɔp-ay   [ˈtɔɸɛ]   'short-3p'
   i-jaman=ay [iˈjamanɛ] '3s-ask=3p'

(373) *tay*   [ˈtaɛ]   'seawater'
   maraɲāy   [maraˈɲaɛ] 'lightweight'
   gaynaka   [gaɛˈnakə] 'sago leaf'

(374) *ɔy*   [ˈɔɛ]   'rice'

(375) boy   ['bóy]   'father'
      aroy   [ə'róy]   'ironwood'

This phenomenon may be captured in two ordered rules.

(376) /y/-lowering (lexical)[48]

$$\begin{matrix} C & V & & V \\ | & | & & | \\ i & \begin{bmatrix} -high \\ +mid \end{bmatrix} & / \ [-high] & \underline{\quad\quad} \end{matrix}$$

(377) /a/-deletion (lexical)

$$\begin{matrix} a \\ [-stress] \end{matrix} \rightarrow \emptyset \ / \ \underline{\quad\quad} \ \varepsilon$$

The /y/-lowering rule changes /y/ to [ɛ] after /a/ or /ɔ/, feeding the /a/-deletion rule. /a/-deletion deletes /a/ from [aɛ] if it carries no stress. If /a/ is not deleted, the sequence [aɛ] is pronounced as two timing units. I leave open the question of whether this vv sequence remains monosyllabic or is resyllabified as two syllables.

9.5. High vowel lowering

Across word boundaries, the verb agreement prefix *i-* (3s) is typically lowered to [ɛ] if the preceding word ends in a [−high] vowel.

(378) *i-nal   pɛar ia   kɔ i-pɔ*   [i'nal 'pɛər 'iə kɔ ɛ'ɸɔ]
      3s-take bow one so 3s-carry
      He took a bow and carried it.

(379) *i-nam tɔpi i   jikala-y i-muy*   [i'nam 'tɔɸi i ji'kalɛ ɛ'muy]
      3s-put hat 3s^to head-3s 3s-again
      He put (his) hat on his head again.

---

[48]In the structural description of this rule, v[−high] comprises the set /a ɔ ɛ/, implying /ɛy/→[ɛɛ]; however, in this dialect either /ɛy/ never occurs or else it is raised to [é] (data is insufficient at present to determine which). These rules apply in the lexical module, i.e., not across word boundaries.

(380) balakalə ia ja i-ma   [balə'kalə 'iə ja ɛ'ma]
     while   one then 3s-come
     Awhile later, he came.

In similar fashion, /u/ is lowered to [o] when following a word ending in /a/.

(381) jɛlay-na uk   ['jɛlɛnə 'ok]
     full-3s   very

Although our data is limited, we might try to capture both of these phenomena in a single rule, as follows.

(382) High vowel lowering (syntactic)

$$\begin{bmatrix} V \\ +\text{high} \\ <-\text{back}> \end{bmatrix} \rightarrow \begin{bmatrix} +\text{mid} \\ <-\text{high}> \end{bmatrix} \;/\; a \;]\; [\;\underline{\hspace{1em}}$$

9.6. Agreement prefix allomorphy

River has the same singular prefix vowel deletion rule as Coast, which deletes the vowel of singular agreement prefixes on vowel-inital verb roots. Unlike Coast, however, the vowels of *ta-* and *da-* are also deleted with vowel-initial verb roots, while *ma-* tends to remain [ma] or [mə], to avoid ambiguity with *m-* (2s).

(383) /ku + ɛkar/   ['kɛkər]   '1s-receive'
     /mu + ɛkar/   ['mɛkər]   '2s-receive'
     /i + ɛkar/   ['ɛkər]   '3s-receive'
     /ta + ɛkar/   ['tɛkər]   '1i-receive'
     /ma + ɛkar/   [mə'ɛkər]   '1e-receive'
     /mi + ɛkar/   [mi'ɛkər]   '2p-receive'
     /da + ɛkar/   ['dɛkər]   '3p-receive'

I posit the following rule, with c specified as [+cor] so as not to delete the /a/ from *ma-*.

(384) Agreement prefix /a/-deletion (lexical)

$$a \rightarrow \emptyset \ / \ \begin{bmatrix} C \\ [+\text{cor}] \end{bmatrix} \underline{\quad} \ ] \ [\ V$$

The remaining [t] or [d] is resyllabified as the onset of the initial syllable of the root; it is then part of the base for reduplication.

This dialect also has a prefix vowel lowering rule, but only *i-* (3s) is affected by it.

(385) *palī* 'turn over'

1s	2s	3s	1e	1i	2p	3
ku-palī	*mu-palī*	*ɛ-palī*	*ma-palī*	*ta-palī*	*mi-palī*	*da-palī*

So for this dialect I frame the rule as follows.

(386) Prefix vowel lowering (lexical)

$$i \rightarrow \begin{bmatrix} -\text{high} \\ +\text{mid} \end{bmatrix} \ / \ \begin{bmatrix} \underline{\quad} \\ [+\text{stress}] \end{bmatrix} \quad \text{AGR}$$

(where [stress] includes both primary and secondary stress)

Although *ku-* (1s), *mu-* (2s), and *mi-* (2p) do not undergo prefix vowel lowering, they do undergo high vowel laxing if verb prefix *r-* closes the syllable.

As in Coast, *mu-* is reduced to *m-* if completely unstressed; however, in River this *m-* remains as a syllabic nasal (rather than being deleted as in Coast) if not preceded by a vowel. As demonstrated above, *m-* undergoes obligatory assimilation to the root-initial consonant. None of the Coast dialect syntactic-module rules affecting agreement prefixes occurs in River.

9.7. Object enclitic allomorphy

In River, as in Coast, adjectives ending in /a/ and /ay/ take the suffix *-in* (pl) before the more specific plural agreement suffixes. However, unlike Coast, *-in* is also affixed (probably as a clitic) before the third-person plural object enclitic *-ay*.

(387) /yɛsa + in + ay/   [jɛsinɛ]   'they don't want'
       /samay + in + ay/   ['saminɛ]   'they are bad'

A Lexical Phonology of West Tarangan

(388) /i+kara=in=ay/ [i'karinɛ] 'it bit them'
/i+waray=in=ay/ [i'garinɛ] 'he/she dries them'

9.8. Compounding

We have in our corpus several instances of two words concatenated and the resulting form reduplicated.

(389) *mata-r-bar* [matar'bar]
eye-DUP-discharge
eye discharge

(390) *mata-b-sɛbar* [matap'sɛbər]
eye-DUP-saliva
eye discharge

(391) *papa-m-jɛm-na* [ɸaɸam'jɛmnə] ~ [ɸaɸan'jɛmnə]
weather-DUP-??-3s
overcast

9.9. Reduplication

The forms of reduplication in this and other dialects have been discussed in detail in Nivens (to appear). Briefly, in River the reduplicative prefix is usually of the form C$_i$C.

(392) /DUP+mɔna+na/ [min'mɔnənə] 'DUP-first-3s'

However, if an open syllable directly precedes the stressed syllable, only the consonant following the stressed vowel appears as the surface form of the reduplicative prefix. (DUP is prefixed to the stressed syllable.)

(393) /DUP+gasira/ [gar'sirə] 'DUP-old'
/DUP+balār/ [bar'lar] 'DUP-garden'

The River form of reduplication provides more evidence for the fricative-to-obstruent rule than is found in Coast.

(394) mɔsin   'sacred 3s'
     mit-mɔsin   'DUP-sacred 3s'
     mat-mɔsan-di   'DUP-sacred-pl'

(395) i-bisak   '3s-mash'
     jɛr-bit-bisak   'NF-DUP-mash'

References

Broselow, E., and John McCarthy. 1983. A theory of internal reduplication. Linguistic Review 3:25–88.

Clements, George, and Samuel Keyser. 1983. CV phonology: A generative theory of the syllable. Cambridge: MIT Press.

Collins, James. 1982. Linguistic research in Maluku: A report of recent fieldwork. Oceanic Linguistics 50:73–150.

Hayes, Bruce. 1986. Assimilation as spreading in Toba Batak. Linguistic Inquiry 17:467–499.

Hughes, John. 1987. The languages of Kei, Tanimbar and Aru: A lexicostatistic classification. In Soenjono Dardjowidjojo (ed.), Miscellaneous studies of Indonesian and other languages in Indonesia, part 9. NUSA 27:71–111.

―――― and Katy Hughes. 1989. A phonology of Dobel. In W. D. Laidig (ed.), Workpapers in Indonesian languages and cultures 7, 43–76. Ambon, Indonesia: Pattimura University and the Summer Institute of Linguistics.

Lass, Roger. 1984. Phonology. Cambridge: Cambridge University Press.

McCarthy, John, and Alan Prince. 1986. Prosodic morphology. ms.

Mohanan, K. P. 1986. The theory of lexical phonology. Dordrecht: Reide.

Nivens, Richard. 1989. Linguistic variation and intelligibility among the dialects of Tarangan. ms.

――――. 1990. The vowels of West Tarangan. ms.

――――. To appear. Reduplication in four dialects of West Tarangan. Paper presented at the Southeast Asian Studies Summer Institute (SEASSI) Conference, 28–30 July, 1989. Honolulu.

Pieter, C., J. M. Watkaat, D. Takaria, D. Jalmaf, and P. Engko. 1984–85. Morfologi Bahasa Aru. Proyek Penelitian Bahasa dan Sastra Indonesia dan Daerah Maluku. Ambon: Departemen Pendidikan dan Kebudayaan. ms.

Pulleyblank, Douglas. 1988. Vocalic underspecification in Yoruba. Linguistic Inquiry 19(2):233–270.

Takaria, D., I. Lemba, Zainuddin, G. H. Persulessy, and J. Sahertian. 1982. Struktur Bahasa Aru. Proyek Penelitian dan Pengembangan Bahasa dan Sastera Indonesia dan Daerah. Ambon: DEPDIKBUD. ms.

van der Hulst, Harry, and Norval Smith. 1982. An overview of autosegmental and metrical phonology. In van der Hulst and Smith (eds.), The structure of phonological representations, Part I.

Wang, William S. -Y. 1968. Vowel features, paired variables, and the English vowel shift. Language 44:695–708.

Zwicky, Arnold. 1977. On clitics. Bloomington: Indiana University Linguistics Club.

www.ingramcontent.com/pod-product-compliance
Lightning Source LLC
Chambersburg PA
CBHW051810230426
43672CB00012B/2675